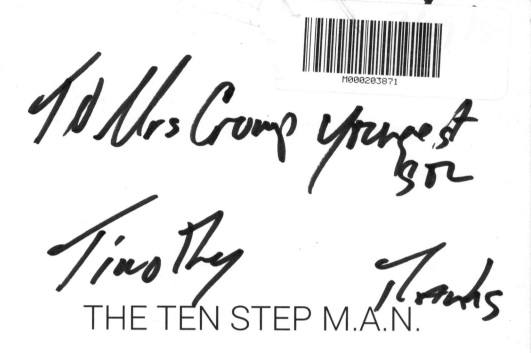

To Mrs Cromp youngest son Timothy Thanks

THE TEN STEP M.A.N.

DEDICATED TO MY SON AND DAUGHTERS AND ALL
THE FIGHTING MEN AND WOMEN OUT THERE

E.A. RAINE PUBLISHING

NEW YORK

7/25/19

Thanks

THE
TEN STEP
M.A.N.

A Practical Guide to Peace, Power, Purpose and Liberation In a World of Women, Wine, War, and Wickedness

BY

EDWARD MULRAINE

THE TEN STEP M.A.N.

A Practical Guide to Peace, Power, Purpose and Liberation
In a World of Women, Wine, War and Wickedness

Copyright © 2018 Edward Mulraine

CONTENTS

Although many books examine the social and moral decline of men, not many books look at the good and potential of men. Yes, deficiencies exist, but they can be fixed. Men make mistakes, but they can learn from them. Men have issues, but they can be remedied. This book starts with the premise that men are good and have the potential to be great.

STEP 1 is Acknowledge the Enemy. It outlines the forces that are behind men's actions by using the biblical text to give a description and understanding of who the enemy is and how the enemy operates in disguise to seduce and eventually hurt men. It also gives men the answer to confront the enemy and regain their standing.

STEP 2 is Integrity. It allows men to be honest with themselves about the various demons that lie within. In being honest, men are asked to call out demons that have overtaken them and disrupted their lives: temper, lust, fear, arrogance, hate and past indiscretions are all dealt with.

STEP 3 is Security. Men must learn to protect themselves inside and out against temptation of the flesh. It begins with the first piece of armor by addressing and confronting sexual issues that men deal with—such as:

sexual temptation, sexual consequences, sexual frustration, sex versus love making. It also addresses issues of: male violations, homosexuality, sexual diseases, marriage and single fathers.

STEP 4 *is Community. It discusses men and politics; equating righteousness with justice. Racism, classism, and sexism are addressed. It teaches men about volunteering their time and not living a hypocritical life which can hurt the community. Additionally it deals with the heart of a man and how men hurt too. Issues of: suicide, domestic violence, death, unforgiveness and men helping men are talked about in detail.*

STEP 5 *is Mobility. It discusses men who find themselves constantly moving in the wrong direction, which often leads to frustration and devastation. The chapter directs men toward social and spiritual mobility, leadership and obedience to leadership. Issues covered include: wrong decisions, getting rid of anything in life that causes temptation and self-destruction, walking away from abusive situations, money management, men balancing their professional and personal lives, and romance.*

STEP 6 *is Resiliency. It addresses tolerance and how men can build up resistance to prevent responding angrily or violently to every big or little thing that happens in their lives. It also discusses being confident and secure, monogamy, starting your own business, staying healthy and how men can* bounce back from disgrace, disasters and allegations and live wholesome lives.

STEP 7 *is Mentally. It deals with the mind and how it can be damaged by what goes in through the eyes. Step 7 deals with lust, mental illness and self-esteem, along with: how to handle disappointments and how men can think and bring out the greatness in themselves.*

STEP 8 *is Effectively. It teaches men how to fight their demons by using the Word of God. It teaches men when to speak, when to be silent and what to say. It also defines and empowers men's role and purpose in the home, on the job and in the streets. This step shows men how to carve out evil and plant good using the Word of God.*

STEP 9 *is Prayerfully. It addresses prayer and how its power has been ignored and underestimated. In this book prayer is given a new understanding that will make men think twice about the necessity and power of talking to God. God is the general and we are the soldiers in God's army and soldiers must keep in touch with the general if they want to live and succeed. It speaks to men in prison, in deceptive situations and powerful positions.*

STEP 10 is *Boldly.* *It encourages men to go forward courageously in the battle. It is the finale, and lets men know that whatever the battle, God is with them.*

The Pledge of Armor, The Principles of Armor, The Purpose of Armor, The Practice of Armor, The Prayer of Armor, The Power of Armor, and The Penalty and Promise of Armor, plus The Psalm of Armor.

AUTHOR'S NOTE

While I was writing this book, a young woman came to me and asked, "Why are you writing a book for men? They don't read."

"Sure they do," I said.

"No, they don't!" she insisted.

I said, "Yes, they do. They read *into* things. They look at the surface, and if they like what they see, they take it a little further and pursue it a little harder. It's the law of *look, like, pursue.*

Men are visual, and the visual works its way to the mental, and the mental works its way to the analytical where men can look deeper into things. This book is designed on those characteristics. Hopefully *The Ten Step M.A.N.* will capture the attention of men with its graphics and title, and then lure men with its content. The content will then lead men to look deeper into their lives and experiences and pursue life changes to become greater men for themselves and others!

I then told the young woman, *"this book is for you too."*

INTRODUCTION

Moving from Good to Great

*The steps of a **good man** are ordered by the* LORD....
Psalm 37:23
*... because **greater is he** that is in you, than he that is in the world.*
1 John 4:4

Aman is distinguished by his character ... How he keeps his word and conducts his deeds. How he lives his life and gains respect with little convincing. How he rises from failure and emerges from disgrace. How he loves and encourages others, embraces family, confronts weaknesses, challenges injustices, and practices ethics. How he adapts to change, envisions the future, dismisses the ignoble, and honors the progressive. How he breathes with ease, speaks with authority, walks with dignity, and addresses the crowd with confidence. A man's character has its own charisma, its own disciples, and they relish hearing him and being around him because he's the same in the light and in the dark.

But a man's character can be tarnished by awful acts of arrogance, selfish ambitions, and relentless drives. He can forsake all others in pursuit of himself. He can reduce others with misogynistic, self-abasing, narcissistic, misguided rhetoric. For this kind of man, there is no humbleness—just power hungriness. He allows his penis to interrupt his mission, his mouth to spew hate, his mind to judge prematurely, his eyes to wander off the path of righteousness, and his brinksmanship to force a fight. He loves money and hates discipline. He loves wrong and does wrong to love. He can succeed in the eyes of others and break down in the sight of God. This can result in public and private failure.

No man wants to fail. Every man wants to succeed. Failure is an institution of family disruption, social disintegration, moral decay, psychological dysfunction, emotional breakdown, financial insecurity, communal chaos, life imprisonment, sexual promiscuity, physical diseases, human shame, and spiritual conflict. It's horrible to feel like a failure and to be perceived as a letdown. Unfortunately the perception and the sentiment of character flaws and personal failures have attached themselves to men in society.

Although many books examine the social and moral decline of men, not many books look at the good and potential of men. Yes, deficiencies exist, but they can be fixed. Men make mistakes, but they can learn from them. Men have issues, but they can be remedied. However, they can't be remedied with just analytical, critical, social, penal, or psychological solutions for the male condition. They can't be improved with just educational journals or statistical manuals that outline more of the problem than the solution. Most men know what the problem is—like most sick people know what the sickness is. And just like the sick, men want the cure. Men want the solution. Men want the medicine so that they can fix what's wrong and live right.

Well, the solution is a spiritual one (please keep reading). I know that for many specialists, spiritual suggestions go against the grain of sound educational practice and are not even considered in social or scientific disciplines. It is too mystical, too unexplainable, and outside the normal understanding of educational research. I know that for many men, spiritual suggestions may sound trite and redundant because many books have been written about God and man. And many men are either tired of or skeptical about God-centered suggestions, and would instead like power answers without spiritual solutions. But the spiritual solution is unique in the way it is presented and the way it connects with other subjects, such as the political, social, and psychological.

The reason the spiritual is so different is because it starts with the premise that men are good, created *"in the image of God."*[1] Being created in the image of God gave men the spiritual, rational, and physical ability to be good rulers, workers, providers, and protectors with good intentions, minds, hearts, and souls. *"God saw all that he had made, and it was very good."*[2] The image of God guides the conscience of men to draw out the best in them.

Additionally, the spiritual suggests that men can be better; that men are good but can be greater. The good started with God; the great is manifested in the son of God. The spiritual seeks to bring greatness to the surface by connecting men with Jesus, who will be *"great and called the son of God."*[3] The greatness of Christ brings out the greatness in men *"because greater is he that is in you, than he that is in the world."*[4] In Christ men have the potential to be great workers, fathers, and leaders. Greatness is not only seen in men's ability but also in men's character. The spiritual indwelling allows men to be conscious of their actions and cognizant of their statements. Greatness takes men to another level of their potential, gives them something greater to look forward to, lifts them to a higher level in the world, and takes them to a deeper level within themselves.

The greatness of Christ allows men to confront their weaknesses by examining the whole of man—not just the "bad" of man—from the psychological to the social, and it provides the necessary dose of power for inner transformation and outer realization.

The spiritual remedy is persistent and allocates more to be effective to move from good to great. If the first dose of spirituality does not work or was not acceptable to your soul or did not connect with your reality or was not up to your doctrinal understanding, then you may require another dose and another dose until it hits the spot where failure and immoral behavior exist.

It's just like water on fire: sometimes the first bucket doesn't work, but if you keep throwing water on fire, it's bound to go out. Men are under fire, from economic hardship to tarnished reputation, and the

---

1: Genesis 1:27
2: Genesis 1:31 (NIV)
3: Luke 1:32
4: 1 John 4:4

more water we put on the fire, the more likely the fire will go out. But this water is not natural; it's spiritual, because there are some things that the natural can't solve. If it could, men wouldn't continue to trip and fall for the same old tricks over and over again, and repeatedly suffer the consequences of those mistakes.

Spiritual water goes deeper than natural water to bring life to the soul. Jesus says, *"If anyone is thirsty, let him come to me and drink. Whoever believes in me, as the Scripture has said, streams of living water will flow from within him."*[5] The souls of many men are dry like the desert and only through living water can the soul be quenched and life fulfilled. Jesus not only promises drops of water, but by faith *"streams of living water."* These streams of living water can cleanse the soul of guilt and refresh the spirit of life. They can wash away the faults of yesterday and the misery of today. And they can bring man from the depths of despair to the shores of hope. The spiritual goes deeper than the natural to release the great in men.

The depth of this book is not only concerned with the male's spiritual connection, as in relationship to God, but also—and mostly—concerned with the male's spiritual strength, as in being prepared and properly equipped to fight against all kinds of character flaws and social failures. Put bluntly, the only way men are going to overturn their situation and social perception, and restore their moral, psychological, and social standing and realize greatness in themselves, is to fight for it.

This fight requires spiritual transformation, personal commitment, and practical action. It is not your typical battle. It is a spiritual battle, and a spiritual battle is deeper than a physical battle, because while the physical battle may hit the surface of failure, a spiritual battle knocks out the root of failure. The root of failure is temptation. Giving into temptation and not being in control of a situation can lead to disaster. Men are good, but they fall short of the good because of temptation. In the beginning man fell to temptation. Falling to temptation is a spiritual plunge that has a calamitous impact on our relationship with God and our personal life, and it diminishes our good character and potential for

---

5: John 7:37-38 (NIV)

greatness. So while the root cause of failure is falling to temptation, the surface symptoms of the fall are seen in divorce, disease, discomfort, disharmony, and disaster in life. Once the root is dealt with, then the surface will bear better fruit in every area: marriage, family, stability, harmony, and peace in life. Men must learn to fight temptation so that they can take control of and responsibility for their lives. The God in us is constantly pulling us toward good even when we fall. When men come back from a fall, they not only have the ability to be good but the potential to be great in the name of Jesus. One thing I've learned is that people may pity and even despise a failure, but they love an overcomer—someone who has conquered weakness and beaten back bad behavior to rise to stability and greatness in life. In the beginning man fell to temptation, but in Christ man can get up in greatness.

Jesus was so strong and successful while on earth as a man because He never fell to temptation. As the Bible says of Jesus, *"For we do not have a high priest who is unable to sympathize with our weaknesses, but we have one who has been tempted in every way, just as we are—yet was without sin."*[6] The greatest leader and example we have is found in Jesus the Christ, who endured what we endure yet showed us that we can fight temptation and succeed in life.

This book not only teaches men to fight, but it also teaches men *how* to fight, *whom* to fight, and *when* to fight. Many men are told to fight: Fight for your country. Fight for your rights. Fight for your lives. But the sad thing is that many men have not been taught how to fight. Many men have not been given the necessary armor and skills to fight their battles, whether it's against cancer or drugs, temper or lust, stubbornness or unforgiveness. Men need guidance in order to confront failure, reverse conditions, and regain control of their lives. This book gives the guiding principles necessary to combat evil, do good, and become great.

This book teaches men that spiritual transformation happens immediately but change happens slowly. It takes understanding and action to live by God's standards. It takes time to be a better man. It's

6: Hebrews 4:15 (NIV)

a constant battle to be great. It takes falling and getting back up to be great. It takes practice to live that change. It takes a series of steps to see and to be that change. This book seeks to pull the good out of men and guide them through the process one step at a time. After each step men should get a better understanding of how they are to live and the changes they ought to make to be that great M.A.N. (read on for what this acronym stands for).

I AM NOT ASHAMED

In the shadow of any writer's work is the sincerity of his own history resulting from a streaming reality. No true writer puts pen to paper void of experience. The choice is whether the writer decides to step out of the shadows and reveal rather than conceal his true identity. As the author of this material, I cannot pursue this discussion regarding the male quest toward wholeness and liberation in isolation of my own biography. "*I am not ashamed of the gospel, because it is the power of God for the salvation of everyone who believes....*"

A sullen feeling came over me as I wrote this book, one that cornered me in the cages of my own male inadequacy. Some years ago I was applying for a passport, which required a birth certificate. I had lost the original years ago and had to get a copy. When I began to read the copy I'd obtained, I noticed plainly there was no name on the father's line. As a wave of grief hit me, I also began to really think about the absent man whose name wasn't on the line and whose presence had never been a part of my life. Although I had a stepfather later in my growing years, I'd often wondered what it would have been like to have had a father, a biological dad around the house or even simply present in my life. Perhaps I would have been a better young man. I might have had a father's style of discipline that would have balanced out a mother's loving instructions.

In his book *Fatherless America,* author David Blankenhorn cites many experts who understand the power of fatherhood in a person's life. Blankenhorn quotes author Michal Lamb, who suggests, "The

---

7: Romans 1:16 (NIV)

characteristics of the father as a parent rather than the characteristics of the father as a man appear to influence child development."[8] Further, Blankenhorn notes that men should be "more sensitive, less rigid, much more flexible," based on the work of author Henry B. Biller.[9] Finally, Blankenhorn cites Andrew M. Greeley, who has called for a measure of androgyny in men, espousing the theory of fatherhood without the masculinity.[10] As if men don't have enough challenges in society to avoid being emasculated! Dangerous thinking …

Yes, there are some traditional characteristics and gender role expectations that men need to modify, but they should never attempt to deny their masculinity or be co-identified as women. There needs to be a distinction in gender even if there is equality in parenting responsibilities. Men, as masculine, have their portion of responsibility in breadwinning, caretaking, disciplining, and child nurturing, and women, as feminine, have their own roles and style. As women have been able to take on dual responsibilities—often out of necessity—men should have no problem showing sensitivity and flexibility in childrearing without losing their sense of masculinity.

We do not want to take the masculinity out of father. We want to add or "incorporate men as they are into family life, in part by giving them distinctive, gendered roles that reflect, rather than reject, inherited masculine norms—such as, for example, the breadwinner role."[11] Androgyny is a fatherless father, and that's like a single-parent home where both parents have the same gender identity. Empowering and uplifting the masculinity of men does not subtract from the power and femininity of women; both genders and roles are needed for the development of the children.

Flexibility not only pertains to a man's family life but to his work ethic. Women such as Hanna Rosin have argued that men are often inflexible. She uses the term "cardboard men" to describe the often rigid

---

8: David Blankenhorn, *Fatherless America: Confronting Our Most Urgent Social Problem* (New York: HarperPerennial, 1995), 109.
9: Blankenhorn, *Fatherless America*, 109.
10: Blankenhorn, *Fatherless America*, 109.
11: Blankenhorn, *Fatherless America*, 109.

man that is stuck in old habits and unable to adjust to an economy that values thinking over muscle building and manufacturing. She argues that as a result of many men's inflexibility, they have been unable to support their families, lead their homes, or find good employment.[12]

There is no doubt more men must become ardent readers, thinkers, and writers to adapt to a changing economic culture. Statistics abound from urban to suburban communities around the country where more and more young men are dropping out of high school. This is dangerous to their family and future, and the alternative to education is often low-paying jobs, incarceration, government dependency, poverty, and death. Unlike other cultures where trade and manufacturing can be a means to financial and family stability, the American culture connects wealth and financial stability to higher education, advanced degrees, and learning. In order to counter the downfall, more men must not only be educated but revolutionary—seeking independent means to create jobs and start employment that cater to their work ethic and mental and physical strength. What made men great historically was their faith and courage to step out and start businesses, to take chances and engage in the unconventional. This included jobs from fixing electronics to selling appliances. Although brute force and muscle may be diminishing in the workplace, faith and courage never go out of style.

PERSONALLY SPEAKING

As for my own life, having a father during my early years might have added the God-appointed masculinity needed in our family and for my insecurities. It would have built into my character the need to be strong and confident. I would have had an additional source for advice. My mother made me think once, but a father possibly would have made me think twice—before I fought in school or hung out with the wrong crowd. I learned what it meant to have a father by listening to other young men at the time, how their fathers would "kill" them (figuratively speaking) if the dads knew what their sons were doing on the streets.

12: Hanna Rosin, *The End of Men: And the Rise of Women* (New York: Riverhead Books, 2012).

If I'd had a father of my own, I might have avoided harmful experiments with drugs, crime, and gangs. I might have avoided the criminal justice system. Even if I didn't avoid it, with a male figure in my life, I possibly would have at least shortened my involvement in those harmful activities. A father would have intervened and at least showed his power and thundered out his requirements. In my mind a father would have been a good protector. On those days when I got beat up by gangs, I would have run home and told my father. I believe a father might have been a good provider, especially on those days when I was hungry and needed a meal. When I needed money to buy the latest fashion, instead of stealing it I would have asked my father. A father would have been a counselor on those days when I needed good advice based upon a man's knowledge and experience. It would have been good to have a father—a man—in whom to confide my secrets and confessions.

I believe that with the absence of a father in my life came the absence of some self-esteem, character, discipline, and basic learning. Manhood was stymied for me. Even if I didn't learn by communication, with a man in the house I would have at least learned by observation. Missing a father was bad enough, but I also lacked any other adult male influences that so often fill the gap in a child's life—uncles, older brothers, or grandfathers—to show the way of male upbringing. Aside from a few of my mother's boyfriends, I had hardly any role models from which to learn. Even the church we went to had a female pastor, which gave us a double dose of motherly love, but little in the way of manly guidance.

With the absence of a male figure came the mandate to navigate the tough terrains of life on my own. And self-navigation results in more mistakes—failures—than does godly, guided instruction. My mother was good at giving direction, but there is a difference between direction and instruction.

Direction shows the way; instruction teaches you how to get there. It's hard to learn how to become a man on your own, from the basics of shaving to the rudiments of dating. I had to learn to work on my own. Learn to drive a car on my own. Learn to fight on my own.

Learn to date on my own. Learn to go to the barbershop on my own. Learn to get in and out of trouble on my own—and there was more getting in and less getting out because of the lack of guidance.

What I've learned through my own experiences with self-navigation through manhood is that men need guidance—plain and clear instruction on everything from parenting to principles of practice. Many women expect men to just know how to be a good man. But if learning how to be a good Christian, Muslim, or Jew requires instruction, how much more do men need instruction and supervision to learn how to be a good man? A young man needs to be taught, by education and strong discipline, how to be a boyfriend and to court a young lady, so that when he grows up, he knows how to be a husband. Men must show young men, by example and instruction, how to be a protector of and provider for their family, community, and nation. How to be disciplined. How to be a father.

How to be honest. Even being a good sex partner is a learning process. Many people will criticize young men (and even some older men) and say, "Since he knew how to make a baby, he should know how to take care of a baby." But the truth is that many young men who make babies made mistakes in having children. A lot of them didn't know what they were doing, from the moment of penetration to the consequences of their sexual action, which can open doors to so many other problems—legal and emotional—after the baby is born. And if young men had known some of this, either by way of fathers or other strong male figures, much of the trouble might have been avoided. A lot of adult men are still in the process of learning about themselves and their partners. Learning requires time and examples, mentors and role models. When young men don't have good male examples in the home, community, or schools, they can attach to the closest model of dominance they see. Unfortunately many times there are more negative examples around than positive ones—the unemployed, heavy drinkers, woman beaters, drug dealers, baby-makers without being caretakers, womanizers. These negative role models teach the worst and perpetuate the cycle of male ignorance, along with their social, moral, and spiritual decline.

Just like pupils need teachers, Christians need preachers, and finders need keepers, so too do men need instructors to grow from boys to men. Men need guidance in learning how to be husbands and fathers. Men need leadership on principles and values. Without guidance men are failing more than they are achieving, hurting more than they're helping, and killing more than they're saving. As the Bible states in Hosea 4:6, *"My people are destroyed for lack of knowledge."*[13]

But the blessedness in my life, even though the male presence was absent, came because of the spiritual guidance that was there. I thank God that I always had a hustler's spirit. I was ready to work hard whether doing bad or good. I thank God for giving me the spirit of discernment to know when to run from danger and the wrong environment. I thank God for the spirit of prayer that my mother taught me. Even when I wasn't doing right by God, I knew how to pray every night before I went to sleep. I just opened my mouth and spoke to God. And I believe it was those prayers through lonely nights, difficult days, and tumultuous times growing up as a young man that made me feel like I had a father to speak to: *"Our Father which art in heaven, Hallowed by thy name."*[14] I thank God for the spirit of learning that He put in me. Even while I was getting into trouble, I acknowledged that I needed education. The streets were basic education in preparation for higher learning. Growing up I went to approximately twelve different schools prior to college, either because of getting expelled or family relocation. None of the teachers ever said I was dumb; they only said I was bad.

It's wonderful when God provides something you need even before you realize that God is filling an absence in your life. Even though I didn't have a dominant male figure in the home, I thank God for sending me godly examples of manhood that taught me well and built my moral character. I thank God for the good man who became a part of our family when I got older. My stepfather, Clarence Nelson, showed me how a man loves a woman and takes care of his family, even when the children are not his own progeny. My mother had four children

---

13: Hosea 4:6 (NKJV)
14: Matthew 6:9

prior to meeting him, and he still took care of us as if we were his own biological children. He has since passed on, but I still carry the lessons he taught me. I thank God for Mr. Brown, my high school teacher who taught me Shakespeare and the love of literature. Nurturing my love of reading helped me to go on to college, which I could have never imagined when I first attended high school. I thank God for a male Muslim professor, Dr. Jimmy Jones, a distinctive black male presence on the Manhattanville College campus. He taught me religious studies from different perspectives. I thank God for an old Jewish businessman, Robert Arnow, for whom I worked during the summer months while in college.

He didn't say much, yet he gave me a whole different perspective of America through his ownership of major corporate buildings in Manhattan. I thank God for the community activism and social involvement modeled by my NAACP mentor, the late Albert V. Tuitt. He taught me the importance of fighting for justice, even in the post-Civil Rights era. He wasn't too religious, but he had the morals and strength of a godly man. Finally I thank God for my spiritual father and pastor, the Reverend Dr. W. Franklyn Richardson. He opened the doors for my preaching and pastoring. His presence, guidance, and inspiration have been immeasurable in my life. He has mentored me to further develop my wisdom, social activism, preaching, and demand for excellence.

Most of all I thank God for being my Father which art in heaven. It is because of Him that I am saved. Throughout this book you will see the words "salvation" and "saved" a lot. Salvation is that gift God has given to "save" us from afterlife condemnation and present-life failure. It feels good when you know you could have died in your mess and drowned in your sin, but God rescued and saved you from darkness and damnation, and brought you into purpose and awareness. God has preserved me for a reason.

Perhaps it was to write this book so that other men can be saved from their destructive ways. So that other men can know there is a God who is a loving Father who sits on high and looks out for the fatherless.

Just maybe He wants them to know that there is a God who loves men and wants to see men grow and succeed so they can build His kingdom on earth and so they can become the fathers and the men to others that they never had themselves.

Although I often have wondered what it might have been like to have a biological father growing up, I have concluded that God knows best. The way my mother was living at the time might have attracted a bad role model in a father, giving me modeling and instruction for my demise rather than for abundant life in Christ. I rest my soul upon the verse, *"And we know that in all things God works for good of those who love him, who have been called according to his purpose."*[15] Although I have a long way to go, I'm satisfied with my life now that I am a man of God. I realize now that God has ordered my life and that God knew the type of man He wanted me to be—a man who can relate to the souls of the broken, the sinful, and the heavy hearted.

Their struggling souls are like those of the apostle Paul: *"When I want to do good, evil is right there with me."*[16] Everybody needs help in being the man that God intends for him to be. I know that I had to go through what I went through in order to relate to brothers in similar circumstances or worse. I thank God for those who helped me, more than they know. It is my hope that through this book, I can help women understand that men are good, and that they, like everyone, need guidance, patience, and help. I hope that I can help other men, young and old, who are struggling to do the right thing; they just need someone to help them find their way and build their character. Jesus is *"the way and the truth and the life."*[17]

My motives for writing this book are not altogether altruistic, however. Just writing this book has made me a better man. Having to think about all the issues that men face has made me realize that men need a continuous course on divine male living. I have tried to be a good father, and evidence of that came some years ago after my son was

---

15: Romans 8:28 (NIV)
16: Romans 7:21 (NIV)
17: John 14:6 (NIV)

born. I don't usually go and get the mail, but one particular day I went to the mailbox. In the mail was my son's birth certificate. On the line for father it read: *Edward Alexander Mulraine.* I was there on the line, and I'm there in his life, for life.

M.A.N.—THE BOOK

The Ten Step M.A.N. seeks to establish those guiding principles so sorely needed to stop failure and to build character. As stated, men are falling all over the place, and someone has got to pick them up. Men face a "hell" of a lot of issues, and many of those issues are either ignored or dismissed. As a result male spiritual, emotional, and physical fatalities persist, leaving dormant and damaged souls around the world. For this purpose we put together a new M.A.N.

M.A.N. is an acronym for "Man of Armor Nation." We expect to create a nation of men built upon the principles of the whole armor of God as recorded in Ephesians 6:11-20. *The Ten Step M.A.N.: A Practical Guide to Peace, Power, Purpose and Liberation in a World of Women, Wine, War and Wickedness,* with its twenty-three chapters, seeks to address the male struggle against evil by inserting the spiritual principles of good one step at a time.

Each step is meant to give understanding and greater strength to battle inner demons and outer failures. Men will be guided from the first to the last step to understand themselves, their challenges, and their ability to fight temptation. This book does not sugarcoat the issues, or try to hide behind leniency for the purpose of decency. We will talk bluntly, because the only way men will overcome their failure is to be real about the issues they are facing. Throughout the book I ask men to examine themselves because there is a lot of corrosion that has built up in our bodies, minds, and souls, and it needs to be removed. And the only way it's going to be eliminated is if we first acknowledge it. So as you read, don't be afraid to call out your enemy. It will set the stage for the battle that you must fight. The entire work is based upon the whole armor of God that Paul prescribed to the church at Ephesus in Ephesians 6:14-18. Those pieces of armor include: **the belt of truth, the breastplate of righteousness, feet fitted with the gospel of peace, the** *shield of faith, the helmet of salvation, the sword of the Spirit, and prayer.* Each piece of armor will be put on step by step and turned into principles to practice on a daily basis. As men put on the armor, they will grow stronger and go higher to live wholesome, decent, and purposeful lives. This book emphasizes solutions to problems, rather than heralding problems over solutions. The principles contained herein are answers that will address and hopefully eliminate any spiritual dysfunction and actual temptation that men are struggling with internally that constantly lead to external failure. The goal is to empower men to take on forces that are tempting, draining, hurting, and haunting them. Men need guidance, and men need power. This book, through examination of the whole armor, will give the needed information that can help guide men to victory over the enemy.

STEP 1 is *Acknowledge the Enemy.* It outlines the forces that are behind men's actions by using the biblical text to give a description and understanding of who the enemy is and how the enemy operates in disguise to seduce and eventually hurt men. It also gives men the answer to confront the enemy and regain their standing.

STEP 2 is *Integrity.* It allows men to be honest with themselves about the various demons that lie within. In being honest, men are asked to call out demons that have overtaken them and disrupted their lives: temper, lust, fear, arrogance, hate and past indiscretions are all dealt with.

STEP 3 is *Security.* Men must learn to protect themselves inside and out against temptation of the flesh. It begins with the first piece of armor by addressing and confronting sexual issues that men deal with— such as: sexual temptation, sexual consequences, sexual frustration, sex versus love making. It also addresses issues of: male violations, homosexuality, sexual diseases, marriage and single fathers.

STEP 4 is *Community.* It discusses men and politics; equating righteousness with justice. Racism, classism, and sexism are addressed. It teaches men about volunteering their time and not living a hypocritical life which can hurt the community. Additionally it deals with the heart of a man and how men hurt too. Issues of: suicide, domestic violence, death, unforgiveness and men helping men are talked about in detail.

STEP 5 is *Mobility*. It discusses men who find themselves constantly moving in the wrong direction, which often leads to frustration and devastation. The chapter directs men toward social and spiritual mobility, leadership and obedience to leadership. Issues covered include: wrong decisions, getting rid of anything in life that causes temptation and self-destruction, walking away from abusive situations, money management, men balancing their professional and personal lives, and romance.

STEP 6 is *Resiliency*. It addresses tolerance and how men can build up resistance to prevent responding angrily or violently to every big or little thing that happens in their lives. It also discusses being confident and secure, monogamy, starting your own business, staying healthy and how men can bounce back from disgrace, disasters and allegations and live wholesome lives.

STEP 7 is *Mentally*. It deals with the mind and how it can be damaged by what goes in through the eyes. Step 7 deals with lust, mental illness and self-esteem, along with: how to handle disappointments and how men can think and bring out the greatness in themselves.

STEP 8 is *Effectively*. It teaches men how to fight their demons by using the Word of God. It teaches men when to speak, when to be silent and what to say. It also defines and empowers men's role and purpose in the home, on the job and in the streets. This step shows men how to carve out evil and plant good using the Word of God.

STEP 9 is *Prayerfully*. It addresses prayer and how its power has been ignored and underestimated. In this book prayer is given a new understanding that will make men think twice about the necessity and power of talking to God. God is the general and we are the soldiers in God's army and soldiers must keep in touch with the general if they want to live and succeed. It speaks to men in prison, in deceptive situations and powerful positions.

STEP 10 is *Boldly*. It encourages men to go forward courageously in the battle. It is the finale, and lets men know that whatever the battle, God is with them.

In addition to the ten steps, I have included **The Articles of Armor**, which consist of the Eight P's Package: *The Pledge of Armor, The Principles of Armor, The Purpose of Armor, The Practice of Armor, The Prayer of Armor, The Power of Armor,* and *The Penalty and Promise of Armor,* plus *The Psalm of Armor.* These articles are to be quoted and followed daily. The package is designed to help lay the foundation to establish a *Ten Step Man of Armor Nation* movement in all communities, houses of worship, and homes, with men who will live by these principles, follow these instructions, and battle their demons. Men may need to dress for the occasion, so the consecration of actual garments for the purpose of unification, presentation, and identification will be developed. But whatever you wear should be consecrated for God's service. The clothing you put on in the morning becomes your armor—not because of the clothes, but because of the man of God in the clothes.

This is a book of spiritual power. It must be read with sincerity and urgency; for the whole armor must be donned now if lives are to be saved and the enemy is to be shamed. Each man who puts on the armor saves another brother and sister from the arms of failure and a wicked ruler. By contrast each man who fails to put on the armor of God allows the enemy to rob, steal, and destroy our families, communities, houses of worship, and world. The more battles the enemy wins, less of humanity will gain eternity. So, yes, this is a fight for the eternal life of God's creation. There is a lot of fixing to do, a lot of issues to confront, and little time to do it. We've wasted too much time. It's time for us to arm ourselves with the whole armor of God.

CHAPTER 1

STEP 1: The Enemy (What We're Up Against)

For we wrestle not against flesh and blood, but against principalities, against powers, against the rulers of the darkness of this world, against spiritual wickedness in high places.

Ephesians 6:12

During the US Civil War from 1861 to 1865, 620,000 soldiers died. The toll was approximately equal to the American fatalities in the Revolutionary War, the War of 1812, the Mexican War, the Spanish-American War, World War I, World War II, and the Korean War combined.[18] Young and healthy men fought and killed each other. Some understood their plight; others were thrown into duty and fought blindly. In the end they were controlled by higher powers that made them fight each other, even to death.

So first let's be real about what we're up against as men. Paul made it clear to the church at Ephesus what all believers are up against: *"For we wrestle not against flesh and blood, but against principalities, against powers, against the rulers of the darkness of this world, against spiritual wickedness in high places."*[19] The description is enough to make anyone cringe and ask, "What the hell does all this mean?"

To the spiritually minded and to those who share the philosophy

---

18: Drew Gilpin Faust, *This Republic of Suffering: Death and the American Civil War* (New York: Alfred A. Knopf, 2008), xi.

19: Ephesians 6:12

of an underlying human cause, it simply means we are not physically fighting against each other. Our humanity, which is flesh and blood, is a cover-up for a deeper systematic dilemma. Like those soldiers during the Civil War, we are controlled by higher powers—wickedness in high places. If we limit our fight to only the flesh, we can attack another person or nation and still miss the fundamental problem.

IDENTIFYING THE ENEMY

Since the first man Adam, men have had to deal with a continuous attack by satanic forces. Satan has been our adversary since the beginning of time. An *adversary* is *an enemy who obstructs or opposes someone's progress in life*. In this case Satan is the enemy that has opposed and obstructed our relationship with God, and caused us to fall to temptation and enter a world of failure and deep character flaws. Disguised as a serpent, Satan tempted humanity and ushered in the fall of man. The fall of man disgraced the good of humanity. Satan behind the serpent is the same demonic force behind negative human actions—forces that make men fight each other, forces that make men kill each other, and forces that seek to ultimately kill all men. More men have died at the hands of Satan than during any war, at anytime, in the world.

Simply put, our struggle is not against human flesh but spiritual wickedness in high places, which seeks to terminate us—mind, body, soul, and, most importantly, our spiritual relationship with God.

Step 1 for every man is *Acknowledge the Enemy*:

He must recognize that Satan is the enemy behind his no-good human actions and that only through the power of God can he beat back wicked forces.

DIFFICULTY IN UNDERSTANDING THE FORCES

Often we look at our battles as purely physical, psychological, emotional, or hereditary, but truth be told, our struggles are much more than we can understand. They're mystical and diabolical, cynical and incomprehensible. It is certainly right at times when men say:

"I don't know why I did what I did. That was stupid!"

"I don't know what got into me!"

"I wish I could go back and do things differently."

"I've never done anything like that before!"

"I keep messing up and I just can't control myself."

We feel terrible when we do things that, in retrospect, cause us to question ourselves and our actions. But we're dealing with forces that are beyond our control, grip, and understanding. Because of the often imperceptible, diabolical forces we battle, it is virtually impossible for us to stop doing the thing that defies logic or understanding on our own. Flesh and blood may hit the tree but won't necessarily strike the root. Spiritual wickedness is at the root of all evil.

NO EXCUSES

And let me interject this before we go any further: the charge of spiritual wickedness in high places and Satan behind human actions is not to suggest that men have excuses for their bad behavior. Rather, this is stated for men to recognize that malevolence lies behind misconduct and to acknowledge that Satan is controlling negative actions. And in order to stop any negative behavior, there must first be an acknowledgement of the root cause—just like alcoholics must acknowledge that alcohol is a problem before they can deal with it. Until then men will constantly suffer the consequences of their evil actions. Now that men know about evil behind their negative actions, there is no excuse why actions can't be taken to eliminate evil. Men are not responsible for the root cause of their actions, but they are responsible for their inactions once they realize Satan is behind their evil thoughts and deeds, and do nothing about it.

HAUNTED BY DEMONS

Many men have succeeded in society. They've attained a good family, are astute politically and strong physically, possess a great personality, are praised morally, and are competitive intellectually and stable financially. The sad thing is, beneath the public personas, many of these men are haunted, and even threatened, by their demons. They know that, if exposed, the revelation will have a calamitous effect on everything they've accomplished, particularly men who are public figures either in church, community, family, work, or school. We've seen great men rise over the years, only to fall once their private demons were exposed. The old adage is true: the bigger you are, the harder you fall. Some men already have fallen to forces and are suffering the consequences of their no-good actions: incarcerated, shamed, publicly disgraced, bankrupted, forced to resign from their position, estranged from their wives, banned from their children, and living with a trail of negative information in their background check. Meanwhile others, as Paul wrote, *"wrestle"* to keep demons under control. Everybody is struggling with something regardless of age or gender, and hoping the something doesn't take them down.

YOU'RE NOT ALONE

If you find yourself battered and confused, conflicted and tempted, beaten, molested, suffering and shattered, don't worry; you're not alone. Men, in biblical and modern times, have always had difficulty wrestling with nefarious forces. Adam had ignorance. Noah had drunkenness. Abraham had fear. Moses had intemperance. Nabal had arrogance. David was a man after God's own heart, yet was guilty of adultery and murder. Solomon had wisdom, yet was a womanizer and idolater. Judas had betrayal. Peter had denial. Even Jesus, for our sake, showed His weakness in anguish over His forthcoming death, requesting God to *"let this cup pass from me."*[20] So in the midst of your struggles, remember that you are not alone—and that God is not dead.

20: Matthew 28:39

THE ENEMY WITHIN

This enemy is real—real hard to understand, real hard to fight, and real hard to beat. Hard because at times we don't know whom we're fighting—ourselves or the enemy—because the enemy is often wrapped up in our humanity. We are actually Satan's "wardrobe." Satan has wrapped himself in our flesh and other physical and emotional entities, like he did with the serpent to tempt Adam. So the rulers, authorities, and powers are often undetectable and hard to target. It's like fighting against your own shadow in the dark: you may swing, but in reality you're not punching a thing.

THE FORCES BEHIND HUMAN ACTIONS

As humans we've made intellectual yet artificial progress by allowing ourselves to dismiss *"principalities," "powers," "satanic forces,"* and *"rulers of darkness"* in favor of more sophisticated, educated language. No longer does society, or even many ministries, label iniquitous behavior, attitudes, and actions as *wicked* or *demonic*. We can't use words like *enemy* and *adversary* to describe our inner foes and bad behavior, because it's too unintelligible and incomprehensible. We rely on more penal, medical, or socially acceptable language—words such as *criminal, immoral, depressed, foul, insane, obnoxious, dreadful,* and *deviant*—to describe the root of our failure. Although these expressions are good and give description to problematic behavior, they can obscure the root and place a solely human and psychological remedy on the issue. A solely human and psychological problem warrants a solely human and psychological answer, such as counseling, medication, prison, hospitalization, and, in the worst cases, the death penalty.

The spiritual application doesn't intend to dismiss the medical or the psychological. It doesn't suggest that these judicial actions and penal enforcements should not be applied. Rather it understands how *"rulers," "authorities," "principalities,"* and *"wickedness"* can be wrapped up in it all, just as Satan disguised himself in a serpent. As deliverance ministers Frank and Ida Mae Hammond have said, "Demons are evil personalities. They are spirit beings. They are the enemies of God and man. Their objectives in human beings are to tempt, deceive, accuse, condemn, pressure, defile, resist, oppose, control, steal, afflict, kill and destroy."[21]

The spiritually minded man sees beneath the physical and psychological issues, and looks at demonic forces involved in the immoral, obnoxious, deviant, and dreadful behavior. The recidivism rate of criminals, relapses of drug addicts and alcoholics, and the recurring failures of everyday people show that the penal system, addiction programs, psychiatric wards, and our own personal strength are insufficient. These systems will always have limited impact because the offenders' actions are coming from a higher authority that masks itself in the psychological, criminal, emotional, and physical being of humans.

So when I hear on the news that a man has killed his family, sure I'm thinking everything from *crazy* to *criminal* and applying any remedy from prison to the death penalty to rid society of this horrible being. But I'm also thinking that rulers and powers of darkness have shrouded themselves in his humanity and overtaken his sanity to make him do the things he does. So society may incarcerate his body and/or medicate his mind, but we should not dismiss the spiritual wickedness behind his actions.

ADDITIONAL REMEDY

If we acknowledge the involvement of spiritual wickedness, then we must also apply a spiritual remedy to the problem. As human problems warrant human answers, so too do spiritual problems warrant spiritual solutions. The spiritual remedy allows men to come into contact with their demons. The spiritual goes deeper into the confines of where wickedness dwells in the mind, heart, and soul, and performs the necessary surgery to carve out the enemy.

21: Frank and Ida Mae Hammond, *Pigs in the Parlor: A Practical Guide to Deliverance* (Kirkwood, MO: Impact Books, 1973), 23.

THE BENEFITS OF THE SPIRIT FOR EVERYONE

Look at the benefits of applying a spiritual remedy. The spiritual man can "arrest" himself when he does something wrong. The spiritual man is "convicted" by his own conscience when he misbehaves. As John 8:9 tells of the men who confronted Jesus about the woman caught in adultery: *"... they which heard it, being convicted by their own conscience, went out one by one."*[22] The spiritual person can deal with his psychological demons with and without psychiatrists, doctors, or psychologists. Minds can be healed, like the demoniac in Luke 8:35: *"Then they went out to see what was done; and came to Jesus, and found the man, out of whom the devils were departed, sitting at the feet of Jesus, clothed, and in his right mind...."*[23]

And these "arrests" and "convictions" go for crimes and also immoral and deviant behavior that is not always enforced by the law or even considered to be unlawful, such as: cheating, lying, deceiving, or hurting someone's feelings.

So those who spread the gospel and those who are saved by the gospel are to be congratulated; they contribute more to society than many would expect. A lot of people are safe in their homes, on the streets, and on the job not only because criminals have been locked up, or the mentally ill have been institutionalized, but also because demons have been cast out. God has arrested, convicted, and transformed the souls of men for a positive impact on family and community. These men have been made new through the power of God and the infusion of the Holy Spirit. No longer failures or immoral monsters, they are great in the sight of the Lord.

WHO ARE YOU TO TAKE ON THESE FORCES? YOU ARE A NEW MAN!

When one comes to Christ, he becomes a new creation: *"Therefore, if anyone is in Christ, he is a new creation; the old has gone, the new has*

22: John 8:9
23: Luke 8:35

come!"[24] The fourth chapter of the book of Ephesians, where Paul spoke to the church at Ephesus, gives an even better description for our purpose: "... *put off, concerning your former conduct, the old man which grows corrupt according to the deceitful lusts....*"[25] The old man is corrupt, vile, vicious, lying, drunken, greedy, depressed, hedonistic, and immoral in character. That is the failing man we used to be before coming to Christ. But by the grace of God through Jesus's sacrifice, we have become new creatures with new characteristics. As Paul wrote, *"But by the grace of God I am what I am...."*[26] With the new creation came a new man. You are a new M.A.N.!

THE NEW MAN

The new man represents God and fights against the forces of evil within and around the world. The new man has a new purpose: *"to be made new in the attitude of your minds."*[27] The new man is given authority to take down demons: *"Behold, I give you the authority to trample on serpents and scorpions, and over all the power of the enemy, and nothing shall by any means hurt you."*[28] The new man can walk without fear: *"Thou shalt not be afraid of the terror by night; nor the arrow that flieth by day"*[29] With the new man comes a new understanding, a new attitude, a new mind, and a new spiritual power. So there is no reason or excuse why men can't fight their demons, because they have been given the knowledge and power from God to do so—the knowledge to know that demons are behind their actions, and the power to fight against, dismiss, and eliminate those demons to regain their standing.

WE CAN'T TAKE ON THESE FORCES ALONE

The reality is that men can neither detect nor fight these evil forces alone. And relying solely on human devices and social sciences to bring us victory against the enemy will only result in calamity. These forces

---

24: 2 Corinthians 5:17 (NIV)
25: Ephesians 4:22 (NKJV)
26: 1 Corinthians 15:10
27: Ephesians 4:23 (NIV)
28: Luke 10:19 (NKJV)
29: Psalm 91:5

have been around far longer than we have existed and have taken down men much stronger than we think we are. We need an alternative; a more effective solution must be applied. An additional remedy must be prescribed, and a stronger power must be acquired. Paul told the Ephesians to be strong, but with an admonition: *"Be strong in the Lord, and in the power of his might."*[30] This caveat points to our connection with a divine power that gives us strength and power to deal with villainous authority. This is not a self-help book; this is a "God's help" book—because we can't battle nor beat demons by ourselves. We cannot succeed or win against Satan on our own. The only way we can stand firm and be strong against the rulers of darkness is to connect with the power of God. Jesus says, *"you will receive power when the Holy Spirit comes upon you."*[31] In other words we can't be strong or successful, or combat demons within and wickedness on high without God. We need the Lord's power and might if we're going to take on diabolical forces. Be strong in the Lord, not in yourself.

THEY GANG UP ON YOU

In human understanding it's as simple as this: When I was younger, I had a bunch of gang members trying to beat me up. They chased me every day. I ran from them because I knew I could not fight all of them by myself. The combined strength of those gang members is like Paul's picture of rulers, authorities, powers, and spiritual wickedness in high places—four against one. But one day I got tired of running and decided to fight. And as one might expect, I got my ass kicked.

The story's not over, though. After my beat-down I went and got my best friend and his crew, all of whom outnumbered the gang members. Plus my boys were stronger than those gang members. The other gang was strong, but the force of my crew against their power was incomparable. We beat them bad.

I'm not advocating physical violence, just using real life to illustrate what holds true in the spiritual realm: one person alone cannot

---

30: Ephesians 6:10
31: Acts 1:8 (NIV)

beat evil forces and powers, and spiritual wickedness. To think so is naïve, pompous, and laughable. To win against evil forces, we need someone bigger, better, and stronger—the Father, Son, and Holy Spirit is your best friend in a battle.

ADDRESSING DOUBTS

The Father, Son, and Holy Spirit will help men to overcome doubts and fears about their life. Some men I know might not admit it, but after having lived wretchedly for so long, they have doubts about God's ability, and even about God's desire to empower and resurrect them over their failure. They've listened to themselves and others tell them they're nothing and will never be anybody. Some men have come to the point of accepting their ill fate, believing they're never going to change. Like the apostle Thomas you may have doubts—perhaps about whether God will raise you up despite your appalling record of past deeds. Will He free you in spite of your fears and calm you in spite of your anxiety? Like Thomas you want Jesus to show you His hands and prove His power over death. The devil has won so many rounds in the boxing match in your life that it's difficult for you to believe God can completely rescue you and bring you back from the dead.

To assure you that God is much stronger than the enemy and that He desires life over death and success over failure for you, just look at the scriptures and the lives of His servants. God *"wants all men to be saved and to come to a knowledge of the truth."*[32] Also, God *"is patient with you, not wanting anyone to perish, but everyone to come to repentance."*[33]

Without God's love and power, David would not have been able to beat Goliath. Abraham would not have had the courage to step out on faith. Moses could not have led his people through the wilderness and toward the Promise Land. Joshua would not have taken over the Promised Land. Lazarus would not have gotten up out of the grave, and Peter would not have become strong and confrontational without the indwelling of the Holy Spirit. And just think about it: you would not

---

32: 1 Timothy 2:4 (NIV)
33: 2 Peter 3:9 (NIV)

have been able to read this book without God's protection on your life. If the devil was so strong, how come he didn't take you out already? The answer: because God wouldn't let him!

EVERYTHING IS PLANNED BY GOD

God has planned everything for your life. God said to Jeremiah, *"Before I formed you in the womb I knew you, before you were born I set you apart; I appointed you as a prophet to the nations."*[34] God foreknew us before we were formed and established us with gifts, talents, and abilities before we were born. That's why when abortionists say that a fetus is not a child, it's not true: God was working on the image before the fetus. The image is the rational, knowledgeable distinction that God gave to humans over animals. The Bible says we were made in his image, God's likeness, while all the animals were made after their kind (see Genesis 1:24-17). God gives His "likeness" to every child before conception. In other words God knew us before we were born and gave us a life before we were conceived. God knew our every move, fault, and fear even before we knew ourselves. God knew when we would fall and when He would pick us up. Look at Acts 9 to see the story of Saul, who became Paul. God had to knock him off of his high horse and blind him before he could see the light. However, the blindness and the light that Paul received were planned before he was born.

GOD CAN KNOCK YOU DOWN TO PICK YOU UP

Many men have lived high on the hog at one time, living a life of sin and its fleeting benefits. But when God knocks you down, He can hit you with everything from prison to sickness and beyond to make you see the light. Not every failure is from the enemy; it may be God trying to get your attention, as He did with Paul. God does not knock us down to utterly condemn us, but rather to save us. Some men have to be knocked down because they won't listen to the Word of God. Their souls are too steeped in the stubbornness and arrogance of the flesh. The only way they can hear is if God hits them with life's hardball,

---

34: Jeremiah 1:5 (NIV)

11

from disease to divorce. As a result of these divine hits, many men have found themselves cradled in the safety of God's arms, doing God's will, and succeeding in society. Only later can they see that it was all part of God's plan.

GOD CAN USE EVIL FOR HIS GOOD

God works in mysterious ways. God can use wicked rulers, powers, and principalities for His own good purposes. While the enemy uses wickedness for your demise, God can use wickedness for your resurrection. Look at how Joseph's own brothers tried to kill him, but by the grace of God, they ended up selling him instead. God then brought Joseph from the pit of prison and raised him up to lieutenant governor of the nation. His brothers then had to come to him for food and forgiveness. In Genesis 50:20, Joseph forgave them and said, *"But as for you, ye thought evil against me; but God meant it unto good...."*[35] Don't think that everything bad that has happened in your life was for your expiry. God can allow you to grow up in poverty to bring you to a path of prosperity and dignity. God can use failure for your good. Look at how evil forces compelled Judas to betray Jesus so that the Savior could be crucified, only to rise from the grave. Look how God used evil against King Saul, so that David could ultimately succeed him as king. Look how God allowed Satan to tempt Job, but didn't allow him to kill Job. Look how many men you know who have similar stories— or maybe even you personally can testify to the difficult yet ultimate success of your journey. You may have endured terrible trials and fierce persecutions, but by the grace of God, you're still here!

The power of God is stronger than the power of rulers and wickedness in high places. However, we have to be *honest* with ourselves about our sins and demons and allow God to empower us toward freedom from the enemy so we can be that greatness for Him.

35: Genesis 50:20

CHAPTER 2

STEP 2: *Integrity (The Honest Fight)*

*The man of integrity walks securely, but he who takes crooked paths
will be found out.*

Proverbs 10:9 *(NIV)*

A uthor Alan Paton has a great line in his book *Cry, the Beloved Country*. In a dialogue between a father and a son, the man asks his boy why he had committed a crime. At first the son blames his troubles on bad companions, but his father does not accept that as an answer. The boy then says it was the devil that made him do it. Then, with awesome poetic pronunciation, the father says:

Oh boy, can you not say you fought the devil, wrestled with the devil, struggled with him night and day, till the sweat poured from you and no strength was left? Can you not say that you wept for your sins, and vowed to make amends, and stood upright, and stumbled, and fell again? It would be some comfort for this tortured man, who asks you, desperately, why did you not struggle against him?[36]

Before we go any further, we must be honest with ourselves. Evil forces do indeed exist, and they are out to tempt and destroy men in every way possible: mentally, physically, governmentally, socially, spiritually, and even racially. Many men need to be honest and admit that these

---

36: Alan Paton, *Cry, the Beloved Country* (New York: Macmillan Publishing Company, 1987), 100.

forces have invaded and even controlled them for a long time. And just like the son in Paton's story, many men cannot honestly say they have put up a good fight against the devil. Many men have not struggled with the enemy or wrestled with wicked forces. As Paul clearly stated, *"For we wrestle not against flesh and blood, but against principalities, against powers, against the rulers of the darkness of this world, against spiritual wickedness in high places."*[37] However, too many men, without a struggle, have allowed the enemy to control their lives.

Step 2 for every man is *Integrity*:

He must be honest with himself about the enemy's negative impact on his life,

and he must fight to kick the enemy out.

GIVING INTO FAILURE

A lot of men fail to be honest. It's a character flaw. A lack of integrity is the greatest trap of the enemy, because the enemy knows once your integrity is gone, you're fair game for just about any trick thrown at you. When Job was being assaulted by Satan, his wife approached him and asked, *"Are you still holding on to your integrity? Curse God and die!"* But Job replied, *"Shall we accept good from God, and not trouble?"*[38] Job fought the devil and maintained his commitment to God in the midst of his adversity. Satan may have taken his family and money, but Job was determined to hold on to his integrity.

Many men have lost possessions, prestige, and power, and often desperately seek to regain authority, even if it means engaging in illegal activity. Many men will sell their soul for a dollar. The true test of a man is this: *Can you maintain your integrity, and be honest with yourself and others in the midst of affliction and temptation?*

37: Ephesians 6:12
38: Job 2:9-10 (NIV)

IT'S HARD TO BE HONEST

And I'm not going to dismiss the difficulty of trying to maintain integrity in the midst of calamity. It's hard to be honest when you're around powerful yet crooked people. It's hard to be honest when your world is falling apart and you're introduced to illegal opportunities. It is hard to stay honest when your wife has to work all kinds of hours to pay the bills and you're not bringing home a dime to help out. It's hard to stay honest when your children need food or tuition to go to school, and if you don't get it, they don't go. No man wants to feel like nothing in his own home.

A lot of people fail to realize that dishonesty is not just men being no good. Many times dishonesty has intentions connected to good deeds: stealing to pay child support, illegal betting to pay the rent, illegal hustling to put food on the table, etc.

All of this is wrong, and as stated earlier, if men only rely upon their own strength and understanding, they will find that the weight, the temptation, the demon is too much to handle alone. But this is where the fight with Satan begins: when you're tempted to do wrong but wrestle to do right. That's the honest fight. Your integrity keeps you from doing wrong and holding on to right.

Some men easily succumb to temptation rather than fight temptation in the midst of affliction. Men need the strength of God to fight temptation and keep them legal, moral, and honest. If a man doesn't remain strong in the Lord, his illegal activities not only will ruin him but the very good he is trying to accomplish, including his reputation.

REPUTATION RUINED AS MEN

The failure to be honest not only ruins our humanity and family, but our standing as well. That's why most if not all men are perceived as dishonest, unfaithful, and, to be blunt, liars. This is true whether preacher or politician, old or young, living or dying. Some men are suffering with a bad reputation as a result of other men's actions. However, most men are stained with a sordid reputation because of their own "mendacity."

(I'll talk more about embarrassment and a ruined reputation in the next chapter.) It is very important that men examine themselves so they can know exactly where dishonesty lies.

EXAMINE YOURSELF

Evil force-feeds issues into humans, and humans house poisonous forces, and forces translate into failures. We must be truthful with ourselves and take a full examination of what forces are ruining our lives. The Bible says, *"let a man examine himself."*[39] Take a minute and examine yourself. No one takes a full medical examination with all his clothes on. The same holds true for a spiritual inspection. Strip yourself naked. Take off your pride. Take off your sham. Take off your game face. Take off your front. Take off anything that we, as men, put on to impress people, to lie to ourselves, to blame others, or to cover our mess. Take it off and be honest with yourself! You can lie to other people but the worst thing you can do is lie to yourself.

As Edgar A. Guest wrote in his poem entitled "Myself":

I never can hide myself from me;

I see what others can never see;

I know what others may never know,

I never can fool myself and so,

Whatever happens I want to be

Self-respecting and conscience free.

IDENTIFY THE FORCE

If you're having a hard time with your self examination, think of those times when you've suffered the consequences of your actions, impulses, or downright stupidity. For example, look at your temper, which is a wicked force. Look at the action: domestic violence, wife abuse, and child abuse. And then look at the possible consequences of

---

39: 1 Corinthians 11:28

your action: jail and unemployment. The examination is to be a true diagnosis of the problem. See if any of the list below applies to you. If not, add one that does.

Force: Action = Consequence

Intemperance: domestic violence, abuse = arrest, divorce

Lust: pornography, infidelity = embarrassment, sexually transmitted diseases

Lying: false information on taxes = audit, penalty

Hate: mean and cruel schemes = people hating you

Thievery: stealing, robbing = can't be trusted, busted

Addiction: excessive drinking, drugs = no longer invited out by friends, loss of family

Gluttony: overeating, overindulgence = obesity, diabetes

Greed: overcharging people = lose support and friends

Stubbornness: unwilling to listen, admit fault = family and friends distance themselves

Arrogance: talking down to others = not liked by many people

Vengeance: hurting and/or killing people = imprisonment, being hurt by someone

EVIL FORCES DO NOT LEAVE EASILY

Since you are dealing with forces that are bigger and stronger than you, it may be difficult to be honest with yourself. Evil forces won't be identified and called out easily. Especially the sin of stubbornness. Stubbornness can be the worst because stubborn people can't even see their wrongdoing to identify it, and if you can't see it, how can you call it out? How can you beg forgiveness if you don't even believe you're doing wrong? You must seek God to dig deep and be honest. Being honest with yourself can be mentally and emotionally draining, so it may take a couple of days or more before you put your complete list together. I would suggest that you go somewhere alone where you can think and confess, then begin to write down those things that have ruined or could ruin your life. You must wrestle and fight with the enemy until he is identified.

LIVING A LIE

If you've been living wicked or addicted for a long time, it's ingrained in your character as a regular part of your life, like an arm or leg. Just imagine if you started on a path of drinking and deviant behavior at age seventeen and you're fifty now. Just think how much time you've had to mature in impiety. A year or two saved in Christ is not going to wash away every unrighteous thought, behavior, and attitude that you've acquired, and perhaps even cherished, over those years. Sanctification—that is, maturing in Christ—takes time. But the first thing men must do if they're sincerely interested in change is to be honest. You have to dig deep, no matter how long it takes to find the fault. Before you can fight it, you have to acknowledge it. David wrote in Psalm 32:

> I acknowledged my sin to You,
>
> And my iniquity I have not hidden.
>
> I said, "I will confess my transgressions to the LORD,"
>
> And You forgave the iniquity of my sin.[40]

GET BUSTED

And if you don't call the enemy out and confess, don't be surprised if you get busted in your mess. Many men know what it's like to get busted lying or cheating or stealing. It's a shock, especially when you thought you'd covered all your tracks. It can leave you scared and scarred when you get caught. But don't think it all bad—because being busted

---

40: Psalm 32:5 (NKJV)

means God had to pull it out since you didn't call it out. Some men don't have the guts to confess their wrongs. Other men think they can hide some stuff and hold on to some sins. NO! That's not how it works. If you want to succeed and fail no more, if you want to live a better life and be great, you have to confess and confront it all. You can't leave little demons hanging around, because they grow up and can pull you back down. Either you're going to confess it all or God's going to blow up your spot. It would have been better for you to admit it than get busted in it.

CONFESSION LEADS TO CONFRONTATION

There comes a time when men must admit that forces, authorities, and rulers have been controlling their lives. They're unseen, perhaps, yet felt. It's okay to admit it: "I have fears. I have regrets. I have pain. I have sorrow. I have secrets. I have insecurities. I have anger. I have hatred. I have arrogance." Keep going—there's plenty more.

The reason it's important to admit the presence of these forces is because true confession is the beginning of transformation and salvation. The Bible says, *"That if you confess with your mouth, 'Jesus is Lord,' and believe in your heart that God raised him from the dead, you will be saved."*[41] Confession is an honest acknowledgment of your sins before God and the beginning of transformation in your life. The good thing is that honest confession leads to confrontation with wickedness in high places, because you're literally and spiritually calling dark forces out of you. Listen to yourself: "I have fear! I have pain! I have sorrow! I have lust!" You actually started something by calling the enemy out from your mouth.

Many men remember the days when they would walk up to the person they didn't like and wanted to fight, call out his name, and say, "Let's step outside!" In the same way, you just called the devil outside by confessing.

Your confession is pushing evil forces out of your house from your mouth. The mere fact that you can speak those pejoratives that you've

---

41: Romans 10:9 (NIV)

denied in the past is a grand first step toward total transformation. The more you say it, the more you confess it. The more you confess it, the more you confront it. You're actually coming into contact with your oppressor, your failure. An "up in your mug," chest-to-chest, hands-pointing-in-your-face verbal confrontation. Look at this: In Mark 5:1-20, when Jesus approached the man who had been demon-possessed, the demons were afraid. Jesus said, *"Come out of this man,"* and the demons ran out into the pigs. Jesus called out the unclean spirits that were in the man. Your confession and honesty is calling all the unclean, unhealthy, dirty spirits out of you, and when you call the devil out, you'd better be ready to fight.

ALL TALK AND NO ACTION

You can't be all talk and no action when you call someone out. You have to be ready to pursue your initial intention. The reason for calling the enemy out is because you want the madness to stop. In this case you want the forces of destruction to stop bothering and controlling you. You want failure to end. You want to annihilate anything that's causing pain, ruining your life, hurting your family, destroying your marriage, trashing your career, or interfering with your spiritual walk with God. And now that you have the power, you can call out the enemy and take him down. Your confession is admitting the problem, and your confrontation is willingness to deal with the cause. The confrontation could be as mild as a conversation or as wild as a wrestling match. Remember, *"We wrestle not against flesh and blood, but against ... spiritual wickedness in high places."*[42] Jesus had a verbal confrontation with Satan after coming out of the desert. He was blunt and dismissive: *"Away from me, Satan!"*[43] Jesus was telling the enemy to get out of his way. Tell the enemy to get out of your way.

BE READY TO SACRIFICE

You have to be ready to sacrifice when you honestly call the enemy out. Remember, a lot of what many men possess comes from their old

---

42: Ephesians 6:12
43: Matthew 4:10 (NIV)

ways of thinking and doing during unrighteous living. The old man was full of schemes and lies, thievery and negligence, which, ironically, produced cars, homes, friends, and jobs. Truthfully the very woman you married might have come as a result of a deal with the devil (but if you are honest, you can save yourself and her). The devil told Jesus in Matthew 4:9, *"All this I will give you … if you will bow down and worship me."*[44] In your former years you worshipped the devil and he gave you all you had. The devil blesses too—for a while.

When you call the enemy out, he can get you back by taking away everything he gave you. The enemy is cruel. He can leave you naked, friendless, homeless, bored, and broke. He can leave you childless, loveless, sick, criticized, and ostracized. Calling the enemy out requires sacrifice. You must be willing to give up everything you have for the love of God. Abraham had to show his love and faithfulness to God through his willingness to sacrifice his son, as seen in Genesis 22. Abraham was willing to give up what he loved. When you are willing to give it all up for God—riches, women, friends, reputation, and even your car—then you are ready to go all the way with the battle. Christ was willing to lose his life so that we can gain life. The Savior says, *"If anyone would come after me, he must deny himself and take up his cross and follow me. For whoever wants to save his life will lose it, but whoever loses his life for me will find it."*[45] To deny yourself is to be willing to give up all that you have for God, and to believe that God will supply your every need. It may take time and it may not come when you want it, but the goal is to be willing to sacrifice to see what God has in store for your new life. If you're willing to lose it for God, you'll gain better in Christ. Although Job lost a lot, the Bible says *"the LORD made him prosperous again and gave him twice as much as he had before."*[46]

YOU CAN DO IT

As a man of God you can go beyond the rhetoric because you have power to pursue your course. Paul continuously told the Ephesians to

---

44: Matthew 4:9 (NIV)
45: Matthew 16:24-25 (NIV)
46: Job 42:10 (NIV)

be strong and stand firm in the Lord. This was a recurring theme in his letter because the total withdrawal of evil forces is a process, and you have to be strong and stand firm in the Lord through it all. You have to go through the loss and pain and everything else that may tarnish you as a result of standing against the enemy. It took strength for you to call the forces out and admit you had issues, and that those issues were causing you problems. But don't stop there. Be strong now that you've called the forces out, and be willing to go all the way. The only way to end failure in your life is to fight to the finish.

DON'T LET THE ENEMY BACK IN

The worst thing you can do is call the enemy out and then allow him to come back in. The Bible says in Matthew 12:43-45 that if you get a demon out of you and then allow it to return, it comes back seven times stronger. A stronger enemy means more guilt, shame, and pain to deal with, which can lead to permanent damage. I knew a man who told me that he was clean from drugs for three years, but then somehow fell back to addiction and lost his family and ruined his life. He felt horrible, and in order to deal with the pain of failure, loss of family, and anxiety of life, he had to stay high all the time. The dope numbed him to the pain, and the enemy came back seven times stronger.

YOU STARTED IT

You may not have realized it at the time, but you started something when you called the enemy out. Listen, when you started talking about bettering your life spiritually, improving your finances honestly, and reaching your goals indefinitely, you called the devil out. When I was in school and got into a fight, the first thing the teacher would say is, "Who started it"? Well, in this case you started it. So don't think the devil is going to just let you kick him and run. When you called the enemy out, the enemy came out to fight. The devil came out to put obstacles in your way. *Darkness* came out to put out your light. *Authorities* came out to pull you over on the road to stop you from getting to your destination. *Rulers* came out to pass laws to make it harder for you to get funding for your vision. And every ruler of darkness, power, and principality is doing what they're called to do. They have a job, and that job is to stop you from evicting them and replacing them with God's plan for your life. They want to keep you at only talking and then ultimately kill your conversation. They want you to live a life of lies, die in your failure, and go to hell for your sin. But because of the power of God, you are better than them.

FINISH THE JOB

You don't want to be a starter and not a finisher, a talker and not a fighter, a dreamer and not a creator. You may know some men like that: every time you see them they're talking about what they're going to be and how they're going to make it happen. And talk is a good start, because it shows that brothers have dreams. And it's good to call out your dreams. But the vision is not the problem; that action is. There is a process involved to get from talk to the top. Some men get frustrated by obstacles and haters. Some men get rerouted and burned by disappointments. It takes hard work to get past the talk and the hate. And that's where a lot of men give up and throw in the towel. They don't want to sacrifice the time, deal with the disappointments, and work to the end. They don't want to fight 'til sweat pours down their face and no strength is left in their body. In Genesis 32, Jacob fought through the night until the morning light, even while his hip was knocked out. Don't stop until you get your blessing!

The Bible says, *"... he who began a good work in you will carry it on to completion until the day of Christ Jesus."*[47] If God started a work in you, He desires to finish it in you. Don't stop. Go all the way. *"Be ye steadfast, unmoveable, always abounding in the work of the Lord, forasmuch as ye know that your labor is not in vain in the Lord."*[48]

THE ENEMY ISN'T PLAYING

When some men realize the enemy came out to fight, they get stuck. They start sweating and stuttering. And these are men who

---

47: Philippians 1:6 (NIV)
48: 1 Corinthians 15:58

were strong and fearless in the world, but who have come to realize this demon is nothing to play with. As long as you're on the devil's side, he'll fool you and make you believe you're invulnerable and all powerful. But as soon as you come out against him, he'll try and cut you down to shreds. The Bible says the enemy comes *"to steal, and to kill, and to destroy,"*[49] and like a gang treats a member trying to leave their gang, the enemy will rob you, kill you, and destroy you—spiritually, emotionally, and physically—before he lets you go. When some men find out the enemy isn't playing, they decide to go back to their original sin. Some get frustrated and return to their vomit because they don't have enough strength to fight the enemy. Others just get tired and leave the path of righteousness. It's a shame how many men we've lost over the years. They gave up because they just couldn't fight the good fight. They couldn't finish the race or keep the faith. They had enough mouth but not enough might. They died in their sin.

But for the men who are ready to go all the way, and the men who are willing to get up, dust themselves off, and give it another try, "Let's get ready to rumble!"

49: John 10:10

BELT OF TRUTH

CHAPTER 3

STEP 3: Security—Part 1

Stand firm then, with the belt of truth buckled around your waist....

Ephesians 6:14 (NIV)

In 1974 boxing great Muhammad Ali took part in a much-publicized match in Africa called "The Rumble in the Jungle." There he would take on George Foreman for the world heavyweight title. Ali prepared for months before the fight and his preparation paid off. He beat George Foreman to regain the title, which came with a belt that symbolized his status as the heavyweight champion of the world.

PREPARATION

Like Muhammad Ali every athlete, singer, soldier, dancer, preacher, lawyer, doctor, etc., must prepare before performing or doing battle. Paul continued in his writing to the Ephesians by telling them to *"put on the full armor of God, so that when the day of evil comes, you may be able to stand your ground, and after you have done everything, to stand."*[50] The protection that Paul admonished them to put on is spiritual armor in preparation for facing opposing forces. The spiritual armor helps men to stand their ground, so that when the enemy comes, they won't waver but be prepared for their own rumble in the jungle.

50: Ephesians 6:13 (NIV)

When God had the Israelites wander in the wilderness for forty years, He was preparing them for spiritual as well as physical warfare, so that when the day of battle came, they would be equipped to engage the enemy. He knew that once they came out of the wilderness, they would encounter temptation and enemy combatants, like Jesus did when He came out the wilderness after forty days. The enemy was standing there waiting to tempt Jesus. But Jesus stood His ground because He had prepared Himself through fasting and prayer, so when the enemy stepped up to Jesus, he got beat like an old drum.

Men, since you called the enemy out, he's waiting for you to engage him, so when the day of battle comes, you want to be able to stand your ground and fight the good fight. But before you go out there, you want to be spiritually covered and prepared for the conflict. The armor of God prepares you for the fight of your life.

LET'S GET DRESSED

You can't fight the enemy without the necessary armor. In order to become a Man of Armor, you have to dress for the occasion. The reason you got undressed was to strip yourself of the old self and put on the new armor. The armor prevents the stuff you called out from getting back in, and gives you power to fight and destroy the stuff that is ruining your life. All through the Bible, whenever men went out to battle, they would get ready by putting on their armor. Jeremiah 46:3-4 states: *"Prepare your shields, both large and small, and march out for the battle! Harness the horses, mount the steeds! Take your positions with helmets on! Polish your spears, put on your armor!"*[51]

The armor that Jeremiah describes is made up of actual garments. The soldiers literally put on their articles of clothing for battle. It is good for us to have actual armor to protect ourselves when we go into battle. It is good for the purposes of distinction, representation, and presentation. How you present yourself says a lot about who you are as a man. Many men fail to present themselves properly on the outside in what and how they wear their clothes. How a man presents himself is not only good

---

51: Jeremiah 46:3-4 (NIV)

for his image but also the image of God. We are made in the image of God,[52] and how we look on the outside is a representation of God on the inside. Men ought to take pride in their physical appearance, from clothes to shoes to grooming and even how one smells. The old saying goes, "Cleanliness is next to godliness."

SPIRITUAL OVER PHYSICAL BATTLE

However, since we wrestle not against flesh and blood but against spiritual wickedness in high places, we're dealing with a spiritual battle, so we must emphasize the spiritual apparel as most important. We don't want to walk around with a fresh suit, clean underwear, and nice haircut, but have a dirty spirit. That's like a good-looking car with no engine; you're not going anywhere, and to think you are is only fooling yourself. The spiritual puts substance behind the actual, giving it power and identity. In 1 Samuel 17, when David fought Goliath, he showed us the power of the Spirit without the clothing. When King Saul tried to put physical armor on David, the young shepherd refused it and instead went out with his slingshot, a bag of rocks, and the anointing of God. He was able to defeat Goliath because of his anointing, not his clothing. It's not the suit that makes the man of God; it's the man of God that makes the suit.

THE ARMOR

In the book of Ephesians, Paul described the armor as an amalgamation of metaphorical military layers and spiritual principles. The description of the military layers was taken from ancient Roman troops' dress code during battle. Each covering was designed for a different purpose and a different part of the body. All components worked as one to protect the soldier and to engage the enemy. In the case of Paul's list of armor, there are seven pieces of protection that cover a believer from head to toe. God has designed the full armor for men who are serious about protecting not only their genitals, but their lust (1. belt of truth); not only their chests, but their hearts (2. breastplate of

---

52: Genesis 1:27

righteousness); not only their feet, but their direction (3. feet fitted with gospel of peace); not only their outbursts, but their temper (4. shield of faith); not only their heads, but their minds (5. helmet of salvation); not only their words, but their intentions (6. sword of the Spirit); not only their talk with friends, but their conversation with God (7. prayer).

THE BELT OF TRUTH

After Ali beat Foreman, he was given a belt to symbolize his victory as the heavyweight champion of the world. Upon our transformation as a new creation, God gives us a belt to engage the heavyweight champion of the wicked world. Although there is no sequential way to put on the armor, I'm glad Paul began with the belt of truth as the first form of protection: *"Stand firm then, with the belt of truth buckled around your waist...."*[53]

Roman troops wore short-sleeve woolen tunics that came to the mid-thigh and were fastened at the waist with a belt. In cold weather Roman soldiers wore leather trousers that reached just below the knee, secured by a belt. The belt also carried weapons for battle. The belt secured and kept everything in place. If the belt fell down, everything else would fall apart and put the soldier's life at risk. If we were to make this plain, it would simply say, "Once your pants fall down, your life can fall apart, too." The fall, in this case, is a spiritual plunge as a result of a sexual encounter.

Step 3 for every man is *Security*:

He must secure himself with the truth of God for the safety and protection of his life.

THE GREAT LOSS OVER A LOOSE BELT

Once the enemy gets you to loosen your belt, he's broken through your security. It's sad because many men lose family, jobs, and freedom,

---

53: Ephesians 6:14 (NIV)

all because of a loose belt. I am reminded of Samson in the book of Judges (chapters 13-16). He went to Gaza, and the Bible says he saw a prostitute and slept with her. His enemies got word that he was there and came for him. Although Samson escaped, he almost got killed over a booty call.

Many of our own men nearly lose their physical and spiritual lives over sex, whether it's with a prostitute or a woman on the side. The enemy is always watching for a time to catch men with their pants down. Like Samson, men have to be especially careful where they drop their pants. A moment of pleasure could result in a lifetime of embarrassment. Many men have lost their families over a one-night fling, and many more have ruined their reputation and brought humiliation to their family by soliciting prostitutes. A loose belt can easily take you from gratification to the grave.

EVERY WOMAN THAT LOOKS GOOD ISN'T GOOD

I guess that's why this is called the "belt of truth," because the truth of the matter is that everything that looks good isn't good. Men are so eager and indiscriminate for sex that they get caught with anyone that looks good. There are a lot of beautiful women out there. They may even walk around with a Bible and talk with a sweet voice. They may make you feel like "the man" by fulfilling your needs, building your esteem, and giving you the pleasure of your life. But truth be told, there are a lot of women out there who are pretty, but very venomous—beautiful, yet deceitful, and they won't hesitate to give you a disease that they know they have. I know many men who have been burned through a sexually transmitted disease, and thank God a pill could take care of it. Others are not so lucky because certain sexually transmitted diseases can be treated but not cured. Syphilis and herpes in its wildest stages can cause grief and anguish and disrupt an active sex life. Evil forces have gotten stronger over the centuries, resulting in incurable diseases like HIV/AIDS.

If you have a sexually transmitted disease, you want to refrain or be very cautious (using condoms) with those whom you get sexually involved with. You don't want to be malicious and as venomous as the person who gave it to you. You want to be truthful with those whom you get sexually involved with and tighten your belt so that you do not do to others what someone did to you. The golden rule in the Bible is to *"do to others what you would have them do to you,"*[54] not do to others what evil has done to you. With the belt of truth securely wrapped around you, your job is to get rid of lies and diseases, not spread them.

EVERY WOMAN THAT LOOKS GOOD ISN'T A WOMAN

The truth is, men get fooled into illicit relationships that can harm them for life. Young (read: *underage*) girls are fooling and intentionally beguiling older men. Educated, reputable, religious men are getting caught out there by young girls posing as older women. A lot of young girls are street savvy and mature, and they know what a lot of men want from women. Many young girls use their looks and their body for financial gain. And many men are excited, and even enamored, by the proposition. They believe they're "the man" because they have a young girl on their arm.

But the girl could be younger than you think. I need not remind men about the law on these matters. Even if you don't know and the girl tells you she is older than she really is, the courts will still hold you responsible for your actions. You could be charged with having sex with a minor; such a conviction can carry five to ten years in prison in some states. Before you loosen your belt, you have to do all you can to find out the age of the woman you sleep with, or else it could result in your ultimate imprisonment. Some of you are shaking right now. Good! The truth is scary. If fear can prevent you from dropping your pants and loosening your belt, then so be it.

GROWN MEN AND YOUNG WOMEN

Even if the young girl is of age, let's say you're forty-four and married, and she's twenty-one and impressionable. Young girls can develop deadly obsessions that can impact you and your family. I knew a man who told me that he could not stop this young girl from calling

---

54: Matthew 7:12 (NIV)

his phone. She became obsessed, following him, showing up at his job, and threatening to tell his wife. He finally had to admit the relationship to his wife. He ultimately confronted the girl, and he and his wife got a divorce. He hasn't been the same since.

CHEATING

Think of all the other calamities that can come with cheating. Young girls and older women not only can become obsessed but can threaten and commit suicide over their "love" for you. Do you really want to be responsible in any way for someone else's death?

They not only can be suicidal, but homicidal. I'm sure you've heard of women hurting or even killing the man they think they love, or hurting or killing the wife, children, and other family members to get back at the man. Do you really want to be responsible for someone in your family getting hurt because of your foolish engagements? Again, think of all the financial expenses that come along with trying to keep up with one or more women. It gets real costly, especially during the holidays. I often think about Solomon in these matters. In 1 Kings 11:3, the Bible says he had seven hundred wives and three hundred concubines.

How in the world do you get gifts for all those women without going broke? Most men find it financially difficult to keep up with one woman. Do you really want to take money from your family's mouth, your savings, and your business ventures to feed your womanizing? Lust can leave you broke. And in many cases, when the money is gone, the women are gone.

THE CONSEQUENCES OF CHEATING: CHILDREN OUT OF WEDLOCK

The worst case of hurt that can come with cheating is having children out of wedlock. This hurt can be devastating to the wife and the other children. And even if a man regrets and feels the guilt and shame that come with his sexual indiscretion, it's nothing compared to the hurt and pain done to the wife who has to endure the agony of a man's sexual mistake. You really don't know how much hurt and tears a person has to live with as a result of something you did by having a child with another woman while you were in a relationship.

It's the same type of hurt and anger many men feel when they find out that the child they've supported and loved for so many years is not theirs. What disappointment and hurt erupts in the relationship! No man wants to have this devastation come into his life. If it does, or if it did, remember in both situations that it's not the child's fault and that they shouldn't have to suffer the consequences of other people's mistakes. The child should never feel unwanted. Every child is a gift from God regardless of how they were conceived. Any hurt that occurs in the relationship as a result of a loose belt must be worked out between the husband and wife, or the man and woman who disrupted the relationship.

This, and more, can happen when the enemy breaks through your security and you drop your pants in the wrong place.

MEN GET INTRODUCED TO OTHER BEHAVIORS

Dropping your pants and loosening your belt can get you into behavior that you never thought possible. Every woman who looks like a woman isn't a female. There are men out there who profess to love women and women only, but are being introduced to other activities because of lust to fulfill their sexual desires. And when the devil gets you, he can get you into all types of behavior that will satisfy your sexual urges. And many a man who once had no interest in another man, and even found such actions vulgar and detestable, has been seduced into a lifestyle that he once abhorred. The devil is shrewd.

Some may say homosexuality was already in such a man. But what was already in him was lust, and lust played into other outlets of pleasure and promiscuity. Some people start out with marijuana and get lured into other forms of drugs. The underlying demonic appetite for substances was there and led to stronger drugs. Men can go from minimal pleasure to major problems because the devil is turning up the heat. The enemy will hook you with one pleasure to reel you in for other detestable behaviors. When you loosen your belt, you open yourself up to the strong forces of the enemy and it can take you on a whirlwind. *Lust is a powerful force from the enemy, and if you don't call it out, it will ruin you physically, mentally, and socially.*

MEN HAVE BEEN VIOLATED

As we speak about what is already in men, we can't ignore the fact that men get introduced to certain behaviors at a young age, and it can leave them spiraling out of control for the rest of their lives. Many young boys are violated by their religious leaders, coaches, uncles, older brothers/sisters, mothers, and even strangers. Read the accounts of gospel singer Donnie McClurkin, who admits to being raped by his uncle. The experience scarred him into certain behaviors for a long time. Chris Gardner, who rose from poverty and abuse to multimillionaire stockbroker, shared in his book, *The Pursuit of Happyness,* about being raped by a male stranger.[55] Even boxing great Sugar Ray Leonard admits to being consistently molested sexually by men in his teenage years.

One of the horrific counseling experiences that I had as a pastor happened with a young man in his thirties. He was suffering from a past of being raped and molested by his uncle. He felt hurt and confused. His biggest question was, "Why did he do this to me?" He hated his uncle because his own sex life was now out of control. He couldn't keep a relationship and was too afraid to reveal his past to any of his girlfriends. He even went so far as to take violent actions against gays and child molesters, and it was tearing him apart. Many men who have been violated suffer a great loss. Their belt of innocence and truth was ripped off of them at an early age; sexual promiscuity got in them and drove them practically insane.

If this describes you, you must seek counseling immediately. God would not want you to hold it in and hurt anyone. It only makes your situation worse, and ultimately hurts you more than anybody else. Please seek help and free yourself.

55: Chris Gardner, *The Pursuit of Happyness* (New York: Amistad, 2006), 101.

DECEPTION AND THE "DOWN LOW" MAN

Male violations, along with other coerced sexual infiltrations, can lead to dishonest relationships. Many men are married to a woman but also sexually involved with men. This "down low" behavior is not only detestable, but deceptive. It shows a great character flaw of lying and cheating, but most of all deceiving. To continue in this practice is to allow Satan to use you rather than to come out of you. God wants everyone to be free, so to live in duplicity is to mislead others and disgrace God—not to mention hurt your own happiness. There has to be a confession, a serious confrontation toward freedom. Sugar Ray Leonard admitted in his book how over the years telling half the truth of his sexual molestation haunted him. However, he found out that to be free from past demons, he needed to tell the whole truth no matter how much it hurt.[56] You must get help and tell the whole truth if you are suffering from past sexual violations.

HOMOSEXUALITY

And just as heterosexual men must take responsibility in freeing themselves from sexual promiscuity and other forms of sexual immorality, so too must homosexual men take responsibility and free themselves from living in silence, lies, and fear about their true identity. Gay people who live in silence, lies, and fear because of social and ecclesiastical expectations of masculinity are doing themselves and others a disservice. Lying about being gay not only hurts the person who is gay, but also those who are fooled by believing the gay person is heterosexual. The belt of truth helps men to live the truth and be free in who they are, and to come into contact with any demons that might hinder them from becoming the person that God wants them to be.

FREEDOM AND THE GAY MAN

Many gay men are looking to free themselves from a pseudo-homosexual lifestyle. This is especially true for those who have been

---

56: Sugar Ray Leonard, *The Big Fight: My Life In and Out of the Ring* (New York: Viking, 2011), 38.

violated or manipulated into the gay life. As we stated, some men have been violated at an early age, which led them into out-of-control heterosexual and homosexual behavior. As an impulse of God's Spirit many gay men are looking to free themselves from the victimization of their past and the homosexual lifestyle of their present. And they should feel free to pursue their course of deliverance without being scorned by the gay community, or the gay community reviling those who suggest that gays can be delivered and set free from homosexuality. If a person is living a gay lifestyle as a result of something that happened to them early or later in life, and they're struggling with themselves and with their lifestyle, then they are not truly a part of the gay community; they're living by trauma rather than by truth. And trauma is open to deliverance, and truth can set the person free from past or even present indiscretions and violations. *"Ye shall know the truth, and the truth shall make you free."*[57]

THE ENEMY MUST GO

If you have been a victim of past sexual molestation, you have to call out the enemy and his lies. God knows it will be tough, but you can't hide behind shame and guilt, and harm yourself and others over past indiscretions. It was not your fault that someone violated you, but it is your responsibility to use the power of God to call out the enemy and free yourself from the physical and emotional harm that is keeping you bound and making you dangerous to yourself and others. It will take time and serious counseling and prayer sessions to get the enemy out, but it must be done. Every morning you must remind yourself that lies must go and truth must prevail. Every time you fall, you must acknowledge it and seek ways to prevent falling again. You must secure your belt, declare your cleanliness and deliverance, and use the belt of truth to fight the enemy. The truth will set you free. If not, you will continue to indulge in sickening behavior, to hurt others, and to suffer the consequences of your evil actions. Go back to Step 2 and start calling the enemy out: "Lust, get out. Lies, get out. Hurts, molestation,

---

57: John 8:32

get out!" And then put on the belt of truth to secure yourself against the enemy.

THE TRUTH WILL BE REVEALED

The belt of truth allows us to carry the truth everywhere we go. The truth deals with reality, prevention, and protection. One thing we can say about Jesus is that He knew the truth. When the enemy came to Him in the desert and promised Him the world, the Savior rejected it outwardly and uncompromisingly: *"the devil took him to a very high mountain and showed him all the kingdoms of the world and their splendor. 'All this I will give you,' he said, 'if you will bow down and worship me."* Jesus quickly and unabashedly said, *"Away from me, Satan!"*[58] Jesus knew the truth. He knew that Satan would give Him the world, but with an attachment of fatal consequences.

When you have the belt of truth, it protects you from lies and secrets, because the belt does not come off until the truth is revealed. It waits and assesses the matter before it engages sexually with anyone. *Truth does not come in one night, especially one-night stands. Truth comes over time.* Men, you want to be absolutely sure where you put your stuff, and you want to use it with the discretion and wisdom that God has given you. If a woman is not clean and has a heart of vengeance, the belt of truth will reveal that to you, because the belt won't come off until the truth is revealed. If she's married and hiding it, the belt of truth will reveal that to you, because the belt won't come off until the truth is told. If she's not a woman but a young girl, the belt of truth will reveal that to you, because the pants won't come down until the truth is known. If she looks like a woman on the outside but is not underneath the clothes, then the buckle won't loosen until the truth is revealed. Keep in mind that whatever the situation, God will expose the truth; you just have to keep your belt secured until the truth is revealed. Don't be so quick to jump into bed or accuse anyone. Allow time to pass and the truth to grow.

58: Matthew 4:8-10

CHAPTER 4

STEP 3: Security—Part 2

THE CONSEQUENCES OF A LOOSE BELT

We often talk about the woman with the issue of blood from the New Testament, but we hardly ever talk about a man with an issue of semen. The book of Leviticus states: *"When any man has a bodily discharge, the discharge is unclean. Whether it continues flowing from his body or is blocked, it will make him unclean."*[59] It further says that anything the man touches becomes unclean, from his bed to his pot. And whoever touches him becomes unclean. As mentioned, and as warrants mentioning again, a man's loose belt can bring disease home to his wife or girlfriend. Then she has to get tested, and if both of them don't get tested, the man and woman can continue to re-infect, or infect others—all because of what one man started.

A bodily discharge is not only dangerous to your relationship, but also to your health. I need not remind men that after any illicit sexual encounter, they should go and get checked. Even if no discharge is present, there can still be an asymptomatic infection. Often men simply choose not to deal with uncomfortable issues, especially those that are health related. But to not check is to spread infection to others and to further infect yourself. And further sexual infections can lead

---

59: Leviticus 15:2-3 (NIV)

to everything from nerve damage and impotence to liver and kidney disease, along with blindness.

MENTAL ANGUISH

As a result of dishonest sexual encounters, mental anguish and jealousy can set in. Just think, even if you don't have a disease or didn't get a woman pregnant, the thought of the consequences can make you paranoid and ruin your mind. In Leviticus 26, God told the Israelites what would happen if they disobeyed him: *"the sound of a windblown leaf will put them to flight. They will run as though fleeing from the sword, and they will fall, even though no one is pursuing them."*[60] Proverbs 28 repeats the sentiment: *"The wicked man flees though no one pursues...."*[61] God promises to inflict fear and paranoia as a result of their falling to temptation. This is the feeling that comes over many men when they have to wait a whole week or hours to find out the results of an HIV/AIDS test. Not that they have it, but the fear and paranoia of thinking that they may have it are enough to make any man go crazy. It's the same as an old girlfriend or casual sexual encounter coming back after all those years to claim child support or claim you sexually violated her. Many men today are still worried and paranoid over something they did twenty years ago. They live with a constant undercurrent of fear and anxiety.

Wearing the belt of truth keeps men secured from disease, paranoia, and jealousy. What should matter overall, regardless of what others are doing, is how *you* are living. Are you living truthfully in spite of your past transgressions? If you're living truthfully, then you won't have to be jealous or paranoid about what someone else is doing, because if someone is doing you wrong, God will reveal the truth. And if you've done someone wrong then the truth will be revealed to you and when the truth is revealed to you it will help you live honestly so you don't repeat those mistakes.

60: Leviticus 26:36 (NIV)
61: Proverbs 28:1 (NIV)

THE BELT AND HONESTY

The belt of truth is not only armor that reveals other people's faults, but it also keeps you honest as a man. The armor helps you to be strong, just as Jesus was during His time of temptation. As a man you must feel comfortable being truthful and admitting that you're married. When you say it, remember, you're calling the devil of lies and deception out of you. Be truthful by admitting, "I'm married!" Be proud to say it. And after you say it, the truth will not only hit them, but also remind you of your vow. That wedding ring you wear symbolizes a bond, a promise between you and your wife.

Many a man has taken off his ring or doesn't bother to wear it. Wearing your wedding ring, even if you are having problems in your marriage, is an outward symbol of your marriage covenant with God and with your wife. Some people need a constant reminder of that covenant. The ring becomes a belt of truth around the finger to remind men of their promise, commitment, and responsibility. So keep the ring on—or put it back on!

THE BELT KEEPS YOU STRONG

Let's be truthful. Some people are undeterred by a declaration of "I'm married," or the presence of a wedding ring, especially if you're a man of status. Once you declare your marital status and the pursuit continues, you have to take further action: *"Away from me, Satan!"* When you wear the belt of truth, you won't stutter when you talk, or trip when you run, because the belt keeps your pants up. Many men don't want to hurt a woman's feelings, so they continue to put up with the pursuit. Other men may even be flattered by it, so they don't take a stand.

But there comes a time when you have to set the record straight and be firm. Your meekness shouldn't be your weakness. You have to take charge of the situation. While you're worrying about hurting her feelings, a woman can ruin your marriage and family. There may be one day you're not as strong as you should be, and her advances may lure you into compromising your vows or your job or your reputation. You have to shut it down. Be strong, stand firm, and end the advances.

The worst thing you can do is reveal that you're married and still fall into the devil's trap. And I'm sure you already know, some women don't care if you're married; they just want to know if you're serious. In fact some women will admit that they prefer to date married men—and think about it: If she has no conscience when it comes to dating a married man, what kind of scruples do you think she will have when it comes time for doing you in? And some men say they're married just to see how women react—if they care or if they don't care. Admitting that you're married but not living up to its standards tells women that you're honest yet open to indiscretion.

Satan loves a hypocrite—and a challenge. He will tempt and make you believe you have the indiscretion under control, and then trap you and reel you into serious consequences. Don't be a fool! You know better now. You must be strong and stand firm upon your commitment. The belt of truth helps you to be honest and truthful, and 100 percent protected against temptation, disease, baby-momma drama, psychological anguish, obsession, and prison.

TRUTH AS YOUR GUIDE

If you're not married, you also must allow the belt of truth to be your guide. No woman is a sex object. Within society our reputation as men is messed up. Our culture of male dominance has fed us the lie that we can harass, take advantage and demean women sexually. We are no longer perceived as being truthful and respectful. We risk our health, happiness, and home over dishonesty and promiscuity. As a M.A.N. we can change all of that. Jesus gave us a great example in John 4:1-42. When the woman at the well met Jesus, He asked her for a cup of water. But she dismissed him as a Jew or just another man trying to get with her. She had a horrific past but probably still looked good. She could get a man but couldn't keep one. Jesus revealed that she'd had five husbands and now was living with a boyfriend, so clearly she had no trouble getting a man. But she couldn't keep a man and stay happy. Her desperation for the water that Jesus was offering showed her soul was empty no matter how many men she'd had.

MEN DON'T DEGRADE WOMEN

A lot of women today are just like the woman at the well. They look good and can get a man, but just can't keep a man. They go in and out of relationships, becoming more warped and damaged after each experience. As a M.A.N. you can wear the belt of truth and deal with women with honesty and integrity so that you don't inflict further damage on those women who already have been bruised and battered by other men. Women should not be used for your sexual entertainment, like strippers, or for your sexual pleasure, like prostitutes. Don't take out your sexual frustration, hunger for power, need for pleasure, or sexual addiction on vulnerable and damaged women. You are further damaging the damaged and will be held accountable not only for their fall, but also for your failure to help them rather than disgrace them. There is no power in damaging the weak. Only weak people seek to destroy other weak people. With power from God your job is to use your strength to resist temptation and strengthen the damaged.

A DIFFERENT LANGUAGE AND INTENT

As men we must learn to have clean, unadulterated conversations with women so that they can see a different man. We don't want to be just another one of their vile and oppressive relationships. Many women, like the woman at the well, are hurt, in need of attention, used, abused, and lonely. They will take any comfort they can get. Jesus spoke a different language to the woman at the well, and with a different intent. His goal wasn't to give her a drink to get her drunk so He could take advantage of her body. He wanted to give her living water that gave her life and a new understanding. As men with the belt of truth, we can speak life into women who are damaged and hurting. We can help them think differently about themselves and about us as men. We don't want to give them a drink so we can get them drunk and abuse their bodies. You have to watch your drinking because drinking can make you do things that you wouldn't normally do if you were sober. Many men filled with intoxication touch woman and make advances at woman without their permission. Need I remind you that sexual harassment charges are real and they could damage the woman and hurt you years later. Be careful drinking and touching women without their permission. Don't touch women without their permission even if you're sober it's disrespectful and degrading and can definitely come back to haunt you.

Just think what would happen if these women encountered a M.A.N. who rejected their sexual offers and advancements. What if you said, "Sister, I'm not trying to get with you like that. I'm just having a good conversation"? What if you said, "I'm not that kind of guy. I respect women more than just for pleasure"? You would blow her mind! You would confuse her understanding! And you didn't say it because she was unattractive or because you're not into women; you said it because you were truthful, you wore the truth, you were the truth, and you told the truth!

Now she can run home with a different perspective of men, because of you. She can run and tell all her girlfriends, "I met a different kind of man the other night." Just like the woman at the well when she left Jesus and told all her friends, she can say, "Come see a man who told me all about myself." Man, you told her all about herself when you confronted her notion that all men are dogs and dishonest. You told her all about herself when you refused to be another one of her sexual conquests or oppressors. You told her all about herself when you gave her worth beyond her body and value beyond her sexuality. As a M.A.N. you're a valuable commodity, because women are looking for men who are different. You just improved the social reputation of men. You succeeded in bringing down Satan's stronghold. God bless you! You killed two demons with one belt. You are THE M.A.N.!

ESPECIALLY IF SHE'S MARRIED

There are some women you should not touch physically, for moral and spiritual reasons. Plainly speaking, stay away from married women! It's offensive to the union and to your future. Some married women out there are going through a phase of darkness. They can be good women in a bad situation. They could be depressed or in midlife crisis, and need friendship rather than a sexual encounter. Joseph knew that he should not touch his boss's wife, no matter how much she threw herself at him (see Genesis 39). It's bad enough getting involved with a married woman, but getting involved with a woman who is married to a man you know is just downright low, detestable, and punishable by death. Many men have died at the hands of other men for their conniving behavior. You could send a good man to jail by messing with his woman. The Bible says, *"You shall not covet your neighbor's wife...."*[62] Stay away from married women or another man's woman!

If you are a real man, you can be a friend by encouraging her and reminding her that she's married, rather than becoming sexually involved with her. After she gets past her phase, she'll be grateful that some Lord-abiding Man of Armor stopped her from making a big mistake. The purpose of the belt of truth is not only to secure you, but also to protect those you come into contact with. Keeping your belt tight will keep you in control and her in respect.

IF YOU DON'T LOVE HER, DON'T DO IT

Here's a question for you men who have a girlfriend you've been dating for a while: If you don't truly feel like she's the one, why get sexually involved or continue to stay physically connected? Why waste her time or your future if you don't feel she is the one? Why loosen your belt if you don't see yourself with her for the rest of your life? When you're a young man in your twenties and early thirties, it's understandable (yet not acceptable) to be confused, play with someone's emotions, and even allow your sexual appetite to get the best of you. But as you get older, there is no need to waste your time, play games, or waste someone else's time with your indecisions and lack of maturity. You have to make up your mind as to whether you want to be in the relationship or not. *You have to be for real, truthful, and good to yourself and the other person. You're not a boy. You're a man who has to make a decision.*

A lot of men know that the woman they're dating is not "the one" but linger in the relationship and end up having a child with her. Even if he didn't plan to have her in his future, now she's there for the rest of his life. Loosening your belt with a woman you don't love or can't

---

62: Exodus 20:17 (NKJV)

commit to can lead to a laundry list of problems, accidents, and hurts for either or both of you. Men often try to play the role of a man of steel, but men get hurt too. (We'll talk about that in the next chapter.) So before you loosen your belt, be truthful with her and yourself. Is she worth it to you?

You don't want to play with a woman's heart by making her believe something that you're not. If you're not in love with her, be a man and say it. She might be hurt, she might be sad, but she'll be worse if she pours all of herself into you and then finds that you're not pouring the same amount of emotions in her. And need I remind you that what you do to others will come back to you.

YOU ARE HURTING HER AND THE CHILDREN

Many men not only hurt the woman when they play games, but if she has children, they're also hurting her children. At a young age children are being introduced to different men in their mother's life, and when the man leaves, he not only hurts the mother but her children as well. So if you're playing games with her heart, you're actually inflicting pain on the whole family. Until you feel like you're serious about the woman you're involved with, you should stay away from her children. Stay away from sleeping at her house. Stay away from dinner at the table and conversations and social interactions with any of her family: mother, father, sisters, brothers, cousins, cat, and dog. If you're not serious, keep your distance, because if you're not true with her, you're not only lying to her but her whole family.

I remember my mother dating a man who seemed nice. He would play with me and my brothers and sister, and take us out. A few months later he was gone. Children don't know the deal between a mother and the man she's dating. The only thing they know is what looks good—and then the disappointment when the good is gone. Although single mothers need to take control and protect their children from their relationships, most men can take charge of their interaction with the family until they're sure about the extent of the relationship with the woman, because men know the truth of their own heart.

And men ought to examine a woman before he brings her around his family, friends, or church. It should not be to show her off as eye candy, or to make others believe you have someone significant in your life. Any woman who meets your family or enters your house should be a serious consideration from the heart of a long-term relationship. Tighten your pants and either wait to meet the children, or, if you're serious about her and love her, then marry her.

WHY NOT MARRY HER?

If she is the one, if she is worth it to you, if you love her, why not marry her? Why not make her your wife? Why not start a family? I know so many men who have been in a relationship for years. They have children with a woman, they proclaim to love her, but they still won't marry her. And no doubt many people have a bad outlook on marriage as a result of what they've seen from other married couples. The sacredness of marriage has been defiled and tarnished, and it is up to God-loving people to bring the reverence back to marriage. Many men think that marriage changes a relationship from one of love to one of bondage. But you must understand marriage as God has sanctioned it: marriage is a spiritual bond between a man and a woman based on love and oneness of soul. *"'This is now bone of my bones and flesh of my flesh.' ... They shall become one flesh."*[63]

Marriage is a happy medium, not an oppressive one. Marriage gives glory to God and allows the two to live in holy matrimony based upon a sacred bond. It allows witnesses, those who are watching the union, to believe that God is love and in the business of uniting His people for life together. One thing I often say when I am performing wedding ceremonies is, "You two inspire other people to know that God is still in the business of bringing couples together in holy matrimony who love each other." I say this because many people want love but have given up on it because either they can't find it, don't believe it, or have been hurt by it. But when couples come together as a result of what God has done, it also inspires others to believe that God, who is the author

---

63: Genesis 2:23

of love, can work in their lives as well. Just like God's salvation can have an impact on others when people come to Christ, so too can God's love when couples come together in holy matrimony. If you love her, secure her by marrying her.

MARRIAGE: NOT FOR EVERYONE

And I'm not pushing that marriage is for everyone. Jesus was not married. Paul was not married, and a host of other godly men never were. It is not necessarily true that God will bring someone into your life for marriage to be possible. God may have other plans for some men that do not include marriage. We cannot be so presumptuous to believe that we know the mind of God for everyone's life. If God has not sanctioned marriage or children for some men, then that ought to be respected.

And some men know they are not ready for marriage and should not fool themselves or others by cursing a holy act. A false act will only result in a ruined relationship which adds to the divorce rate. If you know you are not ready, don't do it. Don't do it because of children. Don't do it to please others. Don't do it for religious or traditional reasons. Some people think because they are living together, they should be married. No! If you are living together, you should be in love, and love should lead to marriage. Examine yourself and see if you are ready for marriage and all the sacrifices that come with it; no one is saying you have to be perfect but you should have a heart that feels perfectly connected to the woman you're with. If God has brought someone into your life and you honest-to-goodness love her, she completes you and you complete her, why not show your love in marriage? Why not give up all others and give yourself totally to her? Why not secure her in marriage with the belt of truth and holy matrimony wrapped around both of you? The saddest man is one who has a good woman he loves and then loses her. After that it's hard to find a good woman again.

CHAPTER 5

STEP 3: *Security—Part 3*

THE BELT WILL CONTROL YOUR SEXUAL URGES

The belt of truth will help men to be strong in the Lord and not give into their sexual urges. Some men, admittedly, have strong sex drives and will use any opportunity to find relief, including constant masturbation. This is the truth: this form of autoeroticism, self-stimulation, is not only unhealthy, but unspiritual. It is a form of weakness, selfishness, and lack of self-control. When young men engage in this type of behavior, it's almost excusable. But when a man continues with such behavior into his thirties and forties or later, it's a problem. Over time such self-induced pleasure can lead to nerve damage, psychosis, and impotence. As you get older, you only have so much strength left in your body, and to waste it on yourself or the bathtub is a disservice and displeasure to the woman you're with or the woman God has for you.

SEX ADDICTION

The belt of truth is a pleasure-saver and self-controller. It helps us to fight against the temptation of the flesh. The flesh desires constant pleasure, but the Spirit of truth demands self-control. Urges are not necessarily going to go away, but men must learn to control their urges, suppress their cravings, and not give into their impulses. Urges are a form of temptation, and you must fight temptation. If you find that you are addicted to sex and can't control yourself, you must seek counseling. You must talk to someone about your urges and find other outlets to reduce the impulse.

Try these simple steps to help with sex addiction:

1. Exercise (such as running, weightlifting, etc.) will help the body relieve and strengthen itself in other areas.

2. Meditation will help strengthen and focus the mind.

3. Bible reading and prayer will help keep your mind and soul on God.

4. Social interaction and spiritual conversation will help you engage with people to do something more creative with your time.

SEX IS GOOD

The truth is, sex is good. It's a blessing from God. You should not be ashamed or upset if you want it and love to have sex five and six times a week. All through the Bible you find sex occurring, and God uses it for the purpose of procreation as well as enjoyment. Some people think just because you're saved that you will no longer want and love sex. NO! God didn't give you the urge or the feeling for nothing. The sex drive doesn't stop when you come to Christ, but the sex direction, discretion, and understanding should change. Your urges should be directed at the one you love, the person God gave you.

Therefore sex is not only sex but lovemaking when done with the woman you love. When you make love with the woman you love, sex isn't reckless. Making love with someone other than the person God gave you is like parking your car in a lot that's not yours. You can get hurt like that. You can get killed like that. You want to love and make love to the one God gave you. You want to satisfy yourself, relieve yourself, and engage yourself as often as you feel, without excuse, with the fullness of potency and passion with the one that God blessed you with. There is nothing wrong with loving sex, but there is everything wrong with having sex with everyone and anyone. Don't be ashamed! Sex is good, and you should want it with the one you love.

SEXUAL FRUSTRATION

I understand that many men can become sexually frustrated because their wife doesn't share their level of intimacy. I've spoken to many men who desire more sexual activity from their woman, only to be rejected over and over again. When men don't get sex consistently, they can feel insulted, frustrated, suspicious, unloved, and unattractive. And sexual frustration can easily lead to sexual temptation.

In addition most men get frustrated because they're always initiating the intimacy, even on their own birthday. Men would love to wake up to their woman kissing them or on top of them, because it shows the woman is in love with her man physically as well as spiritually. But sometimes a woman can put up boundaries in bed: going to sleep with her clothes on, or, as one man put it, his wife putting her knees up between him and her to let him know she's not interested. And the lack of sexual activity can go on for weeks, especially if the woman is upset or has her menstrual cycle, leaving the man sorely deprived.

THE CONSEQUENCE OF A SEXLESS RELATIONSHIP

The lack of sexual activity between a husband and wife can lead to cheating, lusting, constant masturbation, and other deviant and ungodly behavior, not to mention a growing gulf in communication and loving feelings toward each other. Many don't realize how powerful and important lovemaking is between a husband and wife. It is more than sexual. It is a spiritual bonding that unites the social, emotional, and psychological togetherness and development of a couple. To not make love for a considerable amount of time is to lose connection in other areas of the marriage. That's why God said husband and wife shall become one flesh,[64] because they are to be together and stay together in everything, from the sexual to the social. Just as couples make time for eating, it is just as important to make time for lovemaking. The belt of

---

64: Genesis 2:24

truth wraps around them securely and buckles tightly so that they do not lose intimate connection with each other. The longer couples stay apart from lovemaking, they'll also begin to feel comfortable staying apart in raising their children, paying the bills, communicating and living together. This is not God's plan.

This is where men have to tighten their belt real hard. Communication about your dissatisfaction, mixed with self-control, is the best way to handle the situation. You have to talk to your wife, let her know that you want and even need to be with her more than once a week. At the same time remain committed and encourage ways to increase intimacy. You may be frustrated, but arguing, shouting, insulting, and, worse, cheating will do nothing to improve relations. Those things will only prolong the lack of intimacy—from once a week to once a month or year. Seek loving ways through talk and, if really frustrated—because some men can become that frustrated—seek counseling. Some women may not tell you the reason for their lack of interest in sexual intimacy, but they will tell it to someone else, such as a physician or counselor. Women have sexual issues too, ranging from weariness and vaginal dryness to physical changes and emotional distrust of you. And only through communication can you find any of this out.

SEPARATED AND DEALING WITH ANOTHER WOMAN IS WRONG

Let me pause here to elaborate on a serious malevolence that negatively affects the spiritual and ethical life of the marriage community. Many men are finding themselves separated from their wife, and emotionally and physically involved with another woman, as if the other woman is their wife. They're living with them, taking trips with them, and even supporting them financially. This is a serious dilemma that must be addressed for the sake of freeing the man, the wife, and the other woman from both spiritual and moral decay.

Married men are often used to living in a loving and caring relationship, and to the surprise of many, most men would rather be in a committed relationship than to run around with a bunch of women who care nothing about them and whom they care nothing about. Men who are separated and find a woman who replaces their wife feel equally satisfied as if they were married to the new woman. The separated-but-equal union fulfills their desire to be in a committed relationship. Many of these affairs are not initially intentional. However, they evolve into serious and temporarily satisfying relationships that somehow get out of control and turn into what is essentially a natural engagement.

Men, if you are seriously involved with a woman while you are separated from your wife, it is not only wrong, but it is also shameful. *It is wretched! And as a man you must take full responsibility to end the affair*. Really! No matter how in love you are with the other woman or how much she is in love with you, you must end it. It is not a spiritually or morally healthy relationship. There is no way that you, your wife, or the mistress can truly be happy. If you think you are, then you are only fooling yourself and eventually someone is going to get hurt (if they haven't already). Once God comes into your life, you will not only desire to free yourself from hypocritical nonsense, but also free from unethical bondage the woman you are involved with and the wife you took your vows with.

How can you be happy when you can't freely or truly bring the woman you're involved with around family or friends because it would be shameful if you did, knowing that you are still married? You can't take her out without watching over your shoulder, fearing someone will recognize you or her. You can't truly be happy knowing you're treating a woman like dirt rather than a diamond. You may be too selfish to realize some of this, or maybe you don't even care. Well, if you don't care about yourself, then think about her. Do you really think a woman is happy being a mistress—the "other woman" in your life? Do you really think a woman is happy being involved with a married man? Of course not! She may tolerate it and hope for the best to come out of it. She may smile and laugh and cook and clean and do all the things a loving woman would do under the circumstances, but how long do you think that will last? How long do you think she's going to put up with it? Don't you think she will eventually come to her senses and realize that this is wrong and not a genuine relationship for a couple? Don't you think she will eventually wake up and demand more because she believes she's worth more than the crumbs off your plate? Don't you think she has scruples to understand the sacredness of marriage and that being with a married man is wrong?

Man, listen, I know this is hard because many of you have found some really good women that are putting up with your situation, but you have to take care of your business. One thing every man must learn to do is take care of his business, and business starts at home. You need to deal with your wife. You need to find out where you two stand and what the future holds, and if you two can't figure it out, you need to get counseling. If counseling doesn't work and you two are no longer in love with each other, then you must take the necessary steps toward divorce. You can't stay separated forever and be involved with other women in the midst of it, because it will only waste their time and hurt their feelings. Some of you men have no intentions of getting a divorce, and you are manipulating and deceiving women into staying with you. This is wicked. May I remind you, "What comes around goes around," or as the Bible alludes to in Galatians 6:7, "You reap what you sow."

I've known married men who have taken up with women and thought everything was great, only to find out the woman has decided to move on, sometimes with another man. This can leave a man devastated and struck with everything from anxiety to heart attack. Don't think that evil won't sneak up on you if you keep doing wrong to others. If you don't have any intentions of getting a divorce, or can't get one for whatever reason, then free the woman you're dating until you can deal with your situation. No matter how much you love the other woman or she loves you, she doesn't deserve to be trapped in a relationship that has no future promise for her.

And if you decide to get a divorce from your wife, don't do it for the other woman. Get a divorce for you. You need to take care of your business for you to move on freely, for you to decide whether or not you want to be in another relationship, and for you to examine yourself and see what went wrong so you don't make the same mistakes. Don't get forced or threatened or manipulated or trapped into divorce, because it will only result in your unhappiness. You have to pray and be sure it is

God who leads you in the direction to fully remove yourself from the vows you made to your wife, and if so, you should break away for your spiritual betterment. I've seen many men get divorced and discontinue the relationship with the other woman they were dating because they realized it was wrong to be involved in the first place. Man, do the right thing!

CHAPTER 6

STEP 3: *Security—Part 4*

COOKING, CLEANING, AND CHILDREARING

The lack in relationships is not only in sexual intimacy, but because of a changing social and cultural environment, the lack could also be in other areas of the home. No longer can many men expect to come home to a home-cooked meal, a clean house, or a stay-at-home mom. Women are working outside the home and inside the home just as much as men these days, and the demand on couples to be flexible becomes essential in a relationship. So men must be prepared to cook, clean, and do their part in raising the children. This can be difficult and frustrating for some men, because a lot of men are not familiar or knowledgeable in these areas. Some men even feel that this is solely a women's responsibility, but men must be well equipped in all areas, whether at home or at war. Men must be prepared to go beyond the traditional understanding and gender expectations to do what must be done to assure civility and tranquility in the family and survival for themselves. Just as women had to learn to do certain jobs that men traditionally did, men must learn to do certain jobs that women once traditionally did.

If a man cannot cook, he either must take his family to eat out or learn how to cook. Consider that Esau was both hunter and housekeeper. In Genesis 27:2-4, Esau's father asked him to hunt wild game and then prepare it for him. So Esau knew how to hunt for food and also how to cook it.

Men even have to learn to wash and iron their own clothes, or take it to the cleaners. And men must learn to take time with the children (more on that later).

You're not losing masculinity in all of this; instead you're expanding your role and responsibility, as well as your capability and independence to be a man unlimited by tradition and social expectation. You're proving the Bible verse that says, *"I can do all things through Christ which strengtheneth me."*[65] "I can do all things" means a man is not limited to working outside the home, but also working inside the home and in areas once thought off-limits to a man, such as cooking, cleaning, and childrearing. A man's role can be expanded to include any area to show God's will and purpose for his life—from the kitchen to the kids' room.

SINGLE FATHERS

This is especially true with the escalation in single fathers. If fathers are going to raise their children properly, they must learn to work in all areas of the home for the correct upbringing of the children. It's an emotion to love your children; it's a lesson to raise your children. And if you love your children, you're going to have to learn how to raise them. It's a tough job raising children as a single man, but if you have that responsibility, you must learn how to be a good parent, which means: sacrificing time to play, learning how to speak to them, assuring their safety, monitoring their manners, visiting their schools, taking time for homework, and making sure they eat healthy and dress decently.

And as stated earlier, just as you shouldn't go around another woman's children if you're not serious about her, you shouldn't bring women around your children if you're not serious about the woman. You must secure your belt and raise your children. When a man expands his role, he not only proves his skill and shows his openness and independence, but he's actually improving the reputation of males.

65: Philippians 4:13

IMPROVING THE MALE REPUTATION

The tighter the belt, the stronger the man. If you live the truth, it will help not only you as a man, but over time it will also help improve the reputation of all men. The courts are looking at statistics to see how well men are doing when they get custody of their child. If more men do well, it will open the doors for other men to have custody of their children—not only because they have money, but because there is evidence that men can raise children properly, safely, and lovingly. Our ratings are down right now, though. It's like a credit score, and the more you clean it up, the better your interest rates. We want to clean up our credibility with ourselves and with others. Once we clean up ourselves, our social image and our "interest" will improve.

THE BELT OF TRUTH PREVENTS EMBARRASSMENT

Finally let's deal with embarrassment. Wearing the belt of truth securely around your waist is a step in the right direction. It will prevent you from getting into behavior that can bring gross embarrassment to you and to those whom you love. I remember when the late Marion Barry—former mayor of Washington, DC—was caught smoking crack with a woman. The media took notice and exploited the crack use, but he admitted to sex as his problem. His lack of protection around his waist led to his fall from grace. The evil sequence was inevitable: lust led to sex, sex led to women, and women led to crack—and it all led to his downfall. Wickedness in high places sounded the cymbals.

If you keep the belt of truth wrapped around you securely, it will stop you from getting into risky behavior that can embarrass you and leave you publicly disgraced. Fortunately for Marion Barry, God allowed him another chance to get himself together and wrap the belt of truth around himself. But it took more than the belt of truth to keep him. And it's going to take more than the belt of truth to keep us. We need the whole armor of God.

Points to Remember from Step 3

Part 1

1. Step 3 for every man is *Security*: He must secure himself with the truth of God for the safety and protection of his life.

2. The belt of truth secures you from sexual temptation and urges that can ruin your life.

3. Cheating can cause great problems in your life, including: sexual diseases, suicide, homicide, prison, and having children out of wedlock.

4. Allow the truth to lead your relationship.

5. Remember, everything that looks good isn't good.

6. Every woman that looks like a woman is not a woman.

7. If you are a gay male, then live the truth. Don't lie and deceive people about your sexual preference, because it will not only hurt you but also the people who believe in you.

8. If you've been sexually violated, you must seek counseling immediately.

9. The belt will protect you from lies and secrets, because the belt will not come off until the truth is revealed.

Part 2

10. If you are involved sexually with more than one person, you must check your health constantly and encourage the person(s) you are dealing with to do the same.

11. If you are married, don't be afraid to admit it. Keep the ring on as a reminder of your vows to her and to God.

12. Make sure your conversations are pure and truthful. Don't use women for your sexual entertainment and pleasure (such as strippers and prostitutes).

13. Do not touch women without their permission, it is harassment.

14. Do not get involved with married women. It is morally and spiritually wrong.

15. If she's not the one, why get sexually and personally involved? You will end up hurting her, and her children as well if she's a mom.

16. If she is the one, why not marry her? Why not show your love with honesty and holy matrimony?

Part 3

17. Don't allow sexual frustration in your relationship to lead you to sexual temptation. It will only cause more problems. Seek counseling.

18. If you are married but separated and involved with another woman, you must end the affair immediately. You must take care of your business at home before you get involved with another woman. It is wrong and shameful for you to be involved with someone while still married.

19. Loving sex is not bad; having sex indiscriminately is. Stick with the woman God gave you to make love to.

Part 4

20. Cooking, cleaning, and childrearing make you an even better man.

21. If you are a single father, make the best of it.

22. The truth will keep you and your family from a ruined reputation and embarrassment. Do all you can to keep a good reputation. At the end of the day it's all you have.

THE BREASTPLATE OF RIGHTEOUSNESS

CHAPTER 7

STEP 4: Community—Part 1

... and having on the breastplate of righteousness ...
Ephesians 6:14

Ask the majority of men about the political, social, and cultural issues of the day, and I guarantee you they have an opinion on it. Whether highly informed or highly suspect, right or wrong, conservative or liberal, they're unhesitant about expressing their views on current events. Men discuss people like George Washington and Donald Trump to Abraham Lincoln and Barack Obama. Men discuss issues of capitalism, racism, militarism, crime, war, rap and rock music. Men have an affinity for political and cultural issues. Even though a considerable number of men watch sports channels, they constitute an overwhelmingly large segment of viewers on news networks like CNN, MSNBC, and Fox News. On the job, at the barbershop, in church, or at a backyard cookout, you can find men engaged in spirited, opinionated discussions on controversial issues.

MEN AND POLITICAL ISSUES

A Pew Research Publication in 2008[66] noted that women consistently expressed more interest in stories about weather, health

---

66: Pew Research Center Publications, "Where Men and Women Differ in Following the News," February 6, 2008. http://pewresearch.org/pubs/722/men-women-follow-news.

and safety, natural disasters, and tabloid news. However, according to the study, men are more interested in stories about international affairs, Washington news, science and technology, business and finance, and sports. Men are so serious and biologically connected to politics that a recent scientific study determined that men who voted for a candidate that lost found a decrease in their testosterone levels: "The testosterone effect was as if they directly engaged head to head in a contest for dominance and lost. Whereas men whose candidate won fared better. The researchers speculated that there might be a baby boom. Women had no change in testosterone levels, regardless of whom they voted for."[67]

Men also were more likely to get their news from radio talk shows, which increased the number of men who call into talk shows. As we know, the most in-depth coverage of Washington news and issues of international affairs takes place on Sunday mornings. This could be a partial explanation why more women than men attend church each Sunday. Although many churches are skeptical and even reluctant to discuss politics from the pulpit, it probably would help bring more men to church if issues related to politics and social justice were incorporated into sermons and church events. Men have long been leaders in political activism, running for office, and leading high-profile social justice movements. That's why when people say that politics and religion don't mix, I ask them what Bible they're reading. Kings and kingdoms can't be established without God, and justice can't run down as waters and righteousness as a mighty stream if God doesn't permit it. After all, the biblical references to political and social justice movements are undeniable.

MOSES, JESUS, AND SOCIAL JUSTICE

Moses confronting the pharaoh is a famous biblical reference that many social justice activists and religious movements have mimicked in philosophy as well as in strategy. The most prominent were Harriet Tubman, Gandhi, and Rev. Dr. Martin Luther King Jr. Furthermore,

---

67: Sunday Review, *The New York Times,* October 7, 2012.

David is probably Israel's best-known king, and his kingdom ushered in a theocracy for the unification of Israel. God anointed his throne—which was established by war, political dominance, and kingdom-building. There are others—namely Joseph, Ezra, Nehemiah, and all twelve tribes of Israel—who confronted everything from oppression to the census to urban development. Jesus Himself sought to establish God's kingdom on earth. His proclamation in Luke is one of spirit and power: *"The spirit of the Lord is on me, because he has anointed me to preach good news to the poor. He has sent me to proclaim freedom for the prisoners and recovery of sight for the blind, to release the oppressed."*[68]

And there is no doubt that the Spirit of the Lord upon Jesus is the same Spirit of the Lord upon God's people to fight against the *"principalities," "powers," "rulers of darkness,"* and *"spiritual wickedness in high places"* that keep people bound and poor, brokenhearted, segregated, marginalized, captive, blind, and oppressed. Forces of evil can inhabit and influence government institutions and private corporations to hurt and harm people rather than help and free them. Satan took Jesus up the mountain and had Him look over all the land that encompassed both governmental institutions and private corporations, and said, *"All this I will give you … if you will bow down and worship me."*[69] Jesus rejected Satan's offer, but it showed that Satan had power and influence over the land and could put people in powerful positions to carry out his plans and policies of oppression, greed, and injustice.

GOVERNMENTS AND OPPRESSION

Government institutions have passed laws over the years that have been harmful to human progress. Racist and sexist laws that enslaved black people and belittled women in American history are shameful. The impact that those laws still have on many black people and women today cannot be ignored by God's people. After the Israelite enslavement by the Egyptians, they suffered emotional, psychological, social, and economic damage for many centuries. But God continued to fight with

---

68: Luke 4:18
69: Matthew 4:9 (NIV)

them and for them to assure their exit out of bondage and entrance into the Promised Land.

RACISM

Many try to deny and ignore the evil impact of racism and discrimination and their detrimental and dehumanizing effects, particularly on the dignity of black men. Many black men are denied job opportunities and promotions, targeted by police officers, deprived of justice by the court system, and disproportionately make up the prison population simply because of their skin color. As James Baldwin wrote in a letter to his nephew in his book *The Fire Next Time*:

> You were born where you were born and faced the future that you faced because you were black and for no other reason. The limits of your ambition were, thus, expected to be set forever. You were born into a society which spelled out with brutal clarity, and in as many ways as possible, that you were a worthless human being. You were not expected to aspire to excellence: you were expected to make peace with mediocrity.[70]

Undoubtedly wicked systems have worked to undermine and devalue black men. Failure in many men's lives is not only due to their own unrighteous actions, but also an evil, racist, and unjust system. The evil influence upon government institutions, police departments, and educational institutions that deny the rights of people—of any color, gender, or sexual persuasion—is wrong and has resulted in the loss of dignity, family instability, educational inequality, economic inequity, and housing and health-care inadequacy. And just because there has been a black president does not mean that racism has ended. Racism is an evil, persistent force that survives even in times of black progress.

The recognition of evil's influence upon government institutions and private corporations should prompt God's people to take the

---

70: James Baldwin, *The Fire Next Time* (New York: Vintage, 1993), 7.

necessary action to confront Satan for the purpose of political, social, and economic justice. God's people should not allow Satan to divide them and have races fighting each other. Rather God's children of all walks of life, colors, and creeds should recognize the enemy's divide-and-conquer strategy, and unite to beat back the true enemy that influences negative policy in society. You don't have to be black to fight against racism; you don't have to be a woman to fight against sexism; you don't have to be poor to fight against poverty. However, you do have to be God-fearing to fight against injustice, oppression, and greed. *God-fearing* means that you're willing to do what's right to please God regardless of human consequences. This is a fight for all of God's children to join in to assure that the whole of God's human creation is neither rejected nor denied opportunity, freedom, civil or human rights, dignity, or stability in any part of the world. The world is God's community, and injustice disturbs God's territory. As Rev. Dr. Martin Luther King Jr. stated, "Injustice anywhere is a threat to justice everywhere."[71]

GOD'S POLITICS TO TEAR DOWN PRINCIPALITIES

Even America in its quest for freedom from its motherland Britain used religion to justify its escape and independence. During the writing of the Declaration of Independence by Thomas Jefferson, John Adams requested the insertion of, "They are endowed by their Creator with certain unalienable Rights...."[72] The insertion was to be written right after "all men are created equal."

Further, many of the founders of America equated their struggle for freedom and from oppression with Moses leading the children of Israel out of Egypt. As Bruce Feiler wrote:

The echo of the Exodus language widely used in America at the time is haunting. The committee's report, submitted to Congress

---

71: "Letter from a Birmingham Jail [King, Jr.]," Dr. Martin Luther King Jr., African Studies Center, University of Pennsylvania, accessed Oct. 6, 2017, https://www.africa.upenn. edu/Articles_Gen/Letter_Birmingham.html.
72: Toby Mac and Michael Tait, *Under God* (Minneapolis: Bethany House, 2004), 16.

on August 20, 1776, offers vivid, behind-the-scenes evidence that the founders of the United States viewed themselves as acting in the image of Moses. Three of the five drafters of the Declaration of Independence and three of the defining faces of the Revolution—Franklin, Jefferson, and Adams—proposed that Moses be the face of the United States of America. In their eyes, Moses was America's true founding father.[73]

The United States was founded upon biblical characters and righteous principles of justice and freedom for all people—principles that have been at odds with the elite forces of social injustice and economic inequality. Jim Wallis reminds us in his book, *God's Politics*:

When the poor are defended on moral or religious grounds, it is ... a direct response to the overwhelming focus on the poor in the scriptures, which claim they are regularly neglected, exploited and oppressed by wealthy elites, political rulers and indifferent affluent populations.[74]

CLASSISM

Classism is another struggle that evil powers and wicked rulers have influenced to separate people based on money—those "who have" and those who "have not." Those who have are often the ones who acquire more in terms of wealth and power in society. They build up wealth generation after generation, influence economic policy in their favor, sometimes with little remorse for those who have not. They fight against increasing the minimum wage, they fight for lower taxes for corporations, and they fight to increase their wealth at the expense of the poor. And many who are wealthy will give charitably but not sacrificially

---

73: Bruce Feiler, *America's Prophet: Moses and the American Story* (New York: William Morrow, 2009), 67.

74: Jim Wallis, *God's Politics: Why the Right Gets It Wrong and the Left Doesn't Get It* (New York: HarperCollins, 2005), 5.

(to give charitably is to give based on need, while to give sacrificially is to be willing to give up everything for the needy).

Those who have not are often the poor and middle class who constantly struggle to make ends meet. They struggle to pay rent/ mortgage, feed their children, get good health care, house their families, and keep a good-paying job with benefits. These struggles go on for generations. Social mobility—the ability for every generation to rise higher than the last—is often stifled because of the lack of social policies and economic opportunities to help open doors for the poor, seniors, disabled, and middle class. Instead of social mobility, we have social disability, where those who are seeking higher ground are crippled and blocked by unfair and corrupt policies. They are the unemployed and underemployed. They are black and white, brown and yellow and red, Asian, South American, African, European, and Islanders. They are Christian, Jew, Muslim, and Buddhist, amongst others. They are heterosexual, bisexual, and homosexual. The gap in wealth continues to divide people, leaving the rich richer and poor poorer.

This is not to suggest that the rich are by default evil—because both Abraham and David were rich, and Jesus made friends with rich people. It is rather to suggest that Satan uses the system to build up riches and separate people based on their financial ability and inability, which causes war between the classes and conflict in society, and keeps people in conflict against each other rather than working with each other. The consequences of poverty and inopportunity because of an unjust and evil system are obvious.

More poor people are incarcerated and go to jail longer because of incompetent representation. More poor people are uneducated because of low-performing schools. More poor people die from their accidents and diseases because of inadequate health care, doctors, and hospitals. How can God's people be silent during other people's suffering and call themselves Christians? This is Jesus's proclamation to *"preach good news to the poor,"* because their condition needs to be confronted with those who seek to keep them in bondage.

THE BREASTPLATE OF RIGHTEOUSNESS

Let's go back and take a closer look at Moses. This reluctant leader was fighting against Pharaoh to free the children of Israel from an enslaving nation. But more profoundly Moses was fighting against a hard-hearted "ruler" who was dead-set on keeping the Israelites in oppression. Egypt was an example of principalities and wickedness in high places being let loose through a ruler's hard heart. God needed Moses to not only take on the person of Pharaoh, but also the rulers and powers in high places. In other words the whole empire was evil. While Pharaoh's heart was hardened with forces of wickedness, Moses's heart was strengthened through the breastplate of righteousness.

Paul wrote to the church at Ephesus about another piece of needed armor: *"the breastplate of righteousness."*[75] Righteousness is simply doing what's right and just in the Lord's sight. God says, *"Be holy, because I am holy."*[76] The breastplate covers the chest area, and its principal mission is to promote justice and righteousness from the heart. It calls one to social, political, and communal action.

Step 4 for every man is *Community*:

He is to spread righteousness and fight against injustice

for the sake of God's people and property.

The community is the whole of God's earth and everything in it, from its tall trees to its high mountains. It is broken down continentally, nationally, and locally, and filled with people of all different races, cultures, and languages. Every living person on earth is God's creation. God created us all in His image. The breastplate ushers us into the path of righteousness to work on issues on earth for a more beloved community. The heart is protected by the breastplate to prevent any obstruction from disturbing the mission. Without the breastplate of righteousness acts of

---

75: Ephesians 6:14
76: 1 Peter 1:16

defilement can attack the heart, disturb the emotions, and ultimately stop the mission of justice. This is seen in many of our biblical leaders whose hearts were interrupted by the enemy. Samson and David are two glaring examples. Both were divinely appointed leaders with missions to do God's will and guide God's people. Samson was consecrated from birth as a judge over God's people. David was called *"a man after [God's] own heart."*[77] But both allowed their hearts to be infiltrated with the enemy's schemes, which interrupted the communal mission and desecrated the appointed leaders.

JUSTICE IS AN OBLIGATION

In the Old Testament, Israel understood justice and righteousness as closely associated. Both are aspects of the character of God: *"But the LORD of Hosts is exalted by justice, and the Holy God shows himself holy by righteousness,"*[78] and, *"I am the Lord; I act with steadfast love, justice, and righteousness in the earth, for in these things I delight."*[79] The combination of justice and righteousness is one that fuels itself. One feeds off the other. We serve a righteous God who is just. Justice is ushered in by the righteous acts of God. That same righteousness is transferred to humanity so that we may lead justice to victory. Therefore justice is not an option, but rather an inherited heavenly obligation passed down from generation to generation so that all people may live a blessed and wholesome life.

And it must be understood that God is not limited or restricted in who He chooses to speak His word and promote His justice to the world. God can use a preacher or a rapper, a prisoner or a pauper, a woman or a child to do His will.

JUSTICE AS SPIRITUAL CALLING

Justice is not only political involvement but also a spiritual calling. Jesus said, *"The Spirit of the Lord is on me."* The spiritual calling directs the political and social action. When people come to Christ, they are

---

77: Acts 13:22
78: Isaiah 5:16 (NRSV)
79: Jeremiah 9:24 (NRSV)

compelled with the anointing to seek justice for the captives, the poor, and the prisoners; recovery of sight for the blind; and freedom for the oppressed.[80] And the calling comes with a protective covering so that we can carry out the mission without interruption. That covering is the breastplate of righteousness. The breastplate of righteousness gives us a heart for justice. The heart is where justice emanates, and that justice flows throughout the body to take action on behalf of God and the downtrodden.

VOLUNTEER YOUR TIME

A heart of justice will demand a clean community. Many communities are tarnished and broken, with everything from youth violence to senior abuse. Every M.A.N. should find a place where he can give his time and service to cleaning up his community. It is good when the community is protected by people who live and work together in the neighborhood. Young men need to see and learn from good men who work in their community, clean their streets, and patrol their neighborhoods against crime. And you don't have to live in the neighborhood to help a broken neighborhood. Every M.A.N. should find a place he can volunteer his time and talents, whether he lives there or not. To be a volunteer means you're not looking for money; you're looking for change. And in order for change to happen, you have to give freely and humbly of your time, talents, and money to organizations that are making a difference. One of the great commandments in the Bible is, *"love thy neighbour as thyself."*[81] To love your neighbor is to be willing to do something for your neighborhood. What good is it to love your neighbor and watch your neighborhood fall apart?

I've been involved in many community projects. One of my greatest projects was getting pedestrian crossing lights on busy street corners. Prior to the crossing lights, residents crossing the street would have to look at the oncoming cars to determine when they should cross. But when we put the crossing lights up, they were able to look at the signs

---

80: Luke 4:18 (NIV)
81: Leviticus 19:18

that read "stop" and "go" (although they should still look both ways before they cross). This was particularly good for our youth and seniors who were often confused as to when to cross the street.

In many neighborhoods you can find hospitals that need volunteers, nursing homes that need help, youth centers that need coaches, and neighborhood block associations that need financial backing. And if you can't find any that you like, then get together with like-minded people who are committed to uplifting your community and create your own organization. And if you're not fond of organizations or find it difficult to work with people, then go solo and use your creativity, talents, and resources to help someone. You don't have to be part of an organization to help someone learn how to read, or to assist an elderly person on a trip to the grocery store, or to pray for someone in the hospital.

Helping someone not only does something for them, but it also does something for you. It gives you a sense of "somebodiness" in the community and at home. The best honor you can add to your eulogy is when someone says that you helped someone while you were alive. I get the greatest joy when I know I have helped someone, inspired a hopeless soul, or encouraged someone on the brink of giving up. It just feels good.

CIVIC DUTY

And we must remember our civic duty to vote. Many have been turned off by politicians and their false promises. The number of people involved in politics has decreased over the years, and it is understandable, although not acceptable. Believe it or not, there is spiritual power in voting and influencing policy. God sent Moses the prophet to Pharaoh the government head to influence policy that would free the Israelites. Ezra and Nehemiah worked with the kings of their time to build the temple and the walls of Jerusalem.

Voting is absolutely necessary to influence policy, especially on a local level. So the first thing you must do is make sure you are registered to vote and get out to actually vote when elections are held.

Second, you should encourage others to vote. Voting picks up momentum and steam when voters encourage non-voters to vote.

Third, one must organize others around a particular issue connected to a particular candidate. Many people look at national politics as if that's the only level of government. But truth be told, politics is local. Local politics, issues, and candidates have a direct impact on your daily life, and you have easier access to local candidates and elected officials than you do to national ones.

Fourth, many serious issues exist for us today: drugs, crime, high taxes, low wages, housing, etc. Connect those issues to a candidate who will speak on your behalf. Then get involved heavily in the election to assure the candidate succeeds. Once the candidate is elected, stay involved to assure the policies are passed and the neighborhood is improved. If the candidate fails to deliver after some time, then seek another candidate for the purpose of pushing the community agenda.

Do all you can to get involved and change the world one community at a time.

CHAPTER 8

STEP 4: *Community—Part 2*

DICHOTOMY

In order to be consistent, whether in public or private, we have to enlist the support of a higher power. People are skeptical of preachers, politicians, and community leaders because of their duplicitous nature—preaching one thing and doing another. And this is not to suggest that community leaders, elected officials, and preachers are not highly concerned about their constituency and the fight for justice. Many will give their lives and careers for the issues and people. But their private lives can be controversial and corrupt, which means an additional strength and power is necessary to promote consistency in public and private. David was highly concerned with justice for the Israelites. In public he fought valiantly for the nation. He took down foes, and was respected and applauded by his people. But in his private life he fell for Bathsheba, the wife of one of his soldiers. His fall resulted in pain and strife in his public and family life, as seen in 2 Samuel 11–12.

DON'T LIVE A CONTRADICTION

For the sake of the community it's important that you don't live a contradiction in your life. God condemns the hypocrite. Many men come home from work and take out their anger from the job on those closest to them. They can be calm and collected with others, but at home they are abusive, intemperate, and distanced. Many men come home but bring their work with them, never knowing when to stop work and start family (we'll talk more about that in another chapter). When you put on the breastplate of righteousness, you arm yourself against any unholy and unrighteous act that may cause a dichotomy in your life. A dichotomy is simply a contradiction between your walk and talk. Righteousness seeks to mend the differences and eliminate the contradictions. You do not want to be a great basketball coach at school, then a pedophile on the Internet at home, do you? You only ruin your life, not to mention the hopes and dreams of those students who believed in you—not to mention your own family members who thought the world of you. All because you couldn't get your private urges under control. That's why it is important to call out the enemy to free your heart from anything that hinders your future progress and reputation.

EXAMINATION OF THE HEART

Men, we have to deal with ourselves before we can go out into the battlefield and rescue anyone else. It may be time for another self examination. Some jobs require a medical examination at least twice a year. The military is one of them. For this self examination, specifically check your heart. The heart is a vital organ for all other bodily functions. If the heart is not right or not possessing righteousness, then your mission will be unacceptable and false, and have an ultimate death. If your heart is not beating righteous, not only is something wrong with your mission but also your motives. The Bible says, *"For out of the heart proceed evil thoughts, murders, adulteries, fornications, thefts, false witness, blasphemies: These are the things which defile a man."*[82] Is there anything in your heart that is defiling or corrupting you, or holding you down? If so, begin to call it out now: "Lies, get out! Hate, get out! Deceit, get out! Lust, get out! Arrogance, get out! Revenge, get out! Stubbornness, get out! Selfishness, get out!" Then ask God, *"Create in me a clean heart, O God; and renew a right spirit within me."*[83]

82: Matthew 15:19-20
83: Psalm 51:10

The prayer is a cleansing to rid you of anything that has been defiling and polluting your soul. Asking God to create a clean heart in you is to acknowledge you have a dirty and corrupt heart that needs cleansing for a decent and dignified life. The new heart comes with the new man. It's all part of the package. Once you ask God to cleanse your heart, put on the breastplate of righteousness quick! You called the demons out, but if you don't secure yourself, the enemy will come right back in. And remember, if the enemy comes back in, it comes back even stronger. The breastplate of righteousness is a lock that protects the heart and preserves the mission.

YOU JUST HAD A "HEART ATTACK"

By calling the enemy out, you just had a "heart attack." You have attacked any kind of defilement in the heart that's causing you to perform ungodly acts. To attack the heart with righteousness is to use the strength of God to resist temptation. As we see in Judges 13–16, Samson was a Nazirite and therefore called to be in righteous standing with God and man. He was born with the strength to carry out justice as a judge on behalf of the Israelites. He was physically strong but emotionally weak. He fell in love with the wrong woman, Delilah, and she betrayed him. He loved her so much that he allowed her to fool him over and over again. Samson let his guard down, and the enemy was able to get past his breastplate and into his heart, and it weakened his body, wounded his spirit, and delayed justice.

The heart can become corrupted easily if the breastplate is not secured. Samson allowed Delilah to get to his heart and abduct justice. And when the breastplate comes off, the enemy comes in and snatches our strength. Just as he did with Samson, God has called men to be strong in the Lord and the power of His might, and to not allow anyone to take away the strength that God has given us for the sake of justice. As stated, and warrants repeating, it is no wonder why the enemy wants to strip men of their strength, because it is in direct conflict with the plans of principalities, powers, and rulers who want to obstruct progress and derail justice. Evil forces desire to use governmental institutions, corporate entities, and worldly leaders to encourage communal chaos, human oppression, war, military occupation, racism, sexism, materialism, drugs, proliferation of guns, human trafficking, inequality, and heathenism. But God desires to fill men with strength and power to overturn the wickedness of the world, give opportunity to the forgotten and promote justice for the oppressed.

If you do not attack the heart with righteousness, the enemy will corrupt it with wickedness and kill all attempts at justice. The aggrieved forces direct their aim at men of God to weaken their bodies, disrupt their spirits, trouble their hearts, and take away their mission. But when you have a heart attack, your strength is increased, your spirit is renewed, and your mission is clear.

THE WOUNDED MAN

Righteousness is not only a way to promote social reform but also a way to address personal pain. Divorce has reached epidemic proportions for men in America and other Western countries. With divorce comes depression. A 2007 Statistics Canada study showed that men were six times more likely to report experiencing an episode of depression after divorce, compared to women, who were three times more likely to report an episode of depression after divorce.[84]

Men do themselves an injustice when they dismiss or ignore their hurt and pain. Although many women love to monopolize all claims to relational hurt and pain, a lot of wounded men exist in the world. Men don't like to admit it and society likes to ignore it, but like Samson, men hurt, men cry, men get emotionally scarred, and men get used and abused, just like women. Many men put their hearts into a relationship only to find out that the woman is not in love with them or doesn't want to continue the relationship. This can hurt a man—real bad, especially if the woman is in love with someone else, or if she is cheating or has the man's children taken away.

A hurt man is a lifeless man, a man who has lost all direction and power. He feels weak and alone. Sorrow covers his countenance and

---

84: "Marital Breakdown and Subsequent Depression," Statistics Canada, May 5, 2007, www.statcan.gc.ca. (Page no longer available.)

darkness inhabits his character, and his mission for community, family, and himself is halted. He can't get up for work. He can't envision new ideas or pay his bills or handle his career and even his sex life is put on hold. When a healthy man can't have sex or can't keep an erection, something is seriously wrong in his life. He needs help.

A wounded man needs the breastplate of righteousness to re-ignite his passion, for love and for life.

CREATE IN ME A CLEAN HEART

Let's revisit Psalm 51:10, which says, *"Create in me a clean heart, O God; and renew a right spirit within me."* After being wounded, the heart is in need of a serious repair as a result of rejection. Cleansing of hurt from the heart will take time; it's not easy to get over someone you love. So give the breastplate time to clean out all you're feeling. The guilt, the shame, the blame, all of it takes time. Healing is a process. Don't try to rush it by sleeping around or getting involved in another relationship. This can result in even more hurt and confusion for you and the next person. I've known many men who married one woman while still in love with another. They never gave their heart time to heal from the last relationship, and it only caused more pain in their lives. Your heart is not a rope to jump in and out of relationships. You can hurt yourself by doing that. Allow the cleansing to take place and the renewing to be put in shape. Once God creates in you a clean heart, you will get over the hurt and pain from the last relationship. Then you can move on with a renewed spirit for life and for love. God will lead you to the right person because of your renewed spirit. Renewed spirits attract other renewed spirits and dismiss old spirits of guilt and pain. But take your time, because you can end up getting not only hurt, but used as well.

MEN GET USED TOO

I know some of you men are laughing because you're saying, "I've never been used." But men have been used for cash, convenience, and comfort, just as men have used women for cash, convenience, and comfort. Men like to think that only women need comfort and canoodling, but men love and need comfort and canoodling just as much. How many of you love to have a woman cradled in your arms? How many of you love to be cradled in a woman's arms? Samson needed comfort. He lay with his head in Delilah's lap while she stroked his hair—and planned his demise. He was being used. If you feel used, don't go back and retaliate; don't get violent and hurt the person who used you. You have to be strong in the Lord and the power of His might, and resist any temptation that would only make matters worse. Do not submit to the vengeance of your heart, but rather to the cleansing of your soul. The cleansing will help you to move on, and thank God you discovered you were being used before things got worse.

DON'T PUT YOUR HEART INTO PLACES GOD DIDN'T SEND YOU

Men can spend a great deal of time putting their hearts into situations where God didn't send them. We create problems for ourselves. This is what happened to Saul, who became obsessive and highly jealous of David after the death of Goliath. Saul allowed the people to instigate the division: *"Saul hath slain his thousands, and David his ten thousands,"*[85] the people of Israel declared. Saul was king and had been divinely anointed to rule over Israel and protect the people from their enemies. Somehow he got sidetracked, and he aborted his mission of justice. He went from protector to avenger. Instead of protecting Israel, he took off the breastplate of righteousness and spent all his time and resources pursuing David. And David wasn't even his enemy. Saul was his own enemy because he allowed the forces of jealousy, paranoia, disobedience, anger, and revenge to encompass his heart and misdirect his path. As a result he eventually committed suicide and circumvented his mission of justice.

MEN AND SUICIDE

Most people probably don't realize how high the suicide rate is among men. The National Institute of Mental Health reported that in 2007, suicide was the seventh-leading cause of death among males, while

---

85: 1 Samuel 18:7

the fifteenth leading cause of death for females.[86] Almost four times as many males as females die by suicide, meaning that more men commit suicide than women. Although white male suicide rates remain highest, the rate among African American males has increased dramatically over the years. While women get depressed more often, men are more likely to commit suicide in their most dramatic stages of depression (such as after divorce). A lot of this is a result of the access that men have to weapons, such as guns. More men are likely to shoot themselves as an act of suicide. Even younger men are increasing their suicide rates, mostly because of mental disturbance or loneliness of heart.

SUICIDE KILLS THE MISSION

Suicide can definitely halt the mission of justice and leave our community and family in disarray. If you take life into your own hands, you never get to see how God would have worked out your situation or used you to help someone else. Suicide means that you've become desperately hopeless and tired, and can't see beyond your problem or feel beyond your pain. When you're suicidal, it means you have given up on God and given up on life. It's a tough situation to be in, and more and more men are finding themselves in the darkness of their despair, the finale of their failure, and they kill themselves. What a sad loss.

But just imagine if Moses had committed suicide after he killed the Egyptian as recounted in Exodus 2. If there was a time to end it, it was then. Just imagine if David had committed suicide after his family and his soldiers' families were taken by their enemies. In 1 Samuel 30:6, the Bible says the soldiers actually talked of stoning David for their loss. David felt helpless and disturbed, and he had no strength left to confront his army. If there was a time to end it, it was then for David.

GOD HAS PLANS BEYOND YOUR PAIN

But for both Moses and David, God had plans beyond their problems and a mission beyond their pain. Neither Moses nor David

---

86: "Suicide in the U.S.: Statistics and Prevention," National Institute of Mental Health, September 27, 2010, http://www.nimh.nih.gov/health/publications/suicide-in-the-us-statistics-and-prevention/in. (Page no longer available.)

knew it, saw it, or felt it at the time; all they felt was their pain. But God was working it out—just like God is working it out for all of us—and to end life is to never see what God has beyond the agony. The Bible says David found strength in the Lord when they were trying to stone him, which means David realized that his strength, his power, his energy was all used up and not enough to handle their accusations. He couldn't get up and see the light and fight the good fight on his own—he needed an additional power.

As stated earlier, we can't fight darkness and depression on our own. Evil will tell you to kill yourself, and if you don't have enough strength or only rely on your own strength, you can actually end up listening to the enemy. But that's where God steps in: *"Be strong in the Lord, and in the power of his might."*[87] When our strength is gone, God's power kicks in. You have to let go and let God handle the situation. God has plans beyond your problems and possibility beyond your pain, and if you hold on and be strong *in the Lord,* you will see what those plans are. Just stand, don't take any action, don't try anything, find a place and just wait. *"They that wait upon the Lord, shall renew their strength, they shall mount up with wings as eagles, they shall run, and not be weary and they shall walk, and not faint."*[88] Waiting is God working behind the scene on your situation so when the time comes you can step out in a better condition.

YOUR LIFE BELONGS TO GOD: HE WILL TAKE CARE OF IT

The Bible says, *"Eye hath not seen, nor ear heard, neither have entered into the heart of man, the things which God hath prepared for them that love him."*[89] Even in the midst of your darkness, you have to keep some light on to know that God has something *"prepared"* for those who love him. If you're breathing, it's a sign that God still has plans for your life. To take your breath is to take your life, and to take your life is to stop your heart, and to stop your heart is to end the plans that God has for

---

87: Ephesians 6:10
88: Isaiah 40:31
89: 1 Corinthians 2:9

your life. And how could you take something that belongs to God? God gave you life. God brought you into this world. For those who understand salvation in Christ, you acknowledge that the moment you accepted Christ into your life, you gave your life over to God, so how could you take that which belongs to God? And if it belongs to God, you can best believe that God will take care of you and fulfill the plans He has for your life.

YOU STILL HAVE BREATH

Instead of thinking about taking your life, the Bible says, *"Let every thing that hath breath praise the LORD. Praise ye the LORD."*[90] Keep praising God for the one thing you know you do have, and that's breath. The enemy may have taken your money, honey, children, health, and job, but as long as you have breath, you can believe that God still has plans for your life. You may be tired, scared, confused, depressed, or disturbed, but you still have breath. That breath is not yours to take; it's God's to use to get you from gloom to glory. But if you take your breath, how is God going to help your life? Men who have overcome their suicidal thoughts have great testimonies. Men who have succeeded in committing suicide have no story to tell.

ABUSIVE SITUATIONS

Not only can this dilemma lead to suicide, but also homicide, alcoholism, and, most often, domestic abuse. When men have lost control of their lives to unemployment, poverty, drug abuse, and alcoholism—as well as those who are deprived of a sense of power over their lives and family—they are more likely to resort to violence in the family,[91] such as beating their wives and hurting their children. How many of you men never thought you would hit your woman, yet now it seems like a daily ritual? A 2017 report showed that nearly half of all murdered women in the US die at the hands of a current or previous romantic partner.[92] This is a horrific yet real problem in male-female relations—not only for the man, but also for his daughters, sisters, and mother.

90: Psalm 150:6
91: Alex Thio, *Deviant Behavior: Tenth Edition* (New York: Allyn & Baker, 2010), 120.
92: "Nearly Half of All Murdered Women Are Killed by Romantic Partners," *The Atlan-*

DOMESTIC VIOLENCE

Look at what happens: instead of promoting justice, you're involved in a domestic dispute. I don't have to tell men how serious domestic violence charges can be. They not only can ruin your career and send you to jail, but can destroy your family and your life. Even your future relationships can be adversely affected by a past act of domestic violence. A righteous woman, knowing that you've been charged in a domestic violence case, will think twice before she gets involved with you. Now your heart is hurt again.

VERBAL ABUSE

Many men make the mistake of believing that domestic violence is only physical and only affects the woman. But domestic violence can be verbal and affect the whole family, which in turn hurts the whole community. What you say and how you say it can hurt and cut just as bad as if you actually hit someone. A lot of women have never been touched violently by a man, but have been scarred by a man's words: "fat ... ugly ... no good ... stupid ... tramp ... can't cook ... terrible mother." These verbal assaults not only affect the mind but the emotions. Women, children, and family members can feel like nothing and nobody because something a man said scarred them for life. And nothing is as nothing does. Some women will never love again, trust again, or feel good about themselves again because of something a man said. How can a woman be supportive and encourage your career goals and future aspirations, and be a good mother to your children if she feels like nothing? If she feels like nothing, not only will she be nothing to herself, but she'll also be nothing to you. How can you feel like a man of substance when you have a woman of nothing? What does that make you if you make her feel like nothing? It sure doesn't make you a M.A.N. It makes you less than a man.

M.A.N. if you have said anything to hurt a woman (and we all have said something) and you are still involved with her or have access to her, you

---

tic, July 20, 2017, accessed Oct. 11, 2017, https://www.theatlantic.com/health/archive/2017/07/homicides-women/534306/.

should apologize. No matter how long ago it was, call her and apologize. Fight your pride and arrogance and apologize. Say sorry with no strings attached. You're not trying to get back with her, you're not trying to have her relieve you of any debt you owe, you just are sincerely sorry for the things you've said and done that have affected her life in a negative way. Just apologize and keep it going. Seriously M.A.N.

SEXUAL ABUSE

Sexual abuse also takes place, in which men hurt women; rape their wives by causing pain, being overly aggressive, violent, and enforcing during sex; or give their partner a sexual disease. You may never go to jail for some of this, but you sure can go to hell for it. It's wrong. It's not love. It's hate—and a great failure on your behalf. The heart is supposed to do everything it can to love and uplift: emotionally, spiritually, physically, verbally, and sexually. To act contrary to this is to destroy the breastplate of righteousness and to live a life of failure in yourself and in your family. The Bible says:

Love is patient, love is kind. It does not envy, it does not boast, it is not proud. It is not rude, it is not self-seeking, it is not easily angered, it keeps no record of wrongs. Love does not delight in evil but rejoices with the truth. It always protects, always trusts, always hopes, always perseveres. Love never fails....[93]

93: 1 Corinthian 13:4-8 (NIV)

CHAPTER 9

STEP 4: *Community—Part 3*

DESTROYING FORCES WITH THE BREASTPLATE

The breastplate of righteousness protects the heart from submitting to forces of failure, whether aimed at others or directed at self. There is no doubt that King Saul was stressed and depressed when he committed suicide, as seen in 1 Samuel 31. We, as men, need the breastplate of righteousness to help us in times of trouble. Jesus said, *"Let not your heart be troubled: ye believe in God, believe also in me."*[94] And the Psalms declare: *"God is our refuge and strength, a very present help in trouble."*[95] Trouble is always going to be present, so it is not the trouble; it's how strong you are in the Lord to deal with the trouble.

DEATH AND THE TROUBLED HEART

A man's heart can get troubled by a host of issues; one of them is death. This is especially true for men who are close to their mothers. I know a lot of men who are close to their mothers. It tears them apart when their mothers pass on. Men can become secluded, isolated, and even irritable. The breastplate of righteousness is needed in such a situation. It helps men to overcome heart trouble through righteous understanding.

94: John 14:1
95: Psalm 46:1

In 2 Samuel 12, we see that after David's infant son died as a result of his indiscretion with Bathsheba, David recuperated from his depression and hurt. Somehow he realized that he could not bring the child back and was again dedicated to serving the Lord. The realization was another way of seeing things to make his situation better and put his heart at ease.

Men, when your heart is hurting over death, you have to learn to turn the situation around and seek God for a different theological understanding. The dead person cannot come back to you, but someday, because of our finite lives and connection with God, we will go to the dead person. We must believe that life comes after death for those who believe in Christ: *"For God so loved the world, that he gave his only begotten Son, that whosoever believeth in him should not perish, but have everlasting life."*[96] In the meantime we have to learn to live and trust the Lord, knowing that *"all things work together for good to them that love God, to them who are the called according to his purpose."*[97] You may need some help in understanding all of this, because death can really shut some people down to the point where they don't want to listen or talk to anyone. I understand. But everyone needs someone to talk to.

EVERYONE NEEDS SOMEONE TO SPEAK TO

Because many men can be stubborn, arrogant, and proud, they can lock themselves in a box that leaves them distant and alone when feelings of despondency occur. It is often difficult for men to find someone, or the right one, to speak to or get counsel when hurt happens. This private pain can be devastating to the man and to God's mission for his life. The heart of the proud is conjuring up unhappiness and hopelessness—especially after divorce, unemployment, or death. As long as you keep your pain within, your heart will suffer. This not only affects you spiritually but physically as well. Conjuring up hurt in the heart can lead to stress and anxiety, strokes and heart attacks. You have to call demons out to free yourself from misery and melancholy. You

---

96: John 3:16
97: Romans 8:28

have to find someone—preferably older, male, and wiser—who will give you sound advice, or just listen to you communicate your pain. You don't want to keep that despondent demon inside of you. You want to get it out.

TALK ABOUT IT

The more you hold in, the more you go down and the more likely bigger problems will happen in your life. Confession is relief for the soul. You have to pour out your pain and free your heart. Satan seeks to keep you in a box, making you believe you can handle everything by yourself. Be aware that some of life's storms are not only ruinous to the soul, but poisonous to the body. Again, many men suffer from heart attacks and strokes due to stress. Moses was overwhelming himself with his responsibilities and the people's problems. His father-in-law, Jethro, saw his impossible situation and offered him sound and loving advice: *"What you are doing is not good. You and these people who come to you will only wear yourselves out. The work is too heavy for you; you cannot handle it alone."*[98] Jethro gave Moses advice to get some help to relieve himself of his tremendous responsibilities and the burden on his heart.

Men need good, trustworthy people around them, whom they either can call on or who can detect their pain and onerous tasks and seek to sincerely help them out of their heavy load. Men should not get so arrogant that they can't listen to advice, or so proud that they can't seek someone for counsel. It can be hard out there by yourself. Sometimes all you need is a good person to speak to. If you can't find a person, seek Jesus in a way you've never sought Him before. Jesus is a friend who invites us to *"Come to me, all you who are weary and burdened, and I will give you rest."*[99]

YOU HAVE TO CRY SOMETIMES

Righteous living means taking time in prayer and meditation (more on prayer in Step 9), talking to God, and gathering your senses.

98: Exodus 18:17-18 (NIV)
99: Matthew 11:28

Take time to cry. Tears are a cleansing method created by God to free emotions, not to show weakness. You can still be a strong man and cry. David cried. Jesus wept. David said, *"The eyes of the LORD are upon the righteous, and his ears are open unto their cry."*[100] God is listening to your cry! Find a place you can let it out. Especially when it's your child you're missing. Especially when it's your wife you're divorcing. Especially when it's your job, house, or car you're losing. Especially when it's yourself you're abusing. Especially when it's your dreams you're pursuing but not reaching. Find a place to let it out.

The breastplate of righteousness will carry you through all that you inhabit and bring you into a new day. As the Psalms say, *"Weeping may endure for a night, but joy cometh in the morning."*[101] That's the talk of a faithful man crying. It may take many nights before you see the sunlight, but one morning you will get up and feel God's joy. God will comfort and strengthen your heart in the midst of affliction: *"Many are the afflictions of the righteous, but the LORD delivers him out of them all ."*[102] Your cry will open the door to your deliverance. You will see a new day, and you will look back and thank God you didn't give into suicide, homicide, abuse, and/or violence. You fought temptation.

MORE SENSITIVE TO OTHER MEN

Your trials and tribulations will also make you more sensitive to other people's pain, and particularly to the pain of other men, young and old. A lot of men like to dismiss the pain and tears of their sons and brothers. Many men like to laugh at other men in their moment of mourning and call them "chumps," "weak," or "punks" for expressing pain, sorrow, and tears. But until those men have hurt or lost someone—either through death, disaster, or disease—it will be hard for them to understand another man's pain. Some men don't understand the tears of another man until an accusation or an accident hurts them. Sometimes God will break us down with grief and aches so great that we become

---

100: Psalm 34:15
101: Psalm 30:5
102: Psalm 34:19 (NKJV)

more receptive to other people's suffering. No man is too hard to fall or too big to fail. Therefore pain is not only a way to endure suffering, but also a way to sensitize us to others. God desires that we be open to each other's pain.

UNFORGIVING

Unforgiveness is another heartbreaker. Too many men harbor unforgiveness. Having an unforgiving heart can be perilous and highly destructive. Many men stay in relationships, caring for their wives but failing to forgive past indiscretions. Maybe it was cheating, lying, abusing, stealing, abandonment, or any transgression that could cause hurt and pain in the relationship. Or maybe it was a mother, father, or best friend who did you wrong. Many men have not forgiven their fathers or another close male relative. The breastplate of righteousness seeks to make an unforgiving heart clean and pardonable. You can't be in a false relationship, because at any moment it could blow up in your face.

An unforgiving relationship is unholy and unjust, not to mention phony and hypocritical. If you're going to be reunited with a transgressor, you're going to have to forgive that person and the transgression committed, just as God forgave you. The Bible states, *"Forbearing one another, and forgiving one another, if any man have a quarrel against any: even as Christ forgave you, so also do ye."*[103] Just as God did not hold back His pardon from you, He expects you to extend the same forgiveness to others. Whatever the quarrel is or may have been about, you have to do your best to forgive. If you're harboring unforgiveness, know that unforgiveness hurts the unforgiving person more than it does the transgressor. If you don't forgive, God will not forgive you: *"But if ye forgive not men their trespasses, neither will your Father forgive your trespasses."*[104] That's why many men are still walking around distrustful, disengaged, and vengeful, because they're carrying around their transgressor's sins—and it's causing more destruction than

103: Colossians 3:13
104: Matthew 6:15

peace in their lives. When the breastplate is tight, it frees you from the trespasses, wrongs, and faults of other people. But when you're still holding other people's faults against them, it sticks with you much harsher than it sticks with the person who did you wrong. And it can cause you to commit unrighteous acts.

ABSALOM NEVER FORGAVE

In 2 Samuel 13, we find a tragic story. Absalom never forgave his brother Amnon for raping his sister, Tamar. They were all offspring's of King David, but Amnon had a different mother. Absalom said nothing to Amnon for two years, but conjured hate in his heart against Amnon during that time. After two years the hatred got the best of Absalom, and he planned the death of his own brother—out of an unforgiving heart.

But God asks us to forgive even something as difficult and painful as rape. There is no doubt it is difficult, but to keep hate in your heart for all those years is painful at the very least and draining at worst, and can cause you to do things that increase the problem, like hurting somebody. Such abhorrence can hurt your mind and body, not to mention lead to actions that make you hate yourself for what you've done.

FORGIVE YOURSELF

And there is no doubt that in the same way God wants us to forgive people who have done us wrong, He wants us to forgive ourselves for the wrong we've done to others. Many men have not forgiven themselves. They have done wrong, hurt people, caused pain, and now feel the wrath of all the wrong they've done. Coming to God can bring on a convicted conscience that can weigh on the emotions. The conscience is like a thousand witnesses. It knows everything. It knows stuff that nobody knows, and it can tear you apart with guilt if you let it. You have to pray and trust God to free you from the wrongs you've done in life. The prayer is that God would *"Forgive us our debts."*[105] You have to

---

105: Matthew 6:12

confess your faults to God and then have faith that God has freed you from your past transgressions against others. You're forgiven. God is a forgiving God.

If you don't forgive yourself and God says to forgive, not only are you burdened by your own emotions but you're troubled by God's condemnation. You have a double whammy against you because you didn't use the power of God to forgive yourself or forgive others. As a result something you did to someone else can haunt you for the rest of your life. Many men are walking around with the regret and torture of their past, and it's literally killing them and driving them insane. When you pray, pray to God to: *"Forgive us our debts, as we forgive our debtors."*[106] You have to have enough faith to believe that God forgave you for the wrongs and failures that you've inflicted on others and that others have inflicted on you. Only then will you feel free from anything you've done wrong.

FORGIVENESS IS POSSIBLE

Let me take this a little further, because I know forgiveness is hard for people. We serve a forgiving God who admonishes His people to forgive as well. And forgiving others is possible if you find the willingness in your heart. Jacob deceived his father, Isaac, and stole the blessing that rightfully belonged to Esau, his twin brother. Esau was furious at Jacob for his deception, and Jacob ran away in fear for his life. Jacob managed to escape his brother's wrath, but after some time the Lord directed him to return to his homeland, as seen in Genesis 32. Jacob became afraid when Esau agreed to meet him—accompanied by four hundred of his soldiers. Jacob prayed to the Lord and begged God's protection, because he concluded that Esau was bringing his soldiers to exact revenge. But when Jacob looked up, Esau was running happily toward him. He embraced his brother and kissed him, and they cried together—a sign of true forgiveness in a hard situation.

Esau did it right: he stayed away from Jacob until he could forgive him. Forgiveness does not always mean you have to stay around

---

106: Matthew 6:12

the person. Sometimes the worst thing you can do is to be in close proximity to the person that hurt you. It can cause a serious dilemma in your spiritual life. If you can't forgive, why convict yourself by staying in a strained relationship, fooling yourself and others? After a time, with the breastplate on, your heart will grow stronger and your forgiveness will be real.

Righteousness acts as a cleansing to unforgiveness. The breastplate protects the heart and also cleanses the heart (*"Create in me a clean heart…"*). A man with a dirty, vengeful, and unforgiving heart is doing damage to himself and his transgressor—but definitely more to himself. It may take time to truly forgive, but it must be done to prove the protection of the heart, the power of God and the reunification of the family and community.

MEN, HELP YOUR BROTHERS

The story of Jacob and Esau shows us that men are able to forgive one another and others. But it wouldn't have been possible if they didn't love each other. Men need help from other men. If you are a M.A.N., one of your major duties is to love your brother and help him. I like Abraham because he did not hesitate to help his nephew, Lot, and love him like a brother. In Genesis 13–14, Lot departed from Abraham and went to live among the sinful and wicked people of Sodom and Gomorrah. Abraham went in the opposite direction, toward righteousness, and blessed the Lord there. War broke out in the land where Lot lived, and the Bible says Lot and his family got caught in the crossfire and were taken captive. When word got back to Abraham that Lot had been taken, without hesitation he assembled over three hundred soldiers who wore the breastplate of righteousness, and went to get Lot and his family back. Abraham and his men attacked the enemy and brought back Lot and his family; not a thing was missing.

GO AND GET YOUR BROTHERS

M.A.N., we have to put on the breastplate of righteousness and go into the community and get our brothers. They need help. They've been taken by the enemy and they're in trouble. Our hearts must feel for them and go to where they are. Some of them are on street corners; others in hospital beds. Some are in gangs; others are in prison. Some are in college dorms; others in professional workplaces. Your mission is to put on your armor and go and get them and bring them to God. As stated earlier, you must use your time, talents, and treasures to reach out to the vulnerable in your community. More men need to become school teachers in public and private schools. Although this field has often been associated with women, it would be good for young boys to see grown men as teachers, guidance counselors, and even nurses in their school. Young men need role models, and teachers are often the first people that teach children outside the home. If God saved you, it is only right—and righteous—that you go and save others. If you've been saved, you have a divine duty and righteous responsibility to go and get your brothers no matter where they are.

GET THEM AND BRING THEM TO THE HOUSE OF GOD

Get them and bring them into the house of God. And when they come in, be patient and attentive. A lot of men are coming in with their old-man ways and attitudes. Some are looking for women. Some can't listen to instruction. Some think they know everything. Some are hurting. Some don't trust anybody, not even the preacher—*especially* not the preacher. Some have been hurt by the church. Some hearts are filled with lust, power, anger, hatred, or unforgiveness. But with the breastplate of righteousness on, you will be able to help your brothers become serious about their salvation. You will be able to teach them and help them without insulting or demeaning them. You will be able to listen to them and value their opinion and remember that you were once unsaved yourself. Just because they are new to the house of God doesn't mean they can't contribute ideas and talents to the house of worship or the community meeting.

Help your brothers. Be patient. Be kind and be encouraging. *"Behold, how good and how pleasant it is for brethren to dwell together in unity!"*[107]

107: Psalm 133:1

Points to Remember from Step 4

Part 1

1. Step 4 for every man is *Community*: He is to spread righteousness and fight against injustice for the sake of God's people and property.

2. Do good for your community—it is God's property.

3. The breastplate of righteousness protects the heart from dirt and defilement. Don't ever allow the breastplate of righteousness to come off once you put it on.

4. Righteousness is doing what is right and holy before God, yourself, and others.

5. Righteous living and seeking justice are not an option; they're an obligation. Seek justice for the wounded, the poor, and the disenfranchised. Fight against racism, sexism, and classism.

6. Volunteer your time and give from the goodness of your heart, and remember your civic duty to vote.

Part 2

7. For the sake of the community it's important that you don't live a contradiction in your life. God condemns the hypocrite. Let your walk and talk be the same in public and in private, in the light and in the dark.

8. Examine your heart to confront any defilement that corrupts your mission. Learn how to constantly clean your heart and rid it of impurity. Say a simple prayer every morning, afternoon, and evening: *"Create in me a clean heart, O God; and renew a right spirit within me."*

9. Get rid of anything that your unholy heart can use to hurt you (e.g., weapons, unethical relationships, poisonous anger, jealousy, revenge, etc.).

10. A hurt heart can be healed. Life is worth living. Suicide not only kills the person but the mission, and leaves our families and communities in disarray and further disintegration. Seek God and fight for your life.

11. Domestic Abuse can include verbal and sexual abuse, don't do it. Apologize to anyone you've done wrong.

Part 3

12. Strong men cry. Don't be afraid to release your emotions, as it can prevent a lot of problems. David cried. Jesus wept.

13. Don't become so proud that you can't listen to other people's advice when you're hurting or in trouble. Life can get hard out there by yourself. Find someone you can confide in when times get hard.

14. If you are the perpetrator of abuse in your family, you must seek God and counseling. Domestic abuse destroys the community.

15. Forgive others and also forgive yourself for past transgressions against others.

16. Men should help one another. Remember Psalm 133:1—*"Behold, how good and how pleasant it is for brethren to dwell together in unity!"*

FEET FITTED WITH THE GOSPEL OF PEACE

CHAPTER 10

STEP 5: *Mobility—Part 1*

... and with your feet fitted with the readiness that comes from the gospel of peace.

Ephesians 6:15 *(NIV)*

I remember watching the movie *Heat* starring Robert De Niro and Al Pacino. The movie was about career criminals who robbed banks and pulled other big jobs for a living. All of the men in the movie had the same problem: they couldn't walk away from trouble. Even when the heat was on and they had the opportunity to get away, they instead pursued crime. De Niro's famous line in the movie was, "Don't let yourself get attached to anything you are not willing to walk out on in thirty seconds flat if you feel the heat around the corner." His discipline was to leave everything for the sake of crime. Pacino, who played a cop, also had problems. He didn't know how to walk away from his job and find balance between his family life and his professional life. His life was obsessed with chasing criminals. As a result many of the criminals were either hurt or died, and Pacino's character himself was left with a broken marriage. They all were compelled by the force of trouble rather than the gospel of peace.

WHY IT'S HARD TO JUST WALK AWAY

Possibly the most difficult challenge for men is to stay away or step away from people, places, and problems that can ruin their lives. Just search the Internet and you'll find a host of men who have fallen victim to their weaknesses by stepping through the door of temptation, from arguing in the boardroom to fighting on the street corner. Many men are not able to walk away from situations that can escalate or get them caught, embarrassed, or killed. When you look at high-profile cases of entertainers, athletes, politicians, and business executives who commit the most embarrassing and shameful acts over and over again, you may ask, "Man, why didn't they just walk away from that stupidity after they got rich, powerful, and famous?" The answer is simple: *You can take the man out of the environment but you can't take the enemy out of the man.* It will take a whole new power, and that power cannot come from the man alone. He needs the strength of God.

The Israelites had the same problem. God brought them out of the land of their enslavement, but they still had the mind-set of an enslaved people. They constantly wanted to go back to Egypt even though God was trying to bring them forward to the Promised Land. They didn't know how to let go of the chains that held their mind and body in bondage. They didn't know how to walk away.

Walking away is about more than physical relocation or moving from one place to the other. It's about moving in the right direction and making the right decisions. It's about gaining a new understanding about life—one that leads to peace and tranquility rather than war and obscenity. It's about social and spiritual mobility—a mobility that leads to progress. And the only way to go forward and not backward is to erase the trail of dirty footsteps that used to bind you and define you. When you erase it, you can't retrace it because there is no trail leading you back. This is what God was trying to do for Lot and his family when he destroyed Sodom and Gomorrah in Genesis 19. By burning the land God was erasing the evil places Lot had trod so he wouldn't go back. Lot's wife looked back and lost her life. However, Lot and the rest of his family moved on. God wants to erase our steps from the places of destruction we used to walk, and wants to move us and our family on to a new understanding, different direction, and place of peace.

THE FEET FITTED WITH THE GOSPEL OF PEACE

Paul gave the Ephesians something to stand on for their journey: *"... and with your feet fitted with the readiness that comes from the gospel of peace."*[108]

The Roman soldiers, when going into battle, would wear special shoes called *caligae* on their feet, enabling them to advance into battle and against their enemy. Paul used the metaphor to equip the soldiers of God so they could advance without fear, arrogance, or eagerness into the battle with the gospel—the good news—of peace guiding their feet. In order to proceed in peace, we must be at peace and in control of ourselves and our actions when certain situations confront us. (Rationale: we cannot always control a situation, but we can control our response.)

If men are not in control of themselves, especially when faced with adverse situations, they may walk by fear rather than by faith, by anger rather than by temperance, and by arrogance rather than by humility. And the negative walk brings more problems than peace.

Step 5 for every man is *Mobility*:

He is to move graciously into places that will advance his life spiritually

and bring him peace wholeheartedly—mind, body, and soul.

Spiritual mobility is that gracious ability to move mentally and physically from one understanding and social environment to another. Spiritual mobility seeks social advancement and forward progress. Spiritual mobility is in the fitted shoes to guide men internally, move men morally, and lead men peacefully into places where God would be proud of them. The feet fitted like this will prevent men from walking with people and going to places that could cause problems and ultimate

---

108: Ephesians 6:15 (NIV)

destruction in their life. With these fitted shoes men know either to move forward or step backward, to step up or stand down, to walk straight or turn around, to walk into or run away from. It's all in the fitted shoes.

REGRET FOR NOT WALKING AWAY

As I told you earlier, men are full of regrets. One of them has to do with the places they've gone when they should have just gotten up, walked away, and left, or turned and went another way. How often have you ever said, "Man, I shoulda just gone the other way"? Or, "Shoot, if I had just listened to my first instinct, I wouldn't be in this mess"? That wasn't you talking; that was God. And what we call *instinct* is really God's whispering to our spirits to lead us on a path *"of righteousness for his name's sake."*[109]

WALKING INTO THE ENEMY'S TRAP

We men often ignore the voice of God and walk right into the enemy's traps. The story is told in Numbers 16 of Korah, Dathan, and Abiram, who became insolent along with 250 of their supporters and rose up against Moses,. They challenged Moses as the head of the Lord's assembly and wanted for themselves more power (*"powers"*) and more leadership (*"rulers"*), and to be ranked higher than Moses (*"spiritual wickedness in high places"*). Moses tried to reason with them, and then warned them that what they were doing was detestable in the eyes of God. Moses challenged them to come before the Lord, along with their censers (incense burners). "*... The LORD will show who belongs to him and who is holy,"* Moses told them.[110] God was on Moses's side, and He destroyed Korah, Dathan, and Abiram, along with their families and possessions. Because of their greed, arrogance, and disobedience, they walked right into destruction that not only obliterated them, but also their families and inheritance. All because they couldn't resist the devil and walk away from evil.

109: Psalm 23:3
110: Numbers 16:5 (NIV)

A LEADER KNOWS HOW TO FOLLOW FIRST

The problem with many men is that they want to be in control and in charge of everything, even if it means challenging others in leadership positions, just as Korah, Dathan, and Abiram did. Although it's good for men to pursue leadership positions, it is also good for them to be disciplined followers and to learn to respect leadership. A real soldier knows how to follow instructions. Disciples are followers of Christ and are willing to follow diligently and honorably.

The problem with Satan is that he didn't want to follow God's instructions and was kicked out of God's kingdom. Satan puts the same rebellious and arrogant spirit in his own disciples, making them move by power hungriness rather than by power humbleness. To be power hungry is to never be full of power. Many men have sold their souls to the devil, by deceiving, scheming, lying, and overstepping their leadership, simply to get into certain positions, only later to realize that a deal with the devil results in little sleep and no peace. That's why Jesus rejected Satan's offer for power: *"All this I will give you … if you will bow down and worship me."*[111] Jesus didn't want to owe or be owned by Satan. Jesus wouldn't lose His soul to gain the world, for *"What good is it for a man to gain the world, yet forfeit his soul?"*[112] Jesus knew that anything Satan gives will never last and will only lead to temporary happiness and ultimate destruction.

Satan may give you the position of authority, but with the position comes the seat of paranoia, insecurity, family disruption, illegal investigation, and general unhappiness. Be careful what you ask for, because you may get more than you expect. Satan offers the option that impatience accepts, even though God says, "Wait." Satan offers the alternative to God's "No."

When God says, "No," Satan says, "Yes." Satan provides reasoning and justification for unrighteous behavior when God says, "Walk away." Satan steps in and gives you power, fame, cars, houses, and

---

111: Matthew 4:9 (NIV)
112: Mark 8:36 (NIV)

jobs in order to pull you away from God and into his trap. And once you accept the offer, Satan uses it to control you, embarrass you, trouble you, demean you, and even kill you.

To move by arrogance, ignorance, stubbornness, or ego will only lead to division in God's kingdom. As the Bible says, *"And if a house be divided against itself, that house cannot stand."*[113] Many cause division in God's house and community because they overstep leadership. If God has called you to lead, He will make a way so that you get the position that you deserve, whether it be on the job, in politics, or in church—but you must wait for the Lord to open the door before you walk in.

Joshua walked with Moses for many years, but only when God gave Joshua permission did he succeed Moses. Elisha walked with Elijah as his assistant, but only after Elijah was taken up by God did Elisha move forward with the same prophetic mission. Same was true for the disciples who followed Jesus. They walked obediently and humbly with the Savior until His departure, and then they continued in His name. But as can be found in every following, Satan found a money-hungry purveyor in Jesus's camp and used him. Satan is always looking for someone he can use to disrupt things. Don't be a Judas and sell out your brothers.

Every man must be able to walk in obedience so that if the time comes, he can lead with dignity. Whatever position God puts you in—whether it is leadership or as an assistant—you should be able to walk with honor. I know many men, from deacons to assistant directors, who serve with the greatest integrity. And they make the leader's job much easier, and they make their souls much lighter because they're serving with purpose and calling. To be a servant is the greatest honor in God's kingdom on earth.

When men learn to humble themselves and submit to godly authority, blessings and healing, justice and peace will come into their lives. And if God has placed a younger man than you in a leadership position then your job is to follow and respect him, help him succeed.

113: Mark 3:25

Men have to find a pastor whom they can respect, a house of God they can worship in, and a congregation they can tolerate regardless of the imperfections of the people. No place of worship is perfect, and neither are you. We're all trying to walk by faith. Nineteenth-century preacher C. H. Spurgeon observed, "The day we find the perfect church, it becomes imperfect the moment we join it."

FITTED FEET, IMPULSES, AND CONSEQUENCES

If a man's spiritual walk were guided by feet fitted with the gospel of peace, it would usurp many impulses and thwart dire consequences. It has been noted by many observers that the Iraq War was a rushed decision on the part of the United States. And although there was a reason to go in, there was no plan to get out. As a result military personnel from the United States and other countries got stuck in a war with no exit plan. Having no exit plan can cost lives.

Many men have paid the cost of having no exit plan. Many men are guilty of rushing into decisions and judgments without considering the long-term consequences. Think about the last car you bought. Did you consider your other financial obligations, or are you now stuck with a bill for a car that's taking most of your check every month? Once you get into a car contract, it's hard to get out, unless you want to ruin your credit and, along with it, your ability to make other major purchases in the future. Employers are even checking credit scores these days for certain jobs. So if you mess up on a purchase, you can mess up on future prospects for employment, home ownership, life insurance, and other major life ventures.

SPONTANEITY AND CONSEQUENCES

Spontaneous actions can cause more grief and suffering than happiness and comfort. Perhaps if men thought more about the consequences of certain dealings, they would not have walked into chaotic situations. But many men tend to focus more on the pleasure than the consequences when pursuing their desires, which often leads to disaster. The Bible is filled with stories about soldiers of the Lord who rushed into battle. They never consulted God, so they went into war without His permission or protection. And without the Lord's permission and protection, your direction can end in tragedy. We generally fail to think about the consequences of our actions when we move impetuously.

And these days it's much easier to research information before walking into bad deals. You can surf the Internet to search just about anything and anybody, including their history and authenticity. If you find any questionable information about a business or individual, you can always walk away from the deal. More often than not, you have no need to rush into situations and feel like you have to make a decision right away.

AN OPPORTUNITY TO GET OUT

Many men's lives are destroyed because they walk into situations they could've walked away from. If you look at the sequence of events involving Korah, Dathan, and Abiram, they had an opportunity to turn from their wicked ways. Moses pleaded with them, and they could have chosen to walk away. Moses warned them, and they could have heeded his words and walked away. When Moses challenged them, they still had an opportunity to walk away. Each time, however, the forces of greed and power pushed them into situations that they didn't turn away from. And the deeper they went in, the harder it was to get out. I'm sure many men have had girlfriends, wives, mothers, aunts, and uncles warn them to stay away from certain people and places, but in their stubbornness, greed, and need for power, they ignored such advice and instead caught the wrath.

The purpose of the feet being fitted is to prevent men from walking into situations that may bring more harm than good to their lives. God does allow us, before we become fully involved, to turn around and go another way. If you see or sense something is not right with the party you're going to, the house you're walking into, the road you're driving down, or the table you're sitting at, walk away! You have the opportunity—before you go any further—to put on your fitted shoes and turn around. Jesus knew when to stay and when to walk away from a bad situation. At one banquet the Pharisees sought to seize Jesus, but His feet were fitted, so He walked away. You may be the only one out of your crew that God speaks to, and says walk away which means you have to be bold and obedient to the voice speaking to you, warning you, to save yourself.

PEOPLE ARE COUNTING ON YOU

And the sad thing is that when men mess up and walk into bad situations or follow the wrong people, they not only ruin their lives but disappoint people who love them, care for them, and are counting on them. In the previously mentioned movie *Heat,* the cook who had come out of jail and was trying to live right got caught up with people who had committed themselves to crime. His girlfriend kept encouraging him and supporting him and stating how proud she was of him. But he was sullen over his own situation, and when the enemy showed up, the cook made the wrong decision to leave the one who loved him and to again run with the people who cared nothing about him. The result was deadly.

When men mess up and fall to temptation, they disappoint so many people who are counting on them to do good and fight the good fight. When you make it to college or get promoted on the job, loved ones are praying for you and proud of you. To run with the enemy is to fail those who care for you. Your actions can leave people who love you sad, lonely, embarrassed, ashamed, and in tears for a long time. I knew a mother who was so proud her son had gone to Harvard University. She told everyone. A couple of months later she confided in me that he had gotten hooked on crack while at school. What a crying shame.

Many tough men are out there, and they may be able to handle prison—but can those who love you handle you going to prison? Some men don't care if they live or die, but can those who love you handle seeing you dead and gone?

Let me just interject this thought: Have you ever wondered what would happen to the people who love you after you've died in your sin? You ever think what would happen to people who depend on you and care for you, like your son, who looks forward to playing basketball with his father? *But now you're gone.* Protecting your daughter from abusers, molesters, and tormentors? *But now you're gone.* Helping your wife and/ or mother in the home? *But now you're gone.* When you're gone, all the good you do—and could have done—is gone too, and those who love you suffer.

A HEAVY BURDEN

This is indeed a heavy burden to carry when so many people are dependent upon you and one little slip-up can hurt you and those who love you. To walk a straight line can be difficult, with so much pressure on the soul, it can cause fear, anxiety, and breakdowns, which can lead to drinking, drugs, sex, gambling, and other unrighteous acts for temporary false relief from all the pressure. However, a better relief is available for those in Christ. When you walk with God, you are not alone. You allow others to depend on you, so when your burdens get heavy and temptation gets strong, don't be afraid or ashamed to lean on Jesus for support and guidance. Nobody can carry every burden alone, which is why Jesus gave us the fitted shoes. God will send you someone to help you as you help others.

EXAMINATION OF THE FEET

Let's deal with bad decisions some more. Have you gotten into situations that, if you'd thought about it, you would not have walked into? Tell the truth. Sounds like it's time for another examination, this time of the feet. Are your feet guilty of leading you to places you shouldn't have gone, stepping on people while they were down, or advancing toward temptation, abuse, or indiscretions? If so, change your shoes right now!

Put on the shoes fitted for the gospel of peace. You don't need old shoes. You need new shoes. Old shoes, which have human stains on them, are for the old man. Your new shoes have the blood of Jesus on them. The theological understanding of the blood of Jesus is that its power cleanses and forgives so that you can purge sin and shame and walk with newness of life, full of grace and truth in your shiny fitted shoes.

I'm glad Paul spoke about the fitted feet, because for many men shoes are a sign of status, attraction, decency, and comfort. There is nothing like a nice new pair of shoes. When I was growing up, it was customary to clean your sneakers by the hour—and having someone step on your sneakers could cause a great deal of commotion. As I got older and switched from sneakers to shoes, I saw how much pride men took in their shoes, whether it was going to a party or going to church. Military personnel must keep their shoes clean and shined, but in war keep their boots tight and fitted. As a M.A.N. we are in a spiritual battle, and it is important to keep our shoes tight, shined, and fitted so we are ready to run over the enemy and advance God's peace.

WALK RIGHT AT ALL TIMES

A man once told me he had a pair of shoes for the club and a pair of shoes for church. He had a suit for the club and a suit for church. He had a cell phone for his family and another one for his mischief. He even had one car he drove to do his dirt and one car that was clean for Sunday-morning service. At least the brother had enough sense to separate the good from the bad! But remember, we're not trying to live both divine and diabolical, because you can't hold dual citizenship in heaven and hell. We're trying to walk right at all times. Living dichotomously will only result in war within the soul. Wearing our fitted shoes will help us walk right at all times with God. We're not trying to paint a picture of hypocrisy; we're trying to live genuinely.

You can't possibly think you can go toe to toe with the devil, wearing his shoes, and win. You need new shoes.

THROW IT ALL AWAY!

I know this is hard, but you must take the old shoes off and throw them away. I'm referring to the actual material. You must rid yourself of anything that causes temptation and, ultimately, sin. Regeneration is a theological understanding of a new creation: everything old has been destroyed, and anything new must be attained. To keep old ways as well as merchandise and goods around after you've been changed is to give the enemy ammunition to tempt you and send you back to your old ways. So old items require trashing and destroying. And it will take more strength and might from the Lord to get up the power to lift those old goods. Those items will seem heavier than a ten-thousand-pound barbell, because it's not about how strong the body is or how heavy the item is; it's about how strong in the Lord you are and how serious you are about change.

We already looked at how Jesus told some demons to leave a man and then He sent them into the pigs. You have to be strong in the Lord and the power of His might and throw those shoes out, no matter how expensive they are—no matter how good they look or you look in them. Throw out that computer that you've been using to send email messages to mistresses as well as to look at pornography and solicit prostitution. Throw out that cell phone that has been used to scheme, make dirty deals, set up booty calls, and hurt people. Change or terminate your account with Facebook, Twitter, and any other social media or email that has been used to tempt you and make you sin. Remember, even if you try to clean the memory of the computer and phone, there is still a way the devil in his determination can retrieve old information and use it for your demise. The best thing you can do is throw it out and get a new one.

Start trashing, smashing, and throwing things out that you know are tempting and threatening your salvation. I remember coming home one day to find my mother throwing out her record collection that she used to dance and groove to. I couldn't understand it then, but I understand it now. Once you get saved, you don't want anything around that could interfere with your salvation and lead you back into disgrace. You have to throw out pornography DVDs, condoms, guns, knives, alcohol, phone numbers, drugs, friends, clothes, music, movies, etc. Do it now!

This is even heavier, but you may have to move out of the home that has been used as a house for your sin and shame, especially if you're thinking about starting a new family. You don't want to bring your new family into your old house, where you possibly did all kinds of stuff. You don't want to bring your new bride into an old bed, where you possibly did all kinds of stuff. If you have invited evil in your house—sleeping with another woman in your bed, getting drunk and abusing the family, killing someone in the house—you have to get out! You don't want to be in a place that's stained with evil spots, bad memories, and vicious thoughts, because it will only lead to war in the soul and there will be no peace in your house. Be obedient, get strength from the Lord to pick those things up or leave those things behind, and start new. Walk away!

This is even heavier, but you will have to get rid of your old friend who tempts you to do no good. When you get saved and become serious about your salvation, you will have to let some people go and move on. I know many men who are really doing well and have changed their lives for the better, but are still hanging around people who can destroy their new walk with Christ. It is the same when men make it out of the hood through music or sports and still hang around no-good people. Many of these people may be really good friends; they help you with finances, they drive you places, they look out for you when you're in trouble, but they still cause you to fall to temptation. I had two really good friends in the ministry, but they were also detrimental to my walk with Jesus and introduced me to corrupt things that could have ruined me, my ministry, and my family. I had to let them go. It wasn't easy because they were really good guys but had bad ways.

You may change internally, but if the external doesn't change, those devilish reminders can jump up and haunt you at any time. The devil (in the guise of old girlfriends, homeboys, dealers, and debt collectors) has your address and phone number, knows where you live, and can come knocking at your door anytime of the night. Some things you can keep and cleanse, but other things you have to smash and trash. Change your phone number, change your email, change your address. It's all part of your spiritual and actual conversion. Walk away now! Now!

Just like the old shoes, some things don't fit your lifestyle anymore. They're too old for your new walk. They're too ugly for your new look. They're the wrong size, so even if you tried to put them on, because of your new life, they won't fit and you won't feel good.

DON'T SLIP

The great thing about these new shoes is they're slip-proof. A lot of men slip up and lose everything they have because they walked through the wrong doorway or did something with the wrong person. Think about it: one slip-up could cost you everything you have. It takes many steps to get to the top but one slip to lose it all. You have to think about whether the thing you're about to walk into is worth losing everything. Shoes fitted with the gospel of peace keep you from slipping up and losing everything over something that's just not worth the risk. I had a friend who was so excited to get invited to a girl's house that he had just met, his eagerness trumped his intelligence and he went in but never came out alive.

CHAPTER 11

STEP 5: *Mobility—Part 2*

HURTFUL AND ABUSIVE RELATIONSHIPS

One difficult yet necessary purpose of the feet being fitted is to strengthen men to advance in battle to bring peace in abusive, hurtful, or unhealthy relationships. If, by measure, you are the victim or the perpetrator of such atrocities, it is your job as a man to examine your path and take the necessary steps to bring sanity to the madness. Ask yourself, "Am I in an abusive relationship?"

As we discussed in the last chapter, men get hurt and men get used, and there is no doubt that men get abused physically, emotionally, sexually, and spiritually by women in their lives and by other people. A survey by the American Bar Association Commission on Domestic Violence reported that from 1995 to 1996, while 1.3 million women reported domestic violence abuses, 835,000 men reported some type of abuse from women. Let me repeat that: 835,000 men reported being abused by their partner. In some cities around the country, a quarter of the arrests for domestic violence are women.[114]

Domestic violence can include many different forms of aggression, from hitting and spitting to stalking and profanity. The

---

114: Carey Goldberg, "Spouse Abuse Crackdown, Surprisingly, Nets Many Women," *The New York Times*, Nov. 23, 1999, accessed Oct. 9, 2017, http://www.nytimes.com/1999/11/23/us/spouse-abuse-crackdown-surprisingly-nets-many-women.html.

increased acts of domestic violence by women could be due to several factors. Women have a lot of responsibilities in the home and on the job too. They are stressed, and stress can lead to verbal and physical abuse. They can get jealous, angry, and vengeful at a man's new living situation. Also, part of the increase can be attributed to the fact that more men report such acts today. More men are taking precautionary steps to file reports with police to protect themselves from being seen as the perpetrator. This may seem extremely harsh, and possibly no man wants to see his wife, ex-wife, girlfriend, or ex-girlfriend or baby mother locked up or charged with assault. But in not filing, the man is taking a risk of walking directly into an argument or physical abuse and escalating the problem. The reality is, men are much more likely—even if the woman initiated it—to be charged with abuse or assault.

WALK AWAY FROM ABUSIVE SITUATIONS

Men must learn to walk away from abusive relationships. If you are in an abusive relationship and are the perpetrator of that abuse, you need to put on your fitted shoes and walk away from the situation. Or, if it's a continual problem, walk away from the relationship. This takes a lot of strength. Be strong in the Lord, because it may mean walking away from your wife, your children, your home, and your comfort zone, so you can get some help. If you feel you have to hit the woman in your life, you have a problem. If you are beating your children and verbally abusing them, you have a problem. If you are smashing furniture or punching holes in the wall and scaring your family every time you get upset, you have a problem. There is no peace in your life and there is no peace in your home. You need to walk away and deal with yourself.

CHILD ABUSE

I need not remind men that child abuse, which is another form of domestic abuse, is a charge that can lead to imprisonment and banishment from the children. Many men think that one little spank, smack, punch, grab, or shake won't hurt the child. Think twice, especially if you put anger and force behind the blow. You're a big man hitting a little child, and even if you don't mean to hurt the child, you can cause bruises and broken bones. Especially if you've been drinking or smoking and mistakenly hit the child too hard, it could result in scars for life. I remember when one of my brothers took something and my younger brother's father disciplined him by putting a match under his hand. It ended up severely burning his fingers. He still has the scars.

Some men think they can discipline their young children by yelling profusely and slinging profanity and threats. Cursing and cussing and threatening a child are forms of child abuse. Men, you have to be careful, particularly these days, how you handle young people. You can damage them for life with verbal abuse. I know many fathers want their sons to be tough, but teaching toughness by way of abuse is more destructive than constructive. Children can be toughened by discipline, by punishment, and by understanding what a father will tolerate and won't tolerate. For some fathers, including myself, all we have to do is look at our children and it gets them straight. I can testify along with many of these men, we have never abused our children or even hit a child in anger.

And you don't want to hit your daughter, making her believe it's alright for a man to hit her. No, you don't want any man hitting your daughter. Most men would kill a man for hitting their daughter. And you don't want to talk down or cuss, threaten, or hurt your daughter's feelings by the words that come out of your mouth. Many girls are sensitive and they should be protected by their father even if the world is cruel. You are her strength, her protector. You don't ever want her to feel bad about herself. The love you show her will be the confidence she shows the world, and men will know to respect her because she knows what respect looks like as a result of her father. If you don't want another man to demean your daughter, don't be the man who does it. Teach her properly, soldier.

Men need guidance in this area (especially young men and stepfathers—many children die at the hands of young men and stepfathers), because most of the men who get into problems arrive there by accident rather than by intent. Men should put on their fitted shoes and find a place where they can train how to be fathers and handle children. More houses of worship and community groups should develop training programs to teach men the basics of being a father—how to handle, speak to, develop, talk to, and discipline a child.

Child abuse is serious and it will affect the child, and can do so in many ways. When a child sees his mother being beaten, he gets scarred mentally by what he is witnessing, and can grow up not only hating the father but repeating the actions. When a child is beaten by a father or a man in the house, that child not only grows up hating the father or the man in the house, but could grow up not wanting to have children. When a child is sexually abused by their father or a man in the house, not only can they grow up hating the father or the man in the house, but also approach adulthood as sexually confused, promiscuous, hurtful, and hateful in their own relationships, being lustful, abusive, and even destructive to others.

It is up to the man to take a stand with his fitted shoes to prevent any of this from occurring or recurring.

MAN, HELP YOUR WOMAN

The reason you may have to walk away and bring peace to your soul as well as to your home is because you may be with a woman who is not strong enough or knowledgeable enough to walk away. They stay and take the physical and/or verbal abuse for years. Many women have a warped mentality about relationships, believing, *The more he hits me, the more he loves me.* And, *The more he argues with me, the more he cares about me.* Women will even accept their abuse and station in a relationship by justifying it biblically, having acquired a twisted theological interpretation of the Bible. And, as stated, children who watch their mother get beaten and verbally abused grow up to be perpetrators or victims in abusive relationships themselves. You don't want to be in a relationship where you are constantly arguing and fighting with your wife in front of the children. Arguing and fighting with your girlfriend in front of the children. It's not healthy for their development. The best thing, yet the hardest thing you as a man may have to do—before you hurt yourself or get hurt—is to walk away.

ABANDON YOUR SITUATION, NOT YOUR FAMILY

Men have been known to walk away and leave their families. But there is a difference between abandoning your family and distancing yourself from your home. Abandoning is to walk away out of neglect, without any healthy sense of shame. These men have no presence within the family, offering no communication, no funding, and no protection. These men must be dealt with differently because this discussion is about leaving the situation, not the family. But if you have left your family or children with a woman to fall into neglect, you need to prayerfully revisit that situation and come to a humble conclusion to re-engage in your children's lives.

By abandoning them, you did an injustice to your children and to yourself as well. Even if you can't get along with the mother, it's up to you to find some neutral ground where you can communicate with your children and have a relationship with them. It may mean court involvement to protect yourself and spiritual involvement to humble yourself. Whatever you have to do as a M.A.N., you should do. It's never too late, whether you left one year ago or ten years ago. Children need fathers, whether in the home or living separately, because the communication and support are what counts.

Also, a lot of men live in the house, yet are not at home. They offer no communication or emotional support for the child. So they are just as much of a deadbeat dad as an absent father. A lot of men know they could be better husbands and fathers themselves, had they had male role models growing up. Having no guidance in parenting and relationships is a burden. It's like learning to cook from scratch. You get burned more than you get fed.

Statistics confirm that children growing up in a one-parent home, usually because of the father's absence, are more likely to do worse in school, join gangs, use drugs, and end up in jail than are children with both parents in their lives. Man of Armor Nation, you can reduce these statistics.

WALK AWAY AND GET HELP

Distancing yourself from the home means walking away to get help while communicating with, supporting, and protecting your family. Men are protectors of the family. When men abandon their responsibility, they renounce their divine calling. In order to reclaim the calling, men need to walk away and get help. Walk away and get counseling. Walk away and relieve some stress. Even though it's hard, you can make the enemy mad when you walk away from the abusive situation.

WALKING IS A SPIRITUAL MOTION

Not every situation calls for you to leave the home or job when things get rough. Most times it requires patience and understanding. The majority of issues (at least 90 percent) can be de-escalated if reason and calm topple insults and anger. So our walk is not only a physical movement, but also a spiritual motion that shifts from an erratic state to a rational understanding. Remember, fitted shoes advance you toward peace, so if someone is moving toward verbal and physical attack, you have to step up spiritually and move toward silence and calm. If someone is moving forward with annoyance, aggravation, and irritation, you may have to step up spiritually with consideration, concern, and awareness. It is necessary that your spiritual motion be put into play the majority of times, so that every argument and disagreement does not become an excuse for leaving the house or escalating a bad situation. *Be a M.A.N. and take the lead to do the spiritual opposite of the present hostile environment.* If you practice this enough, you will definitely see a difference in your home.

WRONG MOVE

I know a man who told me that the only time he could get out the house without an excuse was when he and his wife had a good argument. He knew she would get all upset and he would get all upset and then leave the house. At times he would schematically plan it so he could get his time away. He even had a name for it: "Night of Freedom." (Men, don't get any ideas from this rotten trick, because the story is not over.)

He came home one day and his wife wasn't there. He called her on the cell phone and asked where she was. She calmly told him she was in Las Vegas. With a wave of shock, he said, "Where?" She said, "Las Vegas. That's what I was trying to tell you before you stormed out the house."

Not every tough situation means walking out the front door. The fitted feet will lead you to the right place for help. A walk can be simply shutting the doors in the basement, a drive around the block, or a talk with a good friend to calm your anger. Then go back home and work out the situation. The worst thing you can do when you walk away is go somewhere that can further destroy your spirit and desecrate your peace. Many men run out of the house to the bar and get drunk. Others find women at the club and get laid. Many men will take off their shoes—shoes that are the gospel of peace—and stay over at a woman's house. That is the crevice of war.

May God have mercy on you for falling to temptation, but falling and staying only condemns your soul further. At least after you fall, have enough strength to get up, put your shoes back on, beg forgiveness, and run out of there! Most women will tell you that when they fall to sexual temptation, they don't linger around—they get out. But many men can get so comfortable in the woman's arms—think of Samson—that they lie there, bathe there, shave there, and may end up dying there, both emotionally and physically. *Put your shoes on, get up, and get out of there!* You need to run to the nearest house of prayer where you can pour out your spirit and beg for forgiveness. You don't need to lie around after you've fallen. Many men don't take time to get to know the woman they take refuge with. She may have an ex-husband or a boyfriend who's a cop or a criminal, with a gun. Remember, men get used too. You can be sitting in this woman's house, feet up on the ottoman with the fitted shoes off. Then you hear knocking at the door, or banging at the door, or cussing and shooting at the door. He may even have a key to let himself in. And because you didn't have your shoes on, or your belt buckled, it takes you longer to run or hide, and that little delay can result in your ass on fire. This may be funny if it were a movie. But this isn't the movies. This is real, and real can kill you.

STRENGTHEN YOUR FAMILY

So stay home and fix your home and stand on your feet and say, "This family will not live like animals, fighting and cussing, debasing and disrespecting each other. We will live in love, harmony, and respect in Jesus's name." When you do this, you are taking back your calling. You reclaim your calling in many different ways: by opening your woman's eyes and having her understand that abuse is not a sign of love, but rather one of control and humiliation; by clarifying any flawed misinterpretation of the Bible that says a woman must submit to her man, even if he's abusing her; by helping her and your family. Children always benefit from growing up in a home where their parents are in a healthy, loving relationship. You bring peace to your home and war to the enemy. You can use your fitted shoes to kick the devil's tail better when you're at peace with yourself.

LET HER GO

Sometimes having the feet fitted means you have to stand. Ephesians 6 tells us to put on the whole armor of God so you will *be able to stand against the wiles of the devil.*[115] If you're not strong enough to walk, and instead choose to let the abuse continue, a time will probably come when the Spirit moves your family to leave you. No man wants to see his woman and children gone. God forbid if she leaves with another man! God forbid if she's involved with your brother or best friend! (I had to go there, because if you've sown a bad seed, you will reap a bad weed.)

Under such circumstances things can get real ugly, and instead of walking away in peace, many men have donned the shoes of anger, violence, and even insanity, doing something that can wreck the family and their lives. The alarming statistics on domestic abuse tell us that men are snapping. Good, decent men are flipping out. They have access to guns and are using them to harm themselves, their women, children, and coworkers. The devil has opened a door of family disruption and community annihilation, and men will continue to walk right through it if their feet are not fitted.

115: Ephesians 6:11

DON'T DO ANYTHING STUPID

M.A.N. listen and think about it for a minute. You do have an opportunity to think and assess the situation before you go any further into the madness. As I told you, Korah, Dathan, and Abiram had time to turn away from attacking Moses. In the movie *Heat* there is a segment where all of the bad guys must decide whether to walk away because they know the police are on to them, or go forward with their wicked plans. You still have time before you do the unthinkable and walk away. Yes, she's about to leave. Yes, she's taking the children. Yes, she may even be sleeping with another man. But is it worth it for you to hurt or harm or kill somebody? The devil will tempt you to act impulsively and violently. But wait, M.A.N.! That's your family! Even if she is doing you wrong, that's your child. That's your life. The devil will arouse your anger and jealousy, and make you believe you have to abduct the child, hurt or kill the mother, or go on a rampage.

But stand! Stand, soldier! Put on your shoes—your feet fitted with the gospel of peace—and stand! Don't move. Stand ... and let her go. Stand ... and let her holler. Stand ... and let her take the children. If you've got to say something, make it an apology: "I'm sorry it has to be this way." Stand ... and remain peaceful. Stand ... and hold on to your hope. Speak positively to her. "We'll work it out some other time." If she's walking away from the abusive situation, God is working through her to do something you should have done. You should have put on your shoes fitted with the gospel of peace and walked away. You should have gotten yourself together. But since you couldn't do it, let God allow her to do it. Let God allow you to stand and watch how it should be done. *Stand, soldier!*

And when she leaves, don't proceed with threats and verbal attacks, or steady annoyance and jealous, outrageous actions. Don't constantly call her, send her emails, stalk her, or show up unexpectedly at her job. Don't be malicious and venomous by posting stuff on the Internet and social media about her or her friends. Don't demand that she come back, or threaten to abduct or hurt the children. Don't intimidate the boyfriend or try and get information from her girlfriends. Don't talk dirty or insultingly about her to the children or other people. What kind of man talks nasty about his children's mother? You look foolish. No child wants to hear you denigrate their mother. You only teach your children to disrespect their mother. What kind of man teaches his children to disrespect their mother? Whatever goes on is between you and her, but in front of the children you should show the utmost respect and decency, even if she is attacking and insulting you. Remember, do the spiritual opposite: *Stand! Be still! You be the smart one.*

LEAVE BEFORE IT KILLS YOU

And I know this can be hard because many women turn the children against the father—making the man out to be an animal, disallowing visits and communication. Many women can be venomous and vindictive, deceitful and threatening. I remember a friend told me about a time when he and his wife were having problems. He came home one day to dinner on the table. He ate as he normally did. But after dinner he felt sharp pains in his stomach and had to run to the hospital by himself because his wife wouldn't take him. The doctor told him he had a touch of food poisoning. She denied any connection to it, but to this day he swears she put something in his food. He left her a week later. There is no doubt that women can be used for evil, but just as my friend did, the best thing to do is put on your shoes and leave the situation before it kills you.

If you want to address the situation, there are legal, procedural, and spiritual things you can do.

DON'T KILL ANYBODY!

Anger management and self-control are not only needed in marital or family situations. A number of men are blowing up and going insane on the job, in the church and in the bars and shooting everyone in sight. They have allowed their rage, frustration, and anger at supervisors and other employees—coupled with their damaged family situation, anger at the nation, overwhelming financial obligations, and failed relationships—to get to the lowest part of their soul, walk up to the site where people are, and start shooting. If you are in this situation or thinking about this action—*Stop! Stand!* Before you do something crazy and end up killing others and yourself. If you do this you will take a baby from his mother, a mother from her baby a father from his family, a pastor from his church and children, and children from their parents. Do you know the kind of damage you cause to other people in your moment of hostility, violence and insanity? If you did, you would put the gun down and talk to God. Most men who go on a rampage end up killing themselves or getting killed during the ordeal. *Stop! Stand! Think!* If you're thinking about picking up a gun and hurting people on the job or other places, *stop, drop and pray!* Talk to God. Do it now! Put on your fitted shoes and walk away! There is a better way. You don't want to allow the lowest level of failure to take you out. Fight the devil and walk away from the situation. I guarantee you, tomorrow you will thank God you didn't carry out the insanity, but instead you showed the strength of God to keep you from doing the unthinkable. Praise God!

Brother it's not worth it to kill anyone, think about how much hurt and pain you cause to others who have to see their loved ones dead. I know in a moment of insanity you may not be thinking about anybody, not even what happens to you. But hopefully before you do the unthinkable you will think about the consequences, pray for your strength to resist the enemy, step away and wait for tomorrow to see a better day. We don't read about the men who thought about such actions but turned away from the insanity, and I can tell you they are happy they never did what the enemy urged them to do. Please don't do it, you're better than the enemy.

GOD CAN MAKE SOMETHING OUT OF THE WORST

There is a bright side. I've seen many men get fired only to get hired by someone better. I've seen many men leave a job only to start a new career or start their own business. I've seen many a relationship break down so that God could build it up and start it over. I've seen many women leave, only to come running back when the man gets himself together.

To get yourself better, you have to do the spiritual opposite of what people would expect from you. Walk in another direction. Go to a place of worship and renew your spirit and mind, and confess your sins. Get counseling on anger management, or sex, drug, or alcohol addiction. Seek help to deal with past trauma and anxiety. Get a job that fulfills you and financially helps the family. Go back to school and get training to elevate your skills. Get your body in shape and restore your vitality. Use that downtime to elevate yourself.

The best time for a man to get himself together is when he's been rejected, denied or kicked out. When he's been abandoned, cheated on or fired. When he's alone in his cell or homeless on the streets. You should use that downtime to look inside yourself and pull out anything negative that destroys you. Again, examine yourself, think about what got you where you are. Use that downtime, that alone time, to draw out the best in you, the worker in you, the hero in you. Use that downtime to renew your mind, body, and spirit. The next time someone sees you who let you go, put you down, or kicked you out, you should be a new man, full of energy on the inside and happiness on the outside. When you improve yourself for you, it gets back at people more than your outrageous actions. It may take time before God reveals His plan for your life, but nothing is going to happen until you take steps to make it happen. Get up and make it happen!

CHAPTER 12

STEP 5: *Mobility—Part 3*

NOT READY FOR CERTAIN BATTLES

Men must also realize that there are some battles they're not yet ready to engage in. Having the feet fitted is preparing you for peace. But don't go to war with the enemy if you're not ready. You may be eager and passionate to take on certain issues because you know about them from experience. But if you're not spiritually ready with shoes tied tightly, the enemy can take you down easily. This is evident by the number of men who believe they've overcome their addictions and former relationships.

They go out too soon and get caught up again while on a mission to save drug addicts and alcoholics. They thought they could walk into a crack house after being clean six months and try to convert someone else. You need to be clean longer than six months before you try to save the world! A good deed requires a ready person. Just because you're saved doesn't mean you're fully sanctified. Cleansing is a process. The taste, the smell, the feeling of those old forces can still be in you and can drive you right back into the mess that you left.

I can't tell you how many people, including preachers, have fallen back to their wicked ways because they acted too soon. Jesus even knew there were certain battles He was not ready for because it was not yet time for Him, and so when they came after Him, He got away. There are certain battles that men have to think about before they walk into them. You may have to run before you walk.

As already mentioned, Abraham rescued Lot from his enemies in Genesis 14. But then in Genesis 19, Lot is at the gate of Sodom, and God is seeking to destroy Sodom and Gomorrah for their wickedness. Lot went right back to the place from which God rescued him the first time. Had it not been for mercy, Lot and his family would have been killed. Men can get caught up in the same mess after God has rescued them—"saved" them. They're walking backward on feet fitted with temptation rather than with the gospel of peace.

You don't want to go back. If you feel like the taste is still in your mouth when you walk past alcohol, or the smell is getting to your nose when you smell a cigarette or joint, or the feeling is erupting in your body when you see your ex-girlfriend, tighten your shoes and get out of there! Don't go back until those feelings and sensations are gone.

HITTING ROCK BOTTOM

Too often men have to hit rock bottom before they really learn to walk right. God may have to knock a man down real hard before he wakes up and smells the coffee. Like Lot, it may take two, three, or even more times falling before men really get the message. A lot of men go in and out of the house of God, like it has a revolving door. The recidivism rate of men going in and out of churches is higher than prison. A lot of men just don't know how to be disciplined.

It's sad to watch men who are trying and constantly failing. They cry, they beg, they beat themselves up, but then they fall right back into the same pit. Often they fall due to problems that erupt in their lives while they're saved, sending them right back down. But men must be strong in the Lord and the power of His might. Being strong means that if you fall—no matter how many times you fall—you put on your shoes and get back up again. Falling happens to the best of us—believe me, I know, and so do many other well-established brothers. But just like them you can get back up. God wants you to stand. Connect with people who will help you when you fall. Stay connected with people who will help you to keep from falling in the first place. They may not have money, but as Peter said to the crippled man who lay by the temple asking for money: *"Silver and gold have I none; but such as I have give I thee: In the name of Jesus Christ of Nazareth, rise up and walk."*[116] There are people who can help you rise up and walk after you've fallen.

WATCH WHOM YOU WALK WITH

It's important to be in spiritual agreement with whom you walk. Many men backslide as a result of their association with men who are supposed to be walking with God. Every person who says "Lord, Lord" ain't saved. In 1 Kings 22, Jehoshaphat almost got himself killed going into battle with Ahab. Both were kings of God's chosen people. But Ahab was wretched, while Jehoshaphat was gullible. Even after Jehoshaphat heard God's prophecy against Ahab, he naïvely allowed Ahab to convince him to go to war. But by the grace of God, Ahab was killed in the battle and Jehoshaphat was spared. After that episode Jehoshaphat spent the rest of his life in prayer before making any decisions, as well as with the people he befriended.

That's why you have to be careful whom you walk with, because if your shoes are not tight and their shoes are not tied, both of you will trip and fall to temptation. It's the blind leading the blind. It's not always good to befriend a brother in the church just because he came off the streets and you came off the streets. Or because he's a former alcoholic abuser and you are too. Divorced men shouldn't always hang with other divorced men. It can lead to reminiscent behavior, and reminiscent behavior can lead to resurrecting that no-good, dirty old man. The Bible says, *"... put off concerning the former conversation the old man, which is corrupt according to the deceitful lusts."*[117] Sometimes divorced men are best aligned with saved married men, to begin to learn the tenets of a healthy marriage. Be careful reminiscing about the so-called good old days when you were doing the wrong thing. Those old thoughts can put a desirable taste back in your mouth, where you not only remember it,

---

116: Acts 3:6
117: Ephesians 4:22

but desire to re-engage in it. It is the same with get-rich-quick schemes that can overtake a man's mind and lead him in the wrong direction.

GET-RICH-QUICK SCHEMES

Many men get caught up in get-rich-quick schemes out of a hunger for money. Almost every man, at one point or another, has had a get-rich-quick scheme. Either some crazy business idea, gambling, investment that was going to reap millions, or simply some plan to create the world's first flying car. Whatever, it was a get-rich-quick scheme. And most men have lost more, way more, than they've gained with their schemes. The Bible tells us that *the love of money is a root of all kinds of evil.*[118] Remember, God can strip you naked when you come to Him, and make you start at the bottom before you get to the top. The love of money is one of those roots that God can cut out of you so that you can love Him over money, and the love of God will lead you to financial stability.

Some men get impatient at their penniless situation and decide to take matters into their own hands. They always believe they have something to prove to their woman, their children, and other men, and having money is one way to prove status.

In Joshua 7, Achan's sin was that he couldn't resist the temptation to acquire riches. God had commanded the Israelites not to touch the devoted things. But Achan did it anyway and then tried to hide it from his fellow soldiers. Joshua didn't realize why the Israelites had lost their next battle until God revealed to him that they had been walking with a thief in their midst. And the thief caused the loss of about thirty-six soldiers' lives. Men have to learn to be patient and not give into greed or eagerness for money. Yes, a man has to earn a living and provide for his family. But as the Bible says, *"Some people, eager for money, have wandered from the faith and pierced themselves with many griefs."*[119]

It is important that you work for money but not be eager and chase after money. The love of money can lead you to being broke.

118: 1 Timothy 6:10 (NIV)
119: 1 Timothy 6:10 (NIV)

When you run after money, you begin to serve money. And as the Bible confirms, a man *"cannot serve both God and Money."*[120] Put God ahead of money so that He may direct your path to monetary gain. God will provide, and if it is in God's plan that you become rich and famous, then allow God to lead you on the path of righteousness and earthly riches. There is nothing wrong with being rich. Riches can help you do more for those who are suffering and oppressed, but your allegiance cannot be to riches because if it is it will be all about you and you will forsake others. Rather, your allegiance must be to *"seek … first the kingdom of God, and his righteousness; and all these things shall be added unto you."*[121] The path of righteousness will bring you to the place of riches if it is God's will, and once you get there, you will be secure and firm not only in your riches but also in your walk with God. As the Bible says, *"If the LORD delights in a man's way, he makes his steps firm; though he stumble, he will not fall, for the LORD upholds him with his hand."*[122]

SAVE FOR THE FUTURE

Instead of thinking how to get rich quick, men should learn how to save and invest money. The worst place you can be financially is to be caught off guard with no money in your pocket or bank account. Many men max out their credit cards and know what it's like to not have a dime to their name. And a lot of our troubles financially are due to lack of savings as well as lack of understanding on how to invest. When an emergency or unexpected bill or breakdown comes along, we have to use other bill money to pay for the current crisis, causing late payments on present bills. Men must learn to put aside a little something from each check, even if it starts with a dollar.

Joseph was a great accountant; he knew how to put away resources for the coming crisis (see Genesis 41). God had given Joseph the vision, and Pharaoh had given him the job to store up food and distribute accordingly when the famine hit. Every man should know how to store up in good times and distribute accordingly when hard

---

120: Matthew 6:24 (NIV)
121: Matthew 6:33
122: Psalm 37:23-24 (NIV)

times hits. Don't prepare for war during war; prepare for war during peace. And if you've lived for a little while, you know that unexpected problems can hit anytime. And not only do you have to be spiritually strong, but financially ready. When your home needs fixing, your car breaks down, your children get sick, or someone dies, it's the savings that will help you in those times of trouble.

More houses of worship need classes on financial investments for the future. Men need to learn to put their money in places that will reap financial interest when it comes time to take it out. Learn how to invest in stocks and bonds and retirement funds. Make sure you have life insurance for yourself and your family.

And always have cash stashed somewhere that's accessible when you can't get to the bank. One thing you want to do is balance your life through your finances so you won't have to beg, borrow, and steal for you and your family when times get hard.

THE FITTED SHOES HELP YOU TO BALANCE LIFE

As we looked at earlier, the cop in the movie *Heat* didn't know how to balance his life. He came home one day and found another man in his house with his wife. Men tend to get excited when they get into new business ventures or new jobs. The focus and energy required for new ventures can be overwhelming. God has given us natural feet so that we can balance our body. And God has given us spiritual feet so that we can balance our lives.

Consider this from 2 Samuel 11: Although what David did to Uriah by sleeping with his wife was horrible and despicable, the fact cannot be dismissed that Uriah had a problem too. He didn't know when to walk away from his job and rest his feet at home with his wife. Although David had his own plans in mind when he asked Uriah to come home, Uriah, being committed to his assignment, refused to go home and be with his wife. He chose to sleep on the floor of the palace rather than go home and be with his wife. And although his commitment is commendable, we have to also recognize the imbalance in his priorities.

There is a problem when men become so enthralled with their careers that they find little or no time for family or for rest. Wearing the shoes fitted for peace compels a man to walk away and go home; leave the job, leave the church, take a day off from work, or go on a romantic night out with his wife without the cell phone or tablet. The Bible says, *"For if a man know not how to rule his own house, how shall he take care of the church of God?"*[123] Although this verse was designed for leaders in the church, it certainly applies to every man in the world.

Women and children need attention too. The problem with Adam is obvious. The Bible says that while the serpent spoke to Eve his wife, Adam was right next to her. Yet the enemy was able to influence her and tempt him. The problem was that although Adam was with his wife, he wasn't paying attention to her. Many men are with their wives: sleeping with her, eating with her, and talking with her, yet not paying attention to her. The devil is sneaking up right under their noses and taking control of their homes. Men, you have to pay attention and balance your life with your wife and children. It's a shame when your children feel closer to other men than they do to you. It's a shame when your wife can talk to other people more than she speaks to you. You have to check your shoes and where they're taking you. The wrong shoes can kill romance in your relationship. Look her in the eyes and pay attention to what she says; that's the only way you're going to keep the fire burning in the relationship.

KEEP THE FIRE BURNING

It's easy for most men to be romantic and affectionate before they get married or become intimately involved with a woman. But it's hard to stay affectionate and romantic. Most married people get tired after seven years and bored after twenty years, leading to estrangement and ultimate divorce. It is necessary that relationships stay exciting and interesting to remain strong. Men, you have a responsibility to help keep the fire burning. Don't let the affection go out or the love dwindle.

Although the Bible is good at defining love, as in 1 Corinthians

---

123: 1 Timothy 3:5

13, it is not so good at giving concrete examples of healthy, romantic relationships between a man and a woman. However, Boaz is one good example of a romantic man. He sat with Ruth and ate with Ruth and got to know her and developed a love for her (see the book of Ruth). He respected her and took her when no one else wanted her. Boaz saw that she was a virtuous woman, and more than that, he was a decent man. He kept the fire burning in the relationship and they had a child. Men, find a woman you love, trust, and cherish, a woman who respects and adores you, so that being romantic and affectionate won't be difficult to continue 'til death do you part.

Don't get so caught up in your dreams or your business ideas that you can't come home and have a real, rather than a rushed, conversation with your wife. Have a real rather than a rushed talk with your girlfriend. Have a real, rather than a rushed, talk with your children. Drop everything and listen to your children when they're talking. Pick your head up and look at what they're showing you. Compliment them when they've done well. Laugh with them when they're joking and advise them when they're questioning life. Take time to play ball and do homework with them, and take your family to dinner. The reason so many women get upset at their men after a hard day's work is because they're feeling abandoned, overwhelmed, and lonely. Instead of getting angry because she's upset, get loving, get understanding, get busy, and calm her anxiety.

You should thank God she's still getting on you about your neglectful ways. The day you have to worry is the day she starts ignoring or stops caring about what you're doing. That means there's a breakdown in the relationship, and it's going to take fitted shoes to bring love back to the home again. As many men can attest, there is nothing like a woman gone cold. When a woman's fed up, she becomes despondent, distant, and devoid of any feelings in the relationship. It's going to take a lot of work to warm her back up and make the relationship right again. Some men succeed and others don't, but if you love her, you will do all you can to get her back.

GO BEYOND THE BOUNDARIES

And it's always good to use your fitted shoes to take your family, friends, and even just yourself on trips to get out of the same environment. Men, you have to go places that are unfamiliar. Although trips take a little money, it relieves a world of stress. Too many men make the sad mistake of staying in the same environment and community they have problems in or can't get peace in. There are times you have to expand your horizons, so take your fitted shoes and go beyond the boundaries of your local destinations. Find new places to go out of the state or country. Find new people to engage in different conversations. Find new restaurants beyond the neighborhood. The "same old" can become not only boring, but disheartening. And it doesn't always take money; most of the time it takes sacrifice. A good getaway—either alone, with your family, friends, or just you and your wife—can refresh your mind, relieve stress, renew your spirit, and open up your imagination.

Personally I'm a mountain man. And at times I take my son with me. There is nothing like driving or riding long distances and ending up on a mountaintop. You might be by yourself, but with God you're never alone. You might be heavily burdened, but you're still on top. Jesus often withdrew to the mountain and found peace and renewal for His soul. Moses often spoke to God on the mountaintop. Find someplace beyond the boundaries of your locality, and I guarantee that when you come back, you will be a man of good feelings and good news.

THE GOOD NEWS

The gospel is the good news, and the good news is that it feels good when you can walk into your house and not have to worry about lying to your wife about where you've been. It feels good when the Lord orders your steps. It feels good when you walk into the doctor's office and don't have to worry about having an STD test because you've walked upright and the woman you're with is just as virtuous. It feels good when you can walk proudly into the courtroom and declare your innocence regardless of the accusations being thrown at you because you've been living righteously. It feels good when your children run to you because they're happy to see you. The gospel of peace brings calm to your soul no matter what comes your way. And truthfully it just feels good to be at peace with yourself and to be able to rest at night.

Points to Remember from Step 5

Part 1

1. Step 5 for every man is *Mobility*: He is to move graciously into places that will advance his life spiritually and bring him peace wholeheartedly (mind, body, and soul).

2. Seek spiritual and social mobility. God will lead you to better places and people in life when you desire to live in peace.

3. The fitted shoes are for peace. You must learn to walk away from trouble. It doesn't make you weak; it makes you strong.

4. A leader knows how to follow first. Don't allow your ego to disrespect and surpass leadership. It will only lead to more problems in the future.

5. Use the fitted shoes to guide and redirect your actions and impulses toward righteousness.

6. When you die or go to prison as a result of your sin or foolishness, you not only hurt yourself, but you disappoint those who are proud of you and are counting on you for love and protection.

7. Examine your feet to assure they're leading you up the path of peace rather than down the trail of trouble.

8. Throw out anything that tempts you or sets you back. Get rid of people, phones, computers, and anything that might negatively interfere with your walk with God.

Part 2

9. Don't allow your feet to walk into violence and abuse. Be strong in the Lord and don't allow jealousy, anger, or rage to make you do the unthinkable and hurt yourself and your family. You must control yourself and stand strong, soldier.

10. If you can't control yourself, you should leave the home and get help—but never leave your family. Your job is to continue to protect and provide for them while you get yourself together.

11. Use that downtime to elevate yourself, and improve your body, mind, and soul. The next time someone sees you who let you go, they should see a better man.

12. Don't allow pressure and stress on the job to make you angry and want to hurt and kill people. Stand strong. *Stop, drop, pray, and walk away.* When you wake up in the morning, you will be glad you didn't do the devil's work.

Part 3

13. Don't go into battles you're not ready for. Be patient. Some things take time before you develop the strength to compete with the enemy.

14. Don't be ashamed to go and get help. Everybody needs help sometimes.

15. Be careful whom you walk with. Even so-called men of God can lead you into problems.

16. Don't run after money, but run after God and He will lead you to financial stability—and riches if it's His will for your life.

17. Balance your life with your work, your wife, your children, and your worship.

18. Learn how to save and invest money for unexpected challenges, as well as for your future aspirations.

19. Keep the fire burning in your relationship; it will make life happier and easier.

20. Go beyond the boundaries of your locality. Find different places, people, and food to engage you.

21. The gospel is good news. It feels good to walk in peace and sleep in peace because you've made the right decisions and moved in the right direction. You should feel good about your progress in life.

SHIELD OF FAITH

CHAPTER 13

STEP 6: Resiliency—Part 1

Above all, taking the shield of faith, wherewith ye shall be able to quench all the fiery darts of the wicked.

Ephesians 6:16

Nonviolence was one of the profound principles of the Civil Rights Movement of the 1960s. This principle established a discipline whereby one who was seeking justice would not allow the adversary to discourage the soul nor reject the body, regardless of the insult or attack thrown at him or her. One had to possess genuine spiritual discipline to be insulted and not react, to be humiliated and not respond, and to be physically attacked and not fight back. The discipline was effective as long as the disciples of the nonviolence movement developed tolerance and inner strength not to allow any abuse, whether verbal or physical, to get to them. In order to develop this discipline, they had to be strong and focused, but most of all protected by a personal faith that made them impervious to invectives and violent incursions.

A SLAP ON THE CHEEK

The reason the nonviolence method, although effective, became unpopular with many men is because it advocated the "turn the other cheek" philosophy. Jesus said, *"… whosoever shall smite thee on thy right cheek, turn to him the other also..* "[124] The character of many men cannot withstand such an invitation. Turning the other cheek is associated with weakness and abuse. Historically, and even biblically, turning the other cheek is not in character with a warrior personality. God never told any of Israel's soldiers to allow themselves to be slapped around, then allow being slapped again. But the philosophy of nonviolence and Jesus's logic was more about preventing the enemy from controlling you spiritually.

If a crooked police officer pulls you over for a minor violation and insults you, he's hoping that his insults will provoke you to respond harshly, giving him a reason to arrest you. Jesus's logic was simply that if the police officer insults you, turn the other cheek and allow him to insult you again, but don't let him provoke you into responding the way he's hoping so that he controls you and gets you into more serious complications. If he insults you once and knows that if he insults you again, you're going to talk back, then he's got you.

Turning the other cheek is not about the slap; it's about the trap. Don't let the enemy trap you.

BUILD YOUR DEFENSES

How can one develop such forbearance, particularly men who are not only defending their bodies but their pride and reputation. Bible warriors like David had little tolerance. The slightest sign of disrespect would lead David on a rampage. In 1 Samuel 25, when Nabal would not help David and his men after David had helped Nabal, David felt insulted. He girded up his soldiers to attack Nabal and the men of his household. But God allowed Abigail, Nabal's wife, to intercede and calm David. He withdrew from his plans and went back home. David could block spears and javelins, but he couldn't block insults and rejection. They went past his shield and into his heart. If it hadn't been for God providing a buffer through Abigail, David would have demolished the entire household of Nabal.

This kind of behavior reminds me of the old unrighteous, undisciplined man, the weak man. When the old man gets into an

---

124: Matthew 5:39

argument with somebody, it can get ugly to the point that he and the other person are in each other's face. But hopefully, before you hit him or he hits you, someone—a teacher, friend, coworker, police officer, or church member—will jump in the middle and pull you two apart. However, it would be so good if, instead of someone else interceding to prevent a fight, we used our God-given strength to prevent ourselves from striking back.

ABOVE ALL, THE SHIELD OF FAITH

Paul placed great emphasis on this next piece of protective covering. Paul said, *"Above all...."* Stop there for a minute. The special emphasis that introduces this piece of armor makes it worth the pause. If we were to assess the phrase *"Above all,"* it would simply mean *"especially ... primarily ... particularly ... most of all, don't forget to."* And then proceed with *"... taking the shield of faith, wherewith ye shall be able to quench all the fiery darts of the wicked."*[125]

Step 6 for every man is *Resiliency*:

He is to use faith to block evil and bounce back from the enemy's attacks.

Jesus is a great example of someone who was able to endure attacks without striking back, yet was able to bounce back. After Jesus was accused of blasphemy and arrested, the Bible says they spat in His face, punched Him, and smacked Him with the palms of their hands. In all this Jesus never retaliated physically. He didn't allow their false accusations, nor their spitting and hitting, to get to Him and reverse His stance. Instead He stayed true to the task and faithful to the mission. He did this to show that their insults weren't strong enough and their hands weren't hard enough to break Him from His mission and make Him do the unspiritual. Jesus was resilient; He bounced back from death and humiliation in the resurrection. The resurrection shows the

---

125: Ephesians 6:16

resilient effect of Jesus and all who are connected to Him. Resiliency is that ability to endure attacks from the enemy, get knocked down, and bounce back. In the end the resilient ones always win.

A GREAT SHOOTER

The devil is a great shooter. If he were a basketball player, he would be MVP—Most Vicious Provocateur —because his aims are so precise and his targets are so clear. It's easy for him to hit his target and upset his opponent. Like a skilled archer, the devil can shoot with force that makes it almost impossible to stop his arrow or even control it once he lets loose. It's like a gun in your face: your hands are not quick enough to block a bullet after the trigger is pulled. If there is an opening, Satan will find it. If there is weakness, he'll sense it. If there is a target, he'll hit it. If there is a hoop, the devil will dunk it from a thousand miles away. In other words you're dealing with a wicked hustler and professional hassler who take his craft seriously. And his goal is to provoke you, attack you, and make you respond unrighteously.

EXAMINATION OF OUR FAITH

Men, please read this carefully. This is hard, but important. I need you to go back to the examination room. This time, rather than examining a physical feature like your feet, examine a spiritual principle like your faith. Many men lack faith or even dismiss its significance in their spiritual walk. Remember, we walk (with feet fitted) by faith and not by sight.[126] However, it seems many men lack understanding about the importance of faith, so they fail to apply faith to their life circumstances.

In Mark 4 the disciples were on a boat when a storm began to rage. The boat began to rock and they feared it would capsize. The disciples ran to Jesus in a panic and said, "We're going to drown!" Jesus, who had been asleep, calmed the storm and quieted the raging sea. Then He looked at the disciples and asked, "Where is your faith?" I have this same question for many of my brothers: Where is your faith? The

---

126: 2 Corinthians 5:7

question begs a scale rather than location. Where is your faith on a scale from zero to ten? Be honest. Is your faith sufficient? Usually you can best determine the scale of your faith during times of crisis. The disciples on the boat were in the midst of a crisis, and they demonstrated—and Jesus confirmed—their lack of faith.

WHERE IS YOUR FAITH?

Where is your faith when sickness hits you? Can you trust and believe that God will heal? Or do you respond with sorrow, fear, and overmedication? Where is your faith when your money is gone? Do you wait upon the Lord to provide and guide you or do you do anything you can to survive?

CHECK YOUR FAITH

In order to understand your faith, let's do some calculating. Add up your circumstances, along with the consequences, and subtract it by your faith. For example, are you sick or unemployed or divorced (circumstance)? What's the worst that can happen (consequence) as a result of your crisis? Will you die as a result of your sickness, become homeless as a result of your unemployment, or commit suicide as a result of your divorce? Now subtract your circumstance and consequence from your faith. Your faith should be able to diminish your fears of the worst possibility (consequence). Your faith is supposed to give you strength to stand and trust God in the midst of the storm. Faith and lack of faith both speak to you. Faith trusts in God while a lack of faith allows the enemy to control the conversation and your actions. Look at the chart below.

Circumstance—Consequence—Faith/Lack of Faith

Unemployed—Lose house—God will provide/Do anything to survive

Divorce—Loneliness—God is a comforter/Find anyone for comfort

Cancer—Lose erection—God is a healer/Life is over

Indicted—Jail—God will defend/life sentence

Rather than react to your circumstance with human understanding, your faith is supposed to help you *"Trust in the LORD with all your heart and lean not on your own understanding; in all your ways acknowledge him, and he will make your paths straight."*[127] You should be able to respond to your circumstances with spiritual confidence, like Jesus did on the boat. The circumstance was the storm. The worst possible outcome was they could drown. But faith would not have said, "We're going to drown." That kind of talk surrenders to the storm. Faith would have said, "Jesus will work it out. ... My God is able. ... I will survive." That kind of talk trusts God in the midst of the storm. But the disciples spoke in the direction of their faith: down.

TALK TOUGH BUT BELIEVE SMALL

A lot of men talk tough but believe small. When you're a M.A.N., your strength is in your faith. Again, when you're a Man of Armor, your strength is in your faith. Now please say it aloud: "When you're a Man of Armor, your strength is in your faith." You can't afford to go up against a fifty-dollar problem with a five-cent faith.

The Bible tells us, *"Now faith is the substance of things hoped for, the evidence of things not seen."*[128] When we operate by faith, it is the mode of transportation that we use to overcome our fears and get to our destination regardless of the obstacles. In other words faith sees beyond the current crisis into the future promise. The future promise by faith is that God is always acting on behalf of the faithful—those who trust and believe in Him—which is why it is important for us to build up our relationship with God.

127: Proverbs 3:5-6 (NIV)
128: Hebrews 11:1

WORK ON YOUR FAITH

When circumstances and insults are thrown at a M.A.N., it's the best time to prove whether his faith is strong or weak. You don't know if the wall you've built is strong enough until you throw a brick at it. If it stands, it's strong. If it falls, you need to make it stronger. It's the same with faith. When people and circumstances throw stuff at you, if you stand, it's because your faith can handle it. If you fall to temptation, it's because your faith is weak.

If you lack faith, you need to work on it. The Bible says, *"Faith without works is dead."*[129] It takes work to build your faith. Work on your faith rather than on your distractions. Work on not fussing with everybody you come into contact with. Work on not reacting to or retaliating against everything someone says or does. Work on not trying to be everything to everybody. Work on listening rather than talking and standing rather than reacting. Then work on trusting and believing, and letting go and letting God.

CONTRARY TO SOCIETY

Faith in God can be difficult because society expects just the opposite from men. Society expects men to work out their problems on their own, not trust in God to do their work. Society expects men to manage the house and community, to work hard and pay the bills. Coming to Christ, leaning on Him, and living by faith can seemingly usurp societal and personal expectations of men, and reverse their roles and responsibilities. But faith does not take away from a man's responsibility, but rather adds faith to his work. The Bible says we are co-laborers with God, which means we work with God in order to accomplish our goals.[130]

God does not want to do all the work. God wants us to be participants in the project. And having faith is one way we work with God to accomplish our goals. Men must work hard in life and, at the

---

129: James 2:26
130: 1 Corinthians 3:9

same time, have faith in God for guidance. While men are working hard and paying the bills, they are also working hard at trusting in God for the bills to get paid. While men are working on not fussing and fighting, they're also working on fighting the good fight by faith. Once a man is able to work on himself and have faith in God, he will build up enough strength to dissolve any darts that come his way from the enemy.

FIERY DARTS

Before we go any further, let's get a clear description and understanding of these fiery darts and how effective they can be. Fiery darts are flaming circumstances—fiery people who throw their full weight behind the attack or insult that is coming at you. It's fiery because it's meant to inflame you and make you react. Make you mad and get you to do and say things that will get you into trouble and take you away from God and your goals.

I remember watching Captain America fight a villain who threw flames at him. The flames were thrown to incite an angry response from Captain America. But Captain America had a shield and was able to block the fireballs and protect his body. Without the shield Captain America would have been, well, done.

THE DEVIL LOVES TO GIVE THEM; PEOPLE LOVE TO THROW THEM

You have fire coming at you no matter where you are or who you are, whether at home or in church, at school or at work. In the gym or in the street, someone's always going to be throwing darts at you. It doesn't matter if you're a janitor or the president of the United States, darts will come. Darts range from people betraying you to people hanging onto your horrible past.

BETRAYAL

The most hurtful are the darts of betrayal. This dart is the worst not only because it hurts, but because it injures. Betrayal is referred to as being stabbed in the back because betrayal literally feels like someone has taken a knife and stuck it right into your back, especially when you didn't see it coming. Betrayal is when someone (usually someone you know) does you wrong, sets you up, lies about you to protect themselves, or sells you out for their own gain. If you've faced the darts of betrayal, you're not alone. Jesus faced them before you did. Judas betrayed Jesus—sold Him out for a handful of coins.

Jesus had enough spiritual insight to know Judas was going to betray him. Most of us are caught off guard when betrayal comes from friend, family member, churchgoer, coworker, fraternity brother, or someone close to us. When betrayed, the first reaction is to want to *kill* the person who did us wrong. And the devil would love for that to be our response, because the reason he caused the person or people to betray us is that he wanted us to respond in an unspiritual, illegal, immoral, and strictly human way so he could further destroy us.

This is where even I have to pause and ask, *What would Jesus do?* I've been betrayed before in my life, so I know the sentiment and desire for revenge are real. Betrayal can cause stress, anxiety, and anger, and make anybody respond viciously. But in order not to fall into the devil's trap and respond to his plan the way he would want, the shield of faith allows us to step back, assess the situation, and see what becomes of their betrayal. One thing I've learned about people who do other people wrong is that their happiness doesn't last. Their plans only progress so far for just so long. Look at Judas, who committed suicide shortly after betraying Jesus. Not that you hope for the worst for anybody, but by faith allow God to let the wicked blow themselves up in their own plans.

People who betray also worry, fear, and are paranoid over the wrong they've done: again, look at Judas. They're worried about how you're going to respond, whom you're going to tell, and what they should do about your response. But they often suffer in their own plans. While Judas died, Jesus rose. And by faith you never know what God is doing when people betray you. Sometimes, as I stated earlier, other people's evil can lead to your rise. Put up the shield of faith, block the enemy, take the knife out of your back, and trust God to take care of your enemies.

The problem with many men is that they react too fast, never giving God time to prove Himself. Faith means being patient and believing that God will intervene. God will give you the necessary response. Don't take action without God's permission.

THE DARTS OF YOUR PAST

Just like the villain who threw fireballs at Captain America, the people who aim at you are the ones to whom the devil distributes darts. The most powerful are the darts about your past. There is nothing worse than people who have ammunition on you and use it against you. Moses had a past as a murderer because he'd killed an Egyptian. A little while later he saw two Israelites fighting and tried to intervene (Exodus 2). One of them called him on his past and said, "Do you intend to kill me, like you did the Egyptian?" Moses got scared and ran away to another country. People love to throw darts, especially if they know it can disturb you. When there's something in your past that you're not proud of, and family and friends know about it, every time you get into a disagreement, they bring it up: "You're a thief. ... You're a liar. ... You ain't nothing but a cheater. ... You're a rapist. ... You're a murderer." Some men have tried to run like Moses, but found out they can't run or hide from the past.

The reason darts disturb you is because the thrower is reminding you of what you used to be rather than rejoicing in who you've become by the grace of God. People remind you by not hiring you or electing you because of a prior conviction. They remind you and throw darts at you after you've cheated. They throw it at you after numerous offenses on your license. You can't buy or rent a car because of the many accidents or incidents you've had with the law. This can hurt, especially if you've been working at improving your image.

MOVE ON

Some offenses take time to clear. You have to admit it, especially if you did it. If you did the crime, you have to do the time and take the hits. I tell men all the time: just because you've been pardoned by God doesn't mean you won't be penalized by the law or other people. God will forgive you but you still have to face the consequences of your illegal and no good actions. The Bible says, *"God is not mocked: for whatsoever a man soweth, that shall he also reap."*[131] You sowed the sin, did the illegal or immoral deed, and will have to deal with the consequences. David slept with Bathsheba and had to pay with his son's life. Moses disobeyed God and missed out on entering the Promised Land. They were forgiven but still faced consequences.

Confession helps you to face the facts and deal with the assaults. When you admit it, there is no need to get upset at what they're saying. Your confession has already moved you past the transgression and into your new life. Put up the shield of faith and block their assaults. If others want to keep bringing up your past, let them, but you should move on. If you respond, you allow them to pull you back. When you allow them to pull you back, your shield of faith is either weak or broken, which leaves you open to failure. However, when you move on regardless of what they say, you have already proven that you are a better man.

FAITH IS PATIENT

Faith is patient. In your waiting, you have to be patient with an understanding that God heals all wounds. The shield of faith blocks impatience, and keeps you calm and hopeful in the midst of accusations, insults, and rejections. The Bible says, *"But they that wait upon the Lord shall renew their strength; they shall mount up with wings as eagles; they shall run, and not be weary; and they shall walk, and not faint."*[132]

You can block the darts of rejection and insults, betrayal and past transgressions, knowing that ultimately you will be cleared of your past mistakes and rewarded for your diligence. The Bible says, *"But without faith it is impossible to please God: for he that cometh to God must believe that he is, and that he is a rewarder of them that diligently seek him."*[133] You will be rewarded if you just wait and continue to seek God's guidance and block the enemy's assaults.

131: Galatians 6:7
132: Isaiah 40:31
133: Hebrews 11:6

The shield is helping you to hold out and hold back the enemy until God shows up and open doors. It could be a month or it could be ten years, but the whole idea is to keep your shield up in the midst of it all. Don't go back or get angry or do something that will add to your waiting. Go all the way. The closer you get to victory, the harder the darts from the enemy. But as Paul wrote in Romans 5, *"suffering produces perseverance; perseverance, character; and character, hope; and hope does not disappoint us...."*[134] Keep hope in the midst of your suffering which is the greatest gift you can have while waiting for release. Hope keeps you seeking and anticipating the good that God has in store for you. Even if you don't recognize it, the mere fact that you're able to wait and hope shows that God is working in you. Hope and patience come from God. Your character is being developed so that your hope can be realized.

And many times it's about developing your character: what kind of person you are and how people see you, how you speak and if you are genuine about changing. Character is about patience, truth, sincerity, hope, and authenticity. Are you truly changed or are you in need of change before anything concrete happens in your life? You can't act like you've changed just to get something good—God knows when you're ready. People can tell whether you're for real or just faking it for the moment to get something. But a truly changed man will wait upon the Lord, knowing that all things work for the good of them that love God.

RESILIENCY

Character building and hope are what marks a comeback. Many men have suffered scandals, convictions, and prison sentences. If you read the paper, follow the Internet, or look at the evening news, you can find men who have been involved in misconduct that has resulted in humiliation and disgrace. This includes those who are in public and not so public life. I'm sure some men who are reading this book have been involved in some type of humiliation, either in the church, community, job or school. Resiliency is about making a comeback from shame and scandal. The shield of faith makes it possible to come back

---

134: Romans 5:3-5 (NIV)

from betrayal, guilt, divorce, prison, and your horrific past. The shield of faith is so connected to resiliency because faith in Christ is built upon the resurrection. The resurrection is about coming back from death and disgrace to live a better and more productive life. *"I have come that they might have life, and have it to the full."*[135] Those men who have failed and fallen to temptation and found themselves in disgraceful positions are prime candidates for the shield of faith and its resilient effect.

People may hate a liar, thief, cheat, or killer, but those who press forward with a convicted soul and a transformed character can go from humiliation to celebration. Even former critics will begin to applaud a man who has made an unusual comeback. I've seen men— from presidents and pastors to athletes, entertainers, and business executives—come back strong from their indignities and be welcomed back into their community, family, and/or job. So you no longer have to be burdened by your past if you are willing to hold up the shield of faith and trust God.

135: John 10:10 (NIV)

CHAPTER 14

STEP 6: *Resiliency—Part 2*

BE READY FOR COMPARISONS

Let's revisit those darts that can make a man retaliate. Nothing irks a man more or arouses his anger quicker than when a woman throws a fiery dart at him by comparing him to another man. It's one of those areas that touch on pride and masculinity, not to mention jealousy and worth.

"Her husband knows how to fix pipes. I wish you knew how to fix something!" Ooo, that was a smack in the face!

"Why are you always so broke? I should have married a banker." Pow, right in the stomach.

"I hope all women don't have this problem in bed." Um, now that's a hit below the belt.

"You ain't got a job."

"You can't have children."

"You ain't got an education."

"You can't communicate well."

"You're an embarrassment."

"The only reason I'm with you is because of the children."

"You ain't nothing and won't ever be nothing."

Bing! Pow! Those are not darts; those are bombs.

THERE'S MORE

Let's paint the full scenario here. When your woman wants to come home and tell you what to do because she's been telling everybody else what to do all day, she wants to administer on the job and at home, making you feel like less than a man. You feel emasculated because you have to wash clothes and do the dishes every night. To make matters worse, she's yelling at you and making you look and sound stupid in front of the children. She has energy to initiate an argument, but when it's time for her to initiate sex, she's tired. Plus every time you turn around, she's asking you about your female coworker. Accusing you of being too friendly with certain women. Questioning where you been and checking your phone, wallet, and computer. Or you haven't been in the house for five minutes before she's screaming about the bills, what she needs from the store, and mowing the lawn.

All of this and you already had a rough day yourself. This can cause a man to blow up and react with everything from shouts and screams to hatred and violence. How can a man remain immovable in the face of all these assaults?

YOU NEED THE SHIELD TO QUENCH

If you didn't think you needed armor and *"above all … the shield of faith,"* hopefully after reading this section, you will reconsider. In order to quench the fiery darts, you need the shield of faith. What the shield of faith does in this instance is allow the fire thrown at you to be extinguished before it gets to you. The Bible says, *"No weapon formed against you shall prosper."*[136] In other words no matter what is said or how it is said, you have the ability and inner strength provided by the shield of faith to dismiss, dismantle, and even ignore the onslaught—rendering words and actions ineffective. They will not prosper, advance, or affect you because the shield of faith will block them before they get to you.

136: Isaiah 54:17 (NKJV)

The shield of faith keeps you confident and self-controlled in who you are and in your abilities. You can laugh in the midst of their insults because you know who you are: you are a mighty M.A.N. of God. You know how to move away or distance yourself from the problem before it gets to you. When you don't retaliate, it doesn't make you weak; it makes you strong. Your character is strong, your relationship with God is strong. Your faith is strong. You don't have to prove anything to anybody—either they love you or they don't—but you should love yourself enough to not allow anyone to make you do something you will regret.

Your ability, behind the shield of faith, to quench the fiery darts is most important. To *quench* is to *extinguish, put out, smother*. When you can extinguish blazing fire and smother striking offenses against you and not retaliate the way they expect, you have not only matured in life, but also grown in Christ. You have become a true Man of Armor. People will see your change.

Nehemiah gives us a perfect example of what it means to be verbally abused yet faithfully strong. *"But it so happened, when Sanballat heard that we were rebuilding the wall, that he was furious and very indignant, and mocked the Jews. ... Now Tobiah the Ammonite was beside him, and he said, 'Whatever they build, if even a fox goes up on it, he will break down their stone wall.'"*[137] They threw all kinds of assaults at Nehemiah, but he just kept on building the wall. He wouldn't allow their cheap shots, ill manners, and bad intentions get to him. He understood that he had work to do for the Lord. So he remained immovable.

Men must learn how to ignore the haters and keep on building. The enemy's main purpose is to take your mind off your work and your faith off of God. If the devil can distract you and irritate you to get you to respond, he can also get you to stop building up your life, your family, and your community. Remember, the enemy is crafty. Many times it's not about the job; it's about interrupting your faith so you can stop doing God's work and bettering your life. Don't get sidetracked. The shield of faith knows how to block out the enemy and prepare for

137: Nehemiah 4:1, 3 (NKJV)

battle if necessary, but you must keep on building in the midst of the madness. If you stop because of the attacks, you will never see your comeback.

I know pastors who have experienced interruptions and fiery darts in their plans to rebuild the church. And the agitators and instigators can't understand the vision, nor do they like the plans for the future. And it doesn't matter how you change it or include their suggestions, they still won't like it. So they do everything they can to stop you. And many pastors make the sad mistake of stopping the work to retaliate and humiliate the agitators, not realizing all they are doing is giving into the devil and preventing God's plans from going forward. When they stop working, they're practically giving their blessings away to the enemy.

It's like a friend I knew who was being robbed. Two guys ran up on him and said, "Give us your coat." He refused and became angry and decided to fight one of the guys. In the midst of fighting he took off his coat and laid it on the ground, and continued fighting. He beat one guy, but when he looked up, the other man had taken the coat and fled. He practically gave it away. When you stop the work, you practically give into the enemy. The best thing a man can do is to show resistance and continue building in the midst of the madness. This goes for pastors, politicians, corporate executives, and anyone else who has people annoying and obstructing their plans while they're working. Put up the shield while working on the wall. You can build the house and tear the devil down all at the same time.

REASON FOR AGGRESSION

The reason why many men are unable to extinguish the flames of the evil one is because they don't like being disrespected. They don't like being criticized even if they're wrong. Men like being praised, being exalted. They act like their nature is one with God, where they inhabit praise and refute criticism. Men are more sensitive than many think. They don't like being disrespected by their children, their women, or by other men. As we already saw, the reason David went after Nabal is because he felt disrespected and wanted to let Nabal know.

Any word or gesture that signifies disregard or debasement triggers a male emotional alert. The alert can go beyond the shield of faith, past the breastplate of righteousness, and into the heart. The feet fitted for peace then instead proceed toward war. Many men believe that in order to maintain respect, they have to respond to the smallest show of contempt. The more the woman talks, the more the man reacts. The louder she gets, the louder he gets, because he will not allow his ego, pride, and feelings to be stampeded or amputated, not by his supervisor on the job, not by a man behind him beeping his horn, and not by a woman. Many men will not let an argument go until they've won or had the last insult.

TICKING TIME BOMB

Some men have personalities that are not as boisterous or readily aggressive, but they allow insults and ill deeds against them to build up inside them. This type can be equally or more dangerous as the outwardly argumentative and belligerent personality. Allowing all those insults and abuses to add up is like consuming food and never having a bowel movement—after a while it will damage your insides. A lot of seemingly calm men are damaged inside and waiting to explode. And when they explode, it's going to be a mess all over the place. All of that poison from suppressed anger, mixed with insults and abuse, irritation and tension, finally will have gotten to them. And, oh, what an eruption it will be! It would have been better if these men had gotten some stuff off their chests, rather than allowing it to pile up to the point of congestion. Whatever the personality type, all men need the shield of faith.

ASSURANCE BY FAITH

Again, *"faith is the substance of things hoped for, the evidence of things not seen."*[138] Faith being *"the substance"* means that faith has retaliatory, resilient, redemptive, and responsible responses to people's words and actions when they come against you. The substance in faith comes with ingredients that actively quench indignities, insults, inadequacies, and

---

138: Hebrews 11:1

insecurities when thrown at you or residing in you. The shield is made up of a substance that gives hope to your situation, evidence to your battle, and confidence to your soul.

Since faith is the substance, you don't have to add anything to it to do the job. You don't have to add your comments, cussing, anger, or insults to faith. Faith is the substance of things you want to say and hope to say, and the evidence of things you don't have to say. Faith proves itself. Your faith speaks for itself. Your faith says and does what others say you are not doing. Faith is your response. You can just walk away by faith.

When others say, "You're no good," your shield of faith is blocking and extinguishing everything they're saying. Hope will block it, and the evidence will be you not responding to it. The shield of faith gives assurance that what they're saying can't hurt you because it can't get to you. It can't hinder you because it can't hit you. Hope has already dealt with it, and evidence has already extinguished it. Faith's ability to reverse situations, forgive transgressions, and resist temptations shows its resilient effect.

Faith keeps you calm and attentive, feeling good and confident, not hollering and abusive, especially to women.

WOMEN HAVE ISSUES TOO

Men, you have to remember that women have their own issues. They have stress. They have menstrual cycles and menopause that can disrupt their emotions. They have low self-esteem and insecurities, doubts, and fears that they want to throw at someone. But even if they throw it, you don't have to catch it; just quench it. Women say things they don't mean. They do things they regret, and they have issues they haven't confronted, just like us. Women are not perfect; they will tell you that. Men will be more understanding and less retaliatory toward women when they realize women are not perfect. They have their issues, so being offended by every word a woman says or by every deed a woman does only makes you look small, her look big, and the situation worse. With the shield of faith you learn to be more understanding and forgiving, regardless of what is said or done. You learn to put up your shield and quench the darts, realizing it's more about your tolerance than her arguing and complaining.

Have you ever had an argument with your wife or the woman in your life and then the next day you're all lovey-dovey and forgiving? The reason you're lovey-dovey and forgiving is because you didn't allow the argument to go to the extreme. You didn't say or do things to make matters worse. Sometimes all it takes is a good hug and kiss and you can love the "hell" out of someone.

The enemy loves confusion and arguing in a relationship. But you can kick the devil's butt when you pull out love, because love conquers confusion. But relationships have a problem when the man and woman can go for two and three days or even weeks without communication and increased tension. The shield is either broken or unused. Ephesians 4:26 says, *"Do not let the sun go down while you're still angry."*[139] If you do go to bed angry, you have to check your shield, because something is seriously broken.

If at any moment you feel like the insults hurled at you are breaking through your shield, get up, put on your shoes fitted for peace, and get out of there! You need time to fix your faith and tie your shoes because the insults are getting to your heart.

MONOGAMY DEFENDED

But after the exit and your return, the nastiest argument can still result in the greatest lovemaking. That's why I say "Nonsense" when some men tell me that having sex with one woman for the rest of your life is like eating chicken every day. In defense of monogamy: in the course of a relationship there are many obstacles, arguments, incidents, good times, and bad times you two go through that have an impact on your emotions and sex life. Each incident or encounter throughout your time together brings a different form of sexual intimacy.

After an argument there is a different feeling of intimacy than

---

139: Ephesians 4:26 (NIV)

after a child is born. There is a difference in lovemaking when you're young and eager than when you're older and more comfortable. When you're exhausted, there is a different lovemaking than when you're well rested. There is a difference in lovemaking when you're stressed than when you're relaxed, a difference when you're at home than when you're on vacation. There is a different sexual experience when it's romantically planned than when it's spontaneous in the middle of the night or day. There is a difference when you have time to yourselves than when you have to rush and get a quickie. It's different in the bedroom than when you're in the bathroom or the living room or anyplace else ... Well, you get my point.

The differences are good. As a M.A.N. you have to make the difference in your sex life with the one you love. You don't always have to lie in the bed. If you still have the stamina, try other places. If you don't have the strength like you used to, be creative; a loss of strength doesn't mean a loss of imagination.

In addition people change physically and hormonally, which can add to sexual intimacy and make it lovingly distinct from any other time you've engaged. So don't allow the devil to make you fall prey to sexual promiscuity in the name of adventure and finding something different. You can have a great adventure on different rides with the person you're already with.

CHAPTER 15

STEP 6: *Resiliency—Part 3*

THE COMBINATION COMING AT YOU

I told you how God allowed a combination of hits to Job's life to come from the enemy. The combination is when situations occur back to back. Before you get over one, another one is coming at you. Job experienced the loss of his children, the depletion of his main investments (servants and livestock), and a stressed-out wife, all right in a row. When the enemy can't get one thing to break you, he'll throw a combination of darts, missiles, and bombs at you. He'll get people and circumstances to come at you. The enemy can hit your health, and when you're sick, it can affect your career and money. And what affects your career and money can affect your home and family. What affects your home and family can affect your confidence and security. And what affects your confidence and security can affect your faith in God.

BILL AFTER BILL AFTER BILL

The shield of faith becomes absolutely necessary when combinations hit. To throw up your hands and not deal with the onslaughts is not the right response. No matter how tiring and trivial it is, you have to deal with it. This statement is truly for the faithful: "God will not give you more than you can handle." Absorb that for a minute, and if you never heard that saying or can't fully comprehend it, go to the nearest churchwoman or preacher and ask them what it means. The reason why Job faced so many problems is because his faith was strong enough to handle it. God didn't give him anything that his faith didn't measure up to. The same is true with us. God knows how much we can handle. And although it may seem like a lot, God believes that it is just enough for who we are in Christ at the moment.

It's like a job. The reason the boss would be willing to promote you and give you more responsibility is because the boss sees ability and potential in you. The same goes for your faith. God sees ability and potential in you for your faith to handle multiple problems. So when combinations come, put up the shield of faith and deal with it. The shield of faith was made for combinations. It allows you to maneuver, so that no matter where the fire is coming from, you can go into action like Captain America and extinguish it. Whatever *it* is, don't run. Deal with it. When there's bill after bill after bill after bill, don't be alarmed. Stay calm and block it. Get on the phone and deal with it. Go to the boss and deal with it. Get to the doctor and deal with it. The worst thing you can do is ignore, run, and hide from darts, because it will only make matters worse. Trust and have faith in God while you're dealing with it all. You'll be surprised how God works it out.

THE DEVIL TRIES TO KEEP YOU FROM YOUR BLESSING

Through the combination of assaults the enemy's hope is that you give up and either break down or do something stupid. But in the shield of faith, you have a friend. Think of it like this: the devil is throwing all kinds of obstacles at you to stop you from getting to something that God has for you. It must be something good, because why else would the devil put all kinds of obstacles in your way? Joshua and his armies fought against the many ferocious enemies that engaged them in battle, and their enemies fought to block the way to the Promised Land. But Joshua kept on fighting until he took the land.

There is something on the other side of those darts, but if you fall or falter or throw up your hands in defeat, then you will never see it. However, if you stay strong and faithful to keep moving in the midst of sadness, madness, and multiple problems, you're bound to see a great blessing. The hotter the darts, the bigger the blessing. The more the attacks, the more the open doors. It could be a new job or a stronger character. It could be a promotion or increased faith. It could be a new home or peace and calm like you've never experienced before in your life. It could be a new spirit or renewed health and strength. Get beyond the enemy lines and you will see what God has waiting for you.

STEP OUT ON FAITH AND START YOUR OWN BUSINESS

The shield of faith works cooperatively with the feet fitted with the gospel of peace. Many men complain and are depressed when they can't get a job because companies won't hire them—either because of their past mistakes, discrimination, lack of qualifications and education, or a bad job market. But the shield allows you to step out on faith and hire yourself.

Men have talents and abilities but wait for others to do for them what God has empowered them to do for themselves. Jesus said to the man who had been crippled thirty-eight years, *"Pick up your mat and walk."*[140] Jesus wanted him to get up and do something for himself. If no one is hiring, you have to get off your couch and seek the Lord for direction to use your God-given talents. Start your own business. If you can sing, sing at different venues. If you can fix cars, become a certified mechanic and work on your neighbors' cars until you get your own shop. If you can cook, start catering events until you are able to open your own restaurant. If you mow lawns, mow your neighbor's lawn, or start a lawn care or landscaping business. If you can sew, start a tailoring business, and sew people's clothes in the church or the house next door.

There are so many jobs beyond the conventional that don't require extensive educational degrees—from various positions in real estate, electrical, computers, and plumbing to owning a barbershop, restaurant, or computer shop. You need to have faith to invest your time in reading, observing, and working with others until you have a

---

140: John 5:8

clear understanding as well as a passion to step out on faith and start your own business. The internet and social media are making it possible to start all kinds of businesses for cheaper and less staff, why wait on anybody but God.

Just make sure you do your homework and research for what it means to own your own business. There is a difference between having the talent and starting the business. Talent is a gift from God; business is a platform of the world. You have to know how to pay bills, file taxes, and keep up on business news and the latest developments related to your particular field. You have to know how to relate to your customers, market your goods, and maintain a good reputation with your services. I've seen a lot of businesses start up, just to shut down a week later, either because of a lack of business knowledge or unrealistic expectations. Start small and work your way up. Educate yourself through formal and traditional means. Seek out professional people who can help you where you lack the ability or knowledge to produce. Seek out degree and non-degree programs and training courses for your own edification and business acumen. The economy is quickly changing from one of manufacturing to one of technology. And you want to be prepared both artistically and intellectually for the changes. The shield of faith gives you strength to block out the impossible and do the probable.

Men have so many talents that can be utilized in different ways beyond the usual. Instead of being the borrower, step out on faith and be the lender. Instead of being the hired, step out on faith and be the one hiring. Instead of being the renter, step out on faith and be the owner. There is nothing like owning your own, whether it is your house, car or business. When a man purchases his own home, many will tell you, it's the greatest feeling of satisfaction and advancement in his life. Men will do all they can, even in the midst of financial difficulty, to maintain their home and car because it's ownership, it's pride, and it's a possession that was earned.

No man should be idle, just sitting around doing nothing. You have to earn your living. You have to earn your degree. You have to earn your possessions. As the old saying goes, "Idle hands are the devil's workshop." King David found this out when he was supposed to go to work and fight battles with his army, but instead he stayed home (see 2 Samuel 11). While he was home doing nothing, he peeked out the window and saw a beautiful woman. The idle time brought the devil crashing into his life. The sequence was as such: David ended up sleeping with another man's wife, she ended up getting pregnant, and David ended up having her husband killed. God ended up punishing David, and most of David's children ended up dead or destructive as a result of their father's sin. If only he had done what he was supposed to do with his time, he wouldn't have had time to do no good.

Men must learn to use their time wisely, network, and market their talents and availability when looking for employment. What good is it to be looking for a job and no one knows about it except your momma, girlfriend, or wife? And the only reason they know is because you're home all day. Put yourself out there. Let people know wherever you go that you are looking for a job. Let them know about your talents, abilities, and past work history.

If you have a job and are looking for something more spiritually and financially rewarding, you have to let people know. The Bible says, *"Cast thy bread upon the waters: for thou shalt find it after many days."*[141] The position may not come right away, but at least you put it out there, and by faith you can be sure that God will give you a return on your investment. Don't be too proud to hang around people and places that can help you get to the next level of your career. If you want to be great, you have to hang around great! Go to network events and get to know people that can help you find your passion and interest. Don't be afraid to speak up to your boss about your interest in certain positions for promotion. No one will ever know what you're interested in if you don't open your mouth. Jesus said, *"Ask, and it shall be given you; seek, and ye shall find; knock, and it shall be opened unto you: For every one that asketh receiveth; and he that seeketh findeth; and to him that knocketh it shall be opened."*[142] You have to open up your mouth, hustle, and believe by faith

---

141: Ecclesiastes 11:1
142: Matthew 7:7-8

that God will answer your request. *"Ye have not, because ye ask not."*[143]

RAPPERS AND FAITH

I know many of us get on rappers because of their foul language and arrogance, but we need to take notice of faithful people in all walks of life while distancing ourselves from filth and self-glamorization. Many rappers stories are filled with courage and faith. Many will tell you they started selling their CDs around the neighborhood before they got a record deal. They stepped out on faith and produced the CD, some with the last few dollars they had. They took it to every friend, family member, nightclub, and street corner and sold it. They put it on the Internet, YouTube, Facebook, streaming services, and other social media sites, and it blew up in popularity. One thing led to another, and some got the big record deal they were striving for. Others didn't need it because they knew how to promote their own goods and get their own sales.

You don't ever have to wait for big companies or corporations or high-profile people to validate you or determine your worth. God is bigger than all of them, and God will make a way for your success. This is true for men from all walks of life, from guys who sell T-shirts to men who start hedge-fund and publishing companies. Many major corporations were started in economically depressed times, and many small businesses grow during times of recession. Many men have stepped out, left a good-paying yet unfulfilling job, and chased their dreams. Some found it, while others didn't. Some gained, others lost. Still others never stopped searching, because many times the joy is in the search, the stepping out, the asking, the seeking, the knocking. Again, *"seek, and ye shall find."* You'll never know what God has in store for you until you step out on faith.

THE SHIELD OF FAITH KEEPS YOU HEALTHY

Let's talk about health and strength. The shield of faith can keep you healthy, especially during combination assaults and while you're

---

143: James 4:2

exercising your talents and abilities, because you're constantly moving and maneuvering so the enemy can't stop you. You have to think of every battle as a spiritual encounter, and you have to be fit spiritually as well as physically to take on the enemy. It's important for men to keep healthy through exercise as well as eating nutritionally. This is an area a lot of men ignore. Some men work out, but eat wrong. Men can be the worst eaters and lose interest even in exercising after a certain age. But you must keep fit.

Ten to twenty push-ups and sit-ups a day, and even basketball or racquetball will do. Bike riding is great exercise. Golf is good for socializing, but it also has its physical advantages it you are walking the path. Jogging and walking aid in weight loss and increased energy. Jesus rode in boats, but He also walked to spread the good news. Paul sailed, but he also walked to spread the gospel. The children of Israel walked hundreds of miles to get to the Promised Land. Being healthy will not only help your spiritual life, but also your internal organs, your sex life, and your mental and emotional balance. And this is important because some men have a family history of certain illnesses and should do everything to prevent that history from taking them out.

Exercise will also help you to relieve stress and take out your aggression in places other than at home or on the job. It's better to hit a punching bag than your children or wife. It's better to run around a track or up and down a basketball court than to run away from home. It's better to kick a soccer ball or football than to kick your boss's butt. Exercise is a stress reliever.

EAT RIGHT

We must learn to eat right. Use the shield to block out unhealthy foods and turn down some plates. You don't have to eat every piece of fried chicken and every piece of bacon coming at you. It may insult some people when you don't eat their food, but if you do eat it, it can hurt you. You can refuse it. If the devil can't get you with words and insults, he will get you with beef and bacon, cakes and ice cream, starch and fast foods that he will throw in your face. And because you can't resist temptation, you'll eat every bit of it and suffer the consequences of your greed. The spiritual challenge to greed is moderation, discretion and balance. We have to watch the foods we eat because men suffer from diabetes, heart disease, vitamin and hormone deficiencies, and high cholesterol at alarming rates. And a large part of our suffering is due to diet. It is absolutely necessary that we monitor the foods we eat to assure health and vitality. Even certain drinks can be just as harmful to the diet as foods. Get rid of those sodas and beers; drink more water and natural juices. It will help replenish the body and invigorate the soul.

FASTING

Fasting can become a great way to block out foods and build resistance. Fasting is a spiritual discipline in which you purpose to let go of some things for a certain amount of time until they are completely out of your life. Some people fast for three days, others for twelve, others for forty days, like Jesus, to build up their resistance to evil. In Matthew 4, Jesus fasted forty days and forty nights, and then resisted the devil's attacks. Fasting teaches you how to resist the fleshly desires; this includes foods as well as lusting after the flesh. The shield of faith is able to build up resistance and block out physical temptations.

For Jesus fasting built up resistance to food and the flesh. The first temptation Jesus faced was about filling the body. *"If you are the Son of God, tell these stones to become bread."*[144] But Jesus had already filled His soul with God's power through fasting and praying, so He was immune to physical temptation. Once you build up your soul by fasting, you can more easily resist the devil—and he will flee.[145]

Fasting also includes resisting temptation in other areas, such as the computer, phone, television, sweets, and even sex. Try fasting for a day or two from things that are consuming you, controlling you, or causing you problems, and I guarantee it will change your behavior as well as your physical structure.

144: Matthew 4:3 (NIV)
145: James 4:7

CELIBACY

Celibacy is the ability to restrain from sex. This includes not interacting sexually in any way with anyone or by yourself. Everything from masturbation to intercourse is rejected. This is a hard discipline for many men. To not have sex is like not breathing. However, I've known men who have made the commitment and kept it until they met and married the right person. Some have gone for days, others for years, but they all can testify to the glorious benefits that it had for them and their partner when the time came—from longer sex to greater intimacy, to spiritual connection and loyalty and more powerful ejaculations. No doubt it is difficult and challenging, but it is possible and calls for a great deal of spiritual strength and physical discipline. Celibacy is especially good if you believe you have a sex problem, as in constantly needing to have sex and being willing to have sex with anyone. Celibacy keeps you in control of your body and not your body in control of you.

CONFIDENT AND SECURE

A big part of blocking the enemy and staying healthy is to be confident and secure in your faith. And your faith makes you confident and secure in who you are as a man. Many men are insecure and lack confidence because of height, sickness, handicap, being less endowed, erectile dysfunction, being overweight, speech impediment, lack of money, lack of education, or an inability to read or write, as well as minimal biblical understanding. Insecurities can make a man lose faith and friends because it shows his weakness. And men don't like to be looked on as weak. As a result men add an increased layer of competitiveness and impressions to offset their insecurities and inabilities.

Many men can't handle their women advancing educationally or professionally because they feel the woman is moving ahead of them. Many men can't submit to a female supervisor, pastor, professor, or elected official because they feel that they as men should be the head and not the tail. These men become intimidated, and some women exacerbate the problem by bashing, downing, and dart-throwing. These men must realize that God calls women to leadership posts as well as men (see Deborah, Esther, and Jesus's mother, Mary). They, just like you, must be respected and exalted for their talent, intelligence, ability, worth, and calling.

When a man is insecure, it turns his relationship into competition rather than friendship. Men, you don't want to be a hindrance out of lack of confidence because of the advancement of your woman, children, friends, or coworkers. It will hurt your family, friends, and your own blessings. In order for you to be comfortable in other people's progress, you have to be confident in your own soul. You have to be appreciative in the talents and gifts that God has given you. Don't allow jealousy and envy to control you and bash others. The way you build up confidence is by faith. Faith is able to overcome weakness and show strength. For God's strength *"is made perfect in weakness."*[146]

Faith gives assurance and confidence, regardless of the limitations in your life. Neither handicap, nor sickness, nor lack of education, nor unemployment should stop you from feeling good about what God has done for you and who you are. You should thank God for you. You should celebrate the gifts God has given you, as it will also help you celebrate others. You don't have to compare or compete with anybody—male, female, not even yourself. You have to seek God to develop your gifts. Where you lack in one area, God can take another part of you and expand it. Ray Charles could not see with his eyes, but his ears were in tune and his gift for playing the piano was enhanced.

Look at the men of the Bible. Paul had a pain in his side. It hurt him and called his faith and ministry into question. But God assured him, without taking the pain away, that *"My grace is sufficient."*[147] Remember, God will never give you more than you can handle. Paul pursued his ministry in spite of his misery. Moses, the great freedom fighter of God, had a stuttering problem (see Exodus 3). His speech was inarticulate. He felt inadequate to carry out the will of God. But God gave him a partner in his brother Aaron to lead the people. And Moses became one of the greatest leaders in the Bible. Naaman was an

---

146: 2 Corinthians 12:9 (NIV)
147: 2 Corinthians 12:9 (NIV)

army commander, but the Bible says he had leprosy, the most despised disease at the time (see 2 Kings 5). But it never stopped him from doing his job. Naaman, with leprosy, was able to carry out his duties as one of the great soldiers in the Bible. God ultimately blessed him and cured him of his disease, and he continued to fight for his king. His abilities overshadowed his sickness.

GOD CAN STILL USE YOU

Whatever deficiency you may have, God can work with it or deliver you from it. So there is no need for you to feel insecure or to lack confidence. Don't focus on your deficiency, because God's grace is sufficient. The shield can block all of that. Instead focus on your abilities and combine it with faith in God, and watch God increase your gifts and talents, and enhance your life and love for self. And when you have love for self, you can appreciate others.

The shield of faith builds up security and confidence, because where you feel ill measured, faith steps in and pulls you up to par and even beyond your wildest expectations. Faith will help you feel comfortable with yourself and allow you to handle your situation. Faith gives you an inner assurance and enrichment. It dilutes any inadequacy you may be feeling inside or perceiving as coming from others. The insults that once affected your sense of security and confidence will be extinguished. When you're secure, you can rejoice and be happy about other people's progress; this goes for your wife and kids as well as for friends and coworkers. You should want to see your children advance. Every generation should go higher than the last. When they advance, rejoice, for a great faith has been realized.

Again, the Bible says, *"Resist the devil, and he will flee from you."*[148] Just imagine if someone or something that used to vex you couldn't get to you anymore. No matter what they say or do, you sit there calmly, yet not stubbornly or selfishly, reading your paper and drinking your coffee. What a Man of Armor you've become! When you're secure in your faith, the winds may blow, the storms may rise, but nothing will

---

148: James 4:7 (NIV)

be able to separate you from the love of God.[149] Your shield has become a great anchor of stability and assurance.

YOU DESERVE SOME PROPS

I want to pause and commend the men who have put on the armor thus far. They have on *the belt of truth, the breastplate of righteousness, the feet fitted with the gospel of peace,* and *the shield of faith*—four stringent and potent pieces of protection. You Men of Armor look really good! Each of you is already becoming a better M.A.N. To come this far isn't easy. Putting on the armor of God has made you look like a new man. Applying this armor should make you feel like a new man. You've made progress in both your personal and spiritual life. From here you should be able to note one or more things you've done to prove the enemy wrong. Note one change you've seen in yourself and in your life, to prove to yourself how God is working on you.

Men need commending. Men need inspiration, encouragement, and affirmation for their good and faithful deeds. Let someone read this part who hasn't said a good word to you in a while. Let them know that it's good to compliment a M.A.N. In Matthew 25:14-30 the Bible talks about an owner who gave talents (money) to three men, and when he returned, two of them had multiplied what had been given them. The owner commended them by saying, *"Well done, good and faithful servant!"*[150]

So let me pause here and say to those who have been given the armor thus far and have acknowledged the necessity of it, practiced it, and struggled with it: *"Well done, good and faithful servant!"*

However, I know there are some reading this book who have not practiced its message or taken seriously its purpose, like the one who did nothing with the talent his boss gave him. To them I say, "Please try again. Please take this seriously." This is not a book for just your enjoyment; this is a book for your survival and salvation. If your home caught on fire, you wouldn't stop throwing water on it. You would keep

---

149: Romans 8:38-39
150: Matthew 25:21, 23 (NIV)

throwing water on it until the fire went out. Your souls are burning. Keep putting the armor on so it can quench the fiery darts. Now finish getting dressed.

Points to Remember from Step 6

Part 1

1. Step 6 for every man is *Resiliency*: He is to use faith to block evil and bounce back from the enemy's attacks.

2. The shield of faith is resilient. It allows you to bounce back from harsh attacks.

3. The shield of faith is a tool for blocking the enemy's darts. Insults, arguments, betrayal, lies, and past indiscretions are all darts the enemy throws at you, and the purpose is to make you retaliate and do something ungodly.

4. Increase your faith so that you do not fall into the trap of the enemy. Satan is shrewd, but God is wiser.

5. Don't allow fiery darts to bring you down or make you do something stupid.

6. Be patient and not ashamed of past mistakes. You did the crime, do the time. Believe that God will deliver and set you free. Once you're free, God can bring you back from disgrace.

Part 2

7. Don't allow anger to build up inside of you. It will only lead to more serious problems when it finally comes out. Say what's on your heart and move on.

8. Don't allow the enemy to stop you from building up your life. Keep building even while darts are thrown at you.

9. Faith is the substance of reversal, forgiveness, and resistance. You don't need to add anything to faith; it speaks for itself. Your faith can calm a situation rather than escalate it.

Part 3

10. Hits are darts from the enemy to keep you from getting to what God has for you. If you give into the hits, you will miss the gift.

11. With faith you can hire yourself. Use your God-given talents to start your own business. Step out on faith and trust God. Don't look for anybody to validate your worth. God is bigger than all of them.

12. Exercise the body and eat healthy. Watch your diet, because overindulgence and greed can lead to sickness.

13. Fasting is a way to build up resistance to control the body so the body won't control you. There are many things that you can fast from: food, computers, sex, etc.

14. Be confident and secure in the abilities God has given you. You don't have to compete or feel intimidated by anybody. Applaud and support others, and thank God for you.

15. You deserve applause: *"Well done, good and faithful servant!"*

16. Please don't give up!

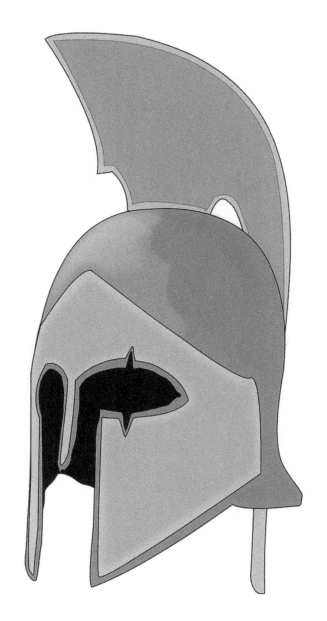

HELMET OF SALVATION

CHAPTER 16

STEP 7: Mentally—Part 1

And take the helmet of salvation....

Ephesians 6:17

When I was younger, my friend's brother was riding on a motorcycle and went over a bump near the sidewalk, which caused the bike to flip and sent him flying through the air. He came down on his head and died. He wasn't wearing a helmet. The ambulance came, and the emergency workers said wearing a helmet could have saved his life. Growing up, I heard stories like this over and over again—men dying in motorcycle accidents because they didn't wear their helmets. You would think that after hearing about so many accidents, men would put on their helmets and protect their heads when riding, knowing that it could save their life.

HARDHEADED

The reason many men die, both spiritually and physically, is because they can be hardheaded, ignoring laws and not following instructions. God often called the Israelites a stiff-necked people because they were stubborn and relentless in their disobedience. God wanted to destroy them many times because of their obstinacy, but instead had mercy and spared them despite their perversity. As men get older, they can get stuck in their position and perspective about life and only a holy act of God can change their minds.

TRANSFORMED BY THE RENEWING OF YOUR MIND

The helmet of salvation protects the head. And Paul was right when he began with *"And take ... "* because no man should be home or leave home without *"the helmet of salvation"* as another piece of armor. The head contains the mind, and the mind contains thoughts, knowledge, wisdom, and understanding. When we came to Jesus, a part of our whole salvation was the transformation of our thinking: *"And be not conformed to this world: but be ye transformed by the renewing of your mind, that ye may prove what is that good, and acceptable, and perfect, will of God."*[151]

Step 7 for every man is *Mentally*:

He must use his transformed mind to resist temptation

and glorify God in what he thinks, says, and does.

The mind is a primary tool of godly living, and its transformational thinking must be protected. The mind helps us to prove the good, acceptable, and perfect will of God. Our transformed thinking and communication is proof of our salvation.

Salvation is a confirmation of our reconciliation with God. It says we are not condemned, but salvaged. What I stated earlier about salvation warrants repeating and elaborating: salvation is God saving us from afterlife condemnation (hell) and present-life desecration, embarrassment, and death. We could have died in our failure, faults, sins, and diseases, but God rescued (saved) us from ignorance, darkness, and despair, and brought us into the light of a new life so that we can see the wrong we were living. Some people who are living erroneously don't even know it and will continue to fail, but when God rescues us— saves us—He opens our eyes to our flaws and gives us an opportunity to reverse our course in life. Same as He did for Paul in Acts 9. The Bible says God knocked Paul off his high horse and blinded him, and then when Paul opened his eyes, he saw the light of his past transgressions

---

151: Romans 12:2

and future promises. Seeing the light caused Paul to correct his present so that he would not have to live with the afterlife punishment of his past. The reason Paul was able to go all the way with Jesus was because his thinking changed. When God brings us out of darkness and into the light, our mind becomes set on fulfilling our salvation by doing His will for the rest of our lives.

The helmet completes our salvation by imparting into our mind the ways, thoughts, will, knowledge, and understanding of God. The helmet keeps filth and forces from entering the head and corrupting the cranium. As a saved M.A.N. you have a head that needs to be protected if you're going to do the will of God. Thinking rationally and critically exerts divine intelligence over any sinful situation. When you can reason well and outsmart the devil, then you know you're saved.

A MADE-UP MIND

The truth is, you can't fully love God without a made-up mind. Jesus said, *"You shall love the Lord your God with all your heart, with all your soul, with all your strength, and with all your mind...."*[152] How can you be saved if you don't love the Savior? If there is any corruption in you, the helmet of salvation provides the purification of your mind to love God with fullness and to look upon Jesus with gratefulness. This is important because when you love someone, you don't disappoint them or cheat on them or leave them. You are true to them. You don't turn away or run away when times get tough; you stay committed regardless of the temptation. The perseverance of the saints is a well-regarded attribute that God has given to those who love Him, which encourages continuation with God regardless of circumstances. This is important because the helmet puts God at the *head* of your life; the *top* of your agenda. No longer will you be led by your own understanding, but rather, in all your ways you will be guided by the Savior. David said it best in Psalm 23: *"The LORD is my shepherd; I shall not want. He maketh me to lie down in green pastures: he leadeth me beside the still waters. He restoreth my soul: he leadeth me in the paths of righteousness for his name's*

152: Luke 10:27

sake.[153] When God is head of your life, He takes the driver's seat and you take the passenger seat. Once you take the passenger seat, you allow God to open your mind to the possibilities that lay ahead.

THE HELMET CAN SAVE YOUR LIFE

Just like a motorcycle helmet, the helmet of salvation can actually save your life. If the enemy can get to your mind after you've been saved, he will corrupt your being and send you right back into the thinking of the world. That's why Paul emphasizes the distinction between being *"not conformed to this world"* and being *"transformed by the renewing of your mind."*

The mind of the world is different from the mind of God. The mind of the world is what we had when we lived with that *old man*. The mind of the world is controlled by forces, powers, and rulers that seek to rob, steal, and destroy. The worldly mind inhabits corrupt thoughts, and the body carries them out. That's why you can find very intelligent men committing heinous crimes. They could have been something great in the world, but instead they used their talents to cheat and deprive people—Ponzi schemes, smuggling millions of dollars worth of drugs and guns into the country, political corruption, racketeering, insurance fraud, etc. It takes intelligence to devise and implement these schemes. However, the mind of God seeks to lift up harmony, live righteously, and do things legally, morally, and intelligently for the sake of salvation. A righteous mind can be just as—and even more—effective in doing good as a wicked mind in doing harm. A righteous man will choose to use his intelligence, protected by his helmet, to do righteous acts.

GOD GAVE US A NEW MIND

A major transformation was needed and given when we got saved. One of the greatest gifts of God is implanting us with new thinking. Worldly thinking is antithetical to God's way, and once we get the new mind—transformed thinking—we must protect it. The helmet of salvation is a major protective covering because it keeps our minds safe

---

153: Psalm 23:1-3

from the enemy and focused on God's will for our lives. The will of God is that we be persistent in our thinking and salvation. In other words nothing should be able to separate us from the love of God. Paul asked the question: *"Who shall separate us from the love of Christ? Shall tribulation, or distress, or persecution, or famine, or nakedness, or peril, or sword?"*[154]A made-up mind would say, like Paul, *"Nay, in all these things we are more than conquerors through him that loved us."*[155]

Paul not only showed his confidence and his commitment, but also his conviction by stating: *"For I am persuaded, that neither death, nor life, nor angels, nor principalities, nor powers, nor things present, nor things to come, nor height, nor depth, nor any other creature, shall be able to separate us from the love of God, which is in Christ Jesus our Lord."*[156] Paul's words give us inspiration for persistence to not allow anything to get in our heads and separate us from God.

He specifically threw in the words *"principalities"* and *"powers"* because those no-good principalities and powers are always trying to separate us from God. Paul presented it as a question, so we can examine our minds to think of those things that will try to separate us from God.

EXAMINATION OF THE MIND

The Bible says in Jeremiah 17:10: *"I the* LORD *search the heart and examine the mind, to reward a man according to his conduct, according to what his deeds deserve."*[157] We can by no means ignore the relationship between the head and the heart. The heart and mind, emotions and thinking work together for the good of God. We must understand how corruption can flow from the heart to the head and from the head to the heart. So as we cleanse our hearts, we also are examining our minds.

What's on your mind that is corrupt or destructive or burdensome that can separate you mentally, intellectually, rationally, emotionally, and spiritually from God? Think about it. What would it be? What is on

---

154: Romans 8:35
155: Romans 8:37
156: Romans 8:39
157: Jeremiah 17:10 (NIV)

your mind more than God? Call it out! Is it money or the lack of money? Is it power or no power? Is it sex or no sex? Is it love or the lack thereof? Is it death or strife? Is it your career or the lack of one? What is the devil putting in your head constantly to make you lose focus on God's will for your life? These things mentioned are not necessarily evil in and of themselves. But they become evil when you mentally overindulge, or they consume most of your time and leave little thought for God to direct your path in these matters. If any of these is a problem, the Bible says, "*seek ye first the kingdom of God, and his righteousness; and all things shall be added unto you.*"[158] You must prioritize your thinking, put God at the top of your yearning, and get rid of anything that is robbing God of His rightful place in your life. The promise in the verse is that if you seek God first, everything else will fall into place (love, money, career, etc.), but you have to first get rid of anything that tops God so you can attain the other promises from God.

GET IT OFF YOUR MIND

If it is not of God, rebuke it right now. Get it off your mind. Let it not consume a great deal of your thinking. Let it not be at the top of your priority list. Separate your worldly desires from your godly thoughts. Throw out your worldly thinking and keep your godly thinking. Then quickly put on the helmet of salvation to prevent the worldly thinking from getting in and to keep the godly thinking from being attacked.

These protective coverings are there to secure you. They're the guard at your door. Once you kick the enemy out, you have to secure the premises so that he does not get back in. If you don't secure the premises, you will have defeated the whole purpose of the covering. Psalm 46 says, "*God is our refuge and strength, an ever-present help in trouble.*"[159] The helmet is a refuge that actually protects you and helps you kick evil thoughts out of your head. The more you think about God, the stronger you get. And anytime you're in trouble, you can believe God will show up and help you. A head that is protected means a devil that's evicted.

158: Matthew 6:33
159: Psalm 46:1 (NIV)

THE MIND AND THE EYES

The helmet of salvation protects us from all types of vices that can run through our minds. The eyes are the entrance to the mind. That's why you have to be careful what you watch. Many of the helmets of the ancient Roman soldiers—and even many helmets for motorcycle riders today—not only covered the head, but everything connected to the head, including the eyes. The eyes must be protected. One look can pollute the soul, tarnish the mind, and tempt the body. That's why Jesus stiffened the law of men's interaction with women. In Matthew 5, He made the law stricter. The law mandated, *"Thou shalt not commit adultery."*[160] But Jesus said, *"... anyone who looks at a woman lustfully has already committed adultery with her in his heart."*[161] Wow! One look and a transgression can transition from the eye to the mind and into the heart, shattering both the helmet and the breastplate.

LOOKING AT WOMEN

It's going to take a lot of discipline to stop men with wandering eyes from looking lustfully at women. This is a hard discipline. Many men have an automatic lust sensor in their brains. Their eyes have to follow every woman that looks good to them. Some men really can't control themselves. Some men try to blame the woman for the way she dresses and looks: the type of shoes she wears, the makeup she has on, or the exposure of her breasts, hips, and legs. But a real M.A.N. won't blame other people for his problem. A real M.A.N. should be able to take responsibility for his actions and control himself regardless of how a woman looks or what she wears.

The problem is not the woman; the problem is a lack of discipline, respect and self-control. The problem is your thinking—what you think about women when you look at them. Even if you believe the woman has no respect for herself, as a M.A.N., you should have enough respect for yourself that you don't fall into the enemy's trap and start lusting after the woman. Just because she gives it, you don't have to take it. Just

160: Exodus 20:14
161: Matthew 5:28

because she shows it, you don't have to lust it. You must take control of your own thinking. You must take responsibility for your own actions. The helmet of salvation helps us to take control of our thinking.

And we can definitely blame society for imparting into generations of men a culture of indecency that produced lusting after women. Many men are taught from an early age to look, lust and even touch women if they like them. But the helmet of salvation reverses our thinking and controls our actions. It challenges social and cultural maladies and produces distinct men that think differently from the world and its crude culture.

Lustful men make the mistake, because of a lack of self-control, of looking at other women while their husbands are present. You can find yourself in a lot of trouble if you look at the wrong man's woman and he catches you. But some men have to take a peek. Their heads have to turn. Their eyes have to wander. It's the result of a lack of discipline, respect, decency, and self-control.

Don't get me wrong: it's not a sin to admire a woman purely and to compliment her genuinely. But most men don't know their limits. Their compliments and admiration quickly turn to flirting and lusting. This is where men must draw the spiritual line in their head.

PRACTICE DISCIPLINING THE EYES

The best thing you can do is discipline your mind so that your eyes don't lead to lust and your mouth doesn't talk temptation. The helmet of salvation teaches you how to be *mindful* of what you say as well as *eyeful* about where you look. It teaches you when you're alone, so that when you're with someone else, you can be mindful and keep your eyes on Jesus rather than on the woman's body. The way to practice is to look at the woman as a person, concentrate on the conversation, and walk away with the conversation in mind rather than the body of the woman. Practice catching yourself when your mind wanders. Yell out *"Jesus!"* in your head when you fall. Talk to yourself about your lack of discipline. Quote scripture in your head when you've mistakenly lusted. No matter how many times you fall, remind yourself of God's will for your mind and eyes. Eventually if you practice discipline, you will get it right. Your mind as well as your eyes will begin to follow God and not her body. Practice immediately turning away when you've slipped up and looked. It takes practice, practice, practice.

PEOPLE ARE ALWAYS WATCHING

Practice when nobody's watching. And keep in mind you never know who's watching you. People are connected whether you realize it or not. A male friend of mine was newly married, and he met a woman in another state while he was on a business trip. He thought it was alright to mess around since he was miles away from home. It turned out that the woman he met was actually a first cousin of his wife, and they met again at a family reunion a year later. He prayed through the whole family weekend that this woman wouldn't say anything.

Men, I say this to show that people are connected. You may think because you're away from home and in another state or country that you can mess around, but you're thinking wrong. The devil can fool you and mess you up. You have to keep in mind everybody knows everybody. There are less than six degrees of separation between you and the next person. And with social networking sites and video cameras everywhere (near bathrooms, the liquor store, in hotels, in cars, in parking lots, on the job, on phones, in lobbies, on street corners, in buildings, etc.), people can see you, set you up, and know where you are at all times. Men get busted all the time—not by contact, but by video or picture. Especially on the job, trying to steal and sneak out with certain items is not going to work in your favor. They have you on camera.

The same is true with law enforcement. You may think a police officer didn't see you run the red light, but the camera did. The camera took a picture of your license plate and sent it home to your mailbox. You just better hope and pray you were somewhere you were supposed to be, because if someone in your house gets that ticket before you do, you're in double trouble.

The helmet protects your head and keeps you aware of where you go, whom you meet, and how you interact with people. People are always watching you. Let me repeat: someone is always watching you—from children and coworkers to neighbors and church members.

Watching you can be good, because if you're mindful that people are watching you, it can prevent you from doing things that ruin your life. Many people are watching, as in looking up to you and seeking you for guidance, so to make the wrong move would be to shatter their image of you. Your daughter is losing respect for you every time you peek out the side window. Your son is getting a lesson on what it means to undress women with their eyes. This type of behavior is unacceptable.

GOD IS WATCHING YOU

Most of all, even if you evade the cameras and fool other people into believing something, God is always where you are. You can't escape God. As the psalmist wrote, *"Where can I go from your Spirit? Where can I flee from your presence? If I go up to the heavens, you are there; if I make my bed in the depths, you are there."*[162] There is nowhere you can go from the sight of God. And it's actually good to know that God is with us everywhere we go, because He protects us when the enemy tries to destroy us. If it had not been for God following us, the devil would have ruined us a long time ago. But thank God for interceding and saving us, rescuing us, keeping us for this moment. Knowing that God is watching us will make us think twice before we go to that motel, steal that computer, run that light, drink that liquor, smoke that joint, or sniff that coke. God watching us becomes our conscience. If we know that God is following us, we believe that He's not only keeping us from trouble, but also from death. As David said in Psalm 23, *"Surely goodness and mercy shall follow me all the days of my life: and I will dwell in the house of the LORD for ever."*[163]

THOUGHTS TAKE UP SPACE

Jesus knew that the eyes feed into the mind, and the mind, if weak, can disprove the will of God. Even if a man doesn't act on it, or can't

---

162: Psalm 139:7-8 (NIV)
163: Psalm 23:6

act on it because of health or physical inabilities, the lustful thought of a woman other than his wife or significant other has already tarnished him. That impious thought has taken up space in his mind that could have been used to glorify God and assist his family. Thoughts take up space in the brain. Our thought space can be used for the good, acceptable, and perfect will of God, or for the awful, imperfect, and unacceptable will of wickedness. A thought used on evil is a thought wasted on life. That thought could have been used for the next business idea, or to think of something nice for your wife, or to consider taking your children somewhere special, or to praise the Lord. Instead you wasted the thought on an evil force. You allowed the devil to consume your time and imagination with unproductive thinking—hell-bound reasoning. As Ezekiel 20:30 says, *"Will you defile yourselves the way your fathers did and lust after their vile images?"*[164]

MEN NEED WAYS TO THINK ABOUT GOD MORE

Think about it: a lot of men spend most of their time outside of church. Many come on a Sunday morning, leave, and don't return until the next Sunday. The Word of God absorbed on Sunday may stay in their heads for a day or two. But after that men are again bombarded by other forms of play and pleasure that can dilute the memory of the Word of God and return them to ungodly thinking. This is why more churches need active men's ministries. Men need a reason to be in church more than once a week. Men need to incorporate the helmet of salvation into their daily lives. This would challenge and even eliminate the glitz and glamour, the violence and lasciviousness of the world that are abusing their brains and taking up so much space.

If you're in the world more than you're in the house of God, that means when you go to the house of God, you're thinking about the world, because that's where you spend most of your time. So you can be *in* the house but not *of* the house. The only way to rid yourself of worldly thinking is to be in the house of the Lord as much as possible.

164: Ezekiel 20:30 (NIV)

As David said, *"I will dwell in the house of the LORD for ever."*[165] This will not only change your thinking, but also your location. A location change will then shift your thinking to the place of your salvation.

PLUCK IT OUT OF YOUR HEAD AS SOON AS IT COMES IN

Salvation helps with mental cleansing. That's why Jesus said, *"And if your eye causes you to sin, pluck it out."*[166] Of course this is not literal, because we're not fighting against flesh and blood, not even our own. We're fighting against spiritual wickedness in high places that causes us to look at things that corrupt us and consume our thoughts. You don't want all kinds of sleaze running through your mind. Through the helmet of salvation, you can cleanse your mind by plucking out sleaze as soon as it comes in.

To *pluck it out* means to *dismiss it, kill it,* and *bury it* with pure thoughts. Start turning your head as soon as you detect wickedness moving in. Kill the thought—immediately—and denounce the sin as soon as it comes in. As soon as murderous thinking hits your head, kill the thought. As soon as hate, revenge, jealousy, or lies come into your head, kill the thought. Pluck it out. Start reciting scripture, start thinking about things that make you happy, start thinking about the consequences if you were to fulfill your messy thinking, start thinking about what God has done and where you have come from. All of this will help you when evil thoughts erupt in your mind. Too much worldly stuff and evil in your head can drive you insane.

165: Psalm 23:6
166: Mark 9:47 (NKJV)

CHAPTER 17

STEP 7: *Mentally—Part 2*

THE MIND AND INSANITY

It is sad to note the number of men, young and old, who are suffering from some form of mental illness. From paranoid schizophrenia to bipolar disorder, men are literally going insane. Their minds have crashed due to stress, depression, and overwhelming burdens, as well as inherited mental disorders. The number of men who commit suicide is four times greater than that of women. The National Institute of Mental Health states that more than 90 percent of people who commit suicide have a diagnosable mental disorder, most commonly a depressive disorder or a substance abuse disorder.[167]

MILITARY MENTAL ILLNESS

Mental disorders have become particularly relevant to men who come out of military service. Due to battle, disease, drugs, alcohol, or injuries, their minds now face great mental disturbance, which has had an impact on their family and future progress. And since guns are so easily accessible, it is easy for the mentally sick to get guns and hurt themselves, or attack innocent people with weapons of mass destruction.

167: "Suicide in the U.S.: Statistics and Prevention," National Institute of Mental Health, September 27, 2010, http://www.nimh.nih.gov/health/publications/suicide-in-the-us-statistics-and-prevention/in. (Page no longer available.)

More has to be done politically and judicially to stop guns from getting into the hands of the mentally ill.

Rulers and principalities have strengthened their stand on constitutional grounds to prevent politicians from going up against pro-gun lobbyists, and it has resulted in weapons of mass destruction being available to really sick people in society. But since the politicians won't act, spiritual people must. Spiritual people will have to take the lead. Every M.A.N. will have to put on the helmet of salvation and take up his spiritual armor to prevent violence from influencing him and destroying others. When spiritual people act, men learn to put guns down. They don't have to wait for Congress to pass a prohibition bill against guns. They can learn to throw the guns away themselves, knowing that their mental condition is not stable.

If you feel you have a mind of destruction that could deteriorate anytime and harm people you love or are angry with, you should take it upon yourself to throw the guns away. Get the guns out of your sight and out of your reach. God will protect you and your family. As I stated earlier, society is not only safer because criminals have been locked up and the mentally ill have been institutionalized, but because minds have been transformed through Christ. And it is because of this transformation that neighborhoods are safer and families are protected.

Many family members in particular see the mental suffering of those who have been in the military. Mental illness after military service can lead to a breakdown in family and personal life. A serious helmet of salvation is needed to intervene and save the minds of men who come out of military service. These methods should include a considerable amount of counseling, with spiritual guidance and biblical understanding at the forefront. We've seen enough of our men die in military service; we want to see more of our men live in God's army.

MENTAL CHALLENGES AND SALVATION

Mental challenges can happen, particularly at the early stages of salvation. Men are caught between the world and the way of God. Being pulled along too fast in Christ from a former life of sin can cause confusion and disappointment. Expectations are high and blessings can be low. The helmet gives balance and allows God to seep in while the world is filtered out. New converts often try to move too fast with God, but salvation is not a race. Ecclesiastes 9:11 tells us, *"The race is not to the swift...."*[168]

Learn what it means to be a man of God and develop those traits in you. Get the knowledge piece by piece; you don't have to rush it. Not even the Bible was put together in one day. Proverbs says, *"... incline thine ear unto wisdom, and apply thine heart to understanding."*[169] It's going to take time, wisdom, and understanding to keep your mind fixed on the Lord—and you can't allow people to rush you into Christian understanding. You have to learn to take it one step at a time.

PEOPLE CAN DRIVE YOU CRAZY

People can overdose you on Jesus: what the expectations are, what you can and can't do, what you can and can't say, how you can and can't live. One slip can invoke criticism or make you feel like a hypocrite. Church people expect you to be at the level of a seasoned believer in Christ as soon as you get saved. For men, in particular, this is difficult. There is a lot of maturing involved in discipleship. You can find yourself trying to do a lot and failing, which can cause confusion and mental anguish, especially if you're doing it for others and not for God. People can drive you crazy or back into the world if you let them. Remember, the primary purpose of being saved is to live spiritually for God—not for politics, not for people, not for programs or social fellowship, but for God.

Putting on the helmet of salvation is like putting earplugs in your ears: it helps you to hear God and block out nonsense. Helmets of ancient days, and even today, covered the ears. Your ears are protected with the helmet of salvation so that you can listen to God. Don't let people damage your head by driving you mad. Remember, even with the helmet of salvation, God's ways are not our ways, and God's

---

168: Ecclesiastes 9:11
169: Proverbs 2:2

thoughts are not our thoughts.[170] We have to live in him. You can go crazy trying to keep up with God. Instead of trying to figure God out, trust God, believe God, worship God, and listen for God. The helmet keeps us grounded in the mind of God so that we can live and listen to his instructions and overcome disappointments. *"... Lean not unto thy own understanding. In all thy ways acknowledge him...."*[171]

BE PREPARED FOR DISAPPOINTMENTS

The helmet not only prepares us for blessings but also for disappointments. This is essential to your salvation and mental calmness. A lot of men can't take disappointments, but you have to be spiritually prepared when things don't go your way. When hopes don't turn out like you thought they would. When you don't get everything you desire.

A lot of men, after being disappointed, turn around and do something crazy or stupid, or end up back in the world – drinking, smoking or allowing depression to get the best of them. But preparing yourself with the helmet means that you are mentally and spiritually prepared for whatever happens, knowing that *"all things together work for good to them that love the Lord, to them who are the called according to his purpose."*[172] Get it in your head that not everything is going to be in your favor or turn out the way you hope. You're not going to win all the time. That doesn't mean God is against you. It simply means that God is ahead of you. If you trust God and believe God is leading your life, you will acknowledge that no matter how much you want something, if you don't get it, God knows what's best. You may want a certain job, but that job may cause more anguish than good for your family. You may want a boat, but that boat could result in a bad accident or financial stress. God sees ahead. Don't try and go ahead of God, but stay behind God and prepare yourself for what He brings you. Going ahead of God can drive you crazy. Stay in the passenger seat and remain faithful despite disappointments.

170: Isaiah 55:9
171: Proverbs 3:5-6
172: Romans 8:28

I've been disappointed many times in my walk with God. He has given me ideas, and I've acted on them only to be disappointed at the outcome. I've lost a lot of money, time, and friends because I really believed that God wanted me to pursue certain dreams, only to discover that He had other plans for my life. I've learned that God can give us ideas and passion and even connections, but can stop short of giving us success for the idea. The ideas I've put my best effort into gave the least results. But I've learned that what God has for me is for me. So while I've been disappointed, I've also been blessed to keep trying until God gives me the desires of my heart.

If you've found yourself constantly disappointed, brush yourself off and act on the next idea God gives you until you succeed. Nothing happens overnight, and disappointments are part of the process to success. Have faith! Your time is coming. God knows when we're ready to go from idea to success. We may be ready for the idea, but it doesn't mean we're ready for the victory. God determines when the increase will come. As 1 Corinthians 3:6 says, *"I have planted, Apollos watered; but God gave the increase."*[173] Keep on planting and keep on watering, and something is bound to grow out of it.

173: 1 Corinthians 3:6

CHAPTER 18

STEP 7: *Mentally—Part 3*

THE MIND AND THE GROWTH OF MEN

A made-up mind shows growth, maturity, and discipline. The Bible says, *"When I was a child, I talked like a child, I thought like a child, I reasoned like a child. When I became a man, I put childish ways behind me."*[174]

NO MOMMA'S BOY

It's sad to see grown men acting like baby boys in the way they handle life, finances, careers, and their families. Some men get good jobs only to lose them a short time later over foolishness, intemperance, or laziness. No woman wants a boy. Let's be real. You have to man up! A lot of men are grown babies because they're momma's boys. Mothers are great, and their nature is to nurture, but there comes a time when a man must grow up and be a M.A.N. That means he must act like a man and think like a man. He must loosen himself from his mother's hold and learn to live like a man and pay bills like a man. He must learn to live on his own and raise his family on his own. And when trouble comes, he must learn to take care of it on his own without running back home to momma and poppa.

A man does not sit home all day and play video games and

174: 1 Corinthians 13:11 (NIV)

watch movies. A man does not stand on the street corner and look at every woman that walks by. A man does not stay at the bar or casino all night and come home in the morning. Rather, a man knows how to hustle and sacrifice for the good of his family. A man knows how to make something out of nothing. A man knows he must grow up so that he can show his sons and nephews and other young men what it means to be a man. A man knows when to leave his mother and be a man on his own.

Men can't blame their mothers for trying to hold on to them, because mothers do what they are blessed to do, which is to nurture. It's good for a man to love his mother, but he must know when it's time to grow up and live as a man. The Bible says that, upon marriage, *"a man will leave his father and his mother and be united to his wife, and they will become one flesh."*[175] Your growth as a man should be seen in connection with your wife, not your mother. And your wife is not your mother. Some men make the sad mistake of trying to turn their wife into their mother. No! Your mother is your nurturer; your wife is your partner. Once married, the bond of the mother is loosened and the bond of the wife is strengthened, and the wife becomes your partner for a new creation and future aspirations in life.

If you're single, then you should be growing as a man, apart from your mother, while loving your mother. Being single allows you to become independent and prepared for manly responsibilities, so when that day of marriage comes, you will live as a man for your own family.

A MAN KNOWS HOW TO MAKE DECISIONS

The helmet of salvation helps with maturity in Christ but also maturity in life. You learn how to make rational, informed decisions. *"… Whatsoever things are true, whatsoever things are honest, whatsoever things are just, whatsoever things are pure, whatsoever things are lovely, whatsoever things are of good report; if there be any virtue, and if there be any praise, think on these things."*[176]

175: Genesis 2:24 (NIV)
176: Philippians 4:8

SOLOMON'S WISDOM

The helmet of salvation helps us to better examine things before we get involved or accept them. This is a sign of wisdom and growth. Your decisions are no longer rushed or based on superficial outcomes or glossy dreams, but rather on wisdom coupled with experience. The greatest example of a mature man in the Bible came from Solomon. He had knowledge before he had wisdom. He was smart enough to know that if he was going to lead God's people and make the right decisions, he needed wisdom. God had told him he could ask for anything, and Solomon chose wisdom. An immature man would ask for riches and women and all the hype that comes with worldly living. But a mature man, a new man, a Man of Armor, asks for wisdom.

Wisdom is that ability to discern right from wrong in tough situations in order to prevent unnecessary problems. Wisdom prevents the devil from fooling you twice. For example, you made a mistake by maxing out that last credit card and not being able to pay it back on time. It not only cost you money but embarrassment and bad credit history. With wisdom, even though you may be in need of cash, you know not to push your credit or even your purchases beyond your limit. You learn to live within your means. Wisdom calls you to remember what happened the last time you made that foolish mistake so that you don't repeat it.

One of my more foolish mistakes as a young man was parking my car in wrong spots and getting ticket after ticket after ticket, which resulted in my car being towed and thousands of dollars in fines. When I became wise, I was determined not to make those foolish mistakes again. I started to examine the situation and the consequences, and then make up my mind not to repeat the actions. The lack of wisdom can cost you everything—time, money, even your life.

WISDOM

Nothing can guide a man like wisdom. It saves men from foolish mistakes, dumb decisions, and recurring regrets. The best thing a man can do is grow up in God. Grow up so the decisions you make are not putting you or your family in jeopardy. Foolish decisions only lead to further frustration. How can anybody trust you if you're a child in a man's body? You're nothing more than a wolf in sheep's clothing, looking like a grown man on the outside, but making childish decisions on the inside. The Bible says, *"If any of you lack wisdom, let him ask of God, that giveth to all men liberally, and upbraideth not; and it shall be given him."*[177] Ask for wisdom right now and God will freely give it to you. When you get wisdom, foolishness and stupidity are evicted.

THINK BEFORE YOU DO

When you have on the helmet of salvation, you think about the consequences of your actions. For many immature men the focus is so much on the pleasure, body, or money that fatal consequences are ignored. The fear of consequences often occurs after the act has been committed. However, the helmet of salvation gives enough wisdom to consider the consequences prior to the act. When you have the helmet of salvation, you think before you do. You think about the consequences of your actions. You think about the people you engage with. You think about how much easier life could be if you just sat back and thought about what moves to make and what route to take before you set forth on your journey.

With the helmet of salvation comes growth, and with growth comes knowledge, wisdom, and understanding. When you have it, not only will others respect you, but you will respect and love yourself for the decisions you make and the direction you take. You will think better of yourself.

THE MIND AND HOW WE THINK OF OURSELVES

A lot of what we do and say is related to how we think of ourselves. The Bible says in Proverbs 23:7: *"For as he thinketh in his heart, so is he."*[178] There must be a balance of the mind in connection with one's spirit and aspirations. As the Bible explains in Romans 12:3, we don't

---

177: James 1:5
178: Proverbs 23:7

want to think of ourselves more highly than we ought to (more on that in a little while). On the other hand we don't want to think of ourselves more lowly than we ought to, either. This goes back to issues of confidence and security. The helmet of salvation provides mental strength and stability. When you think lowly of yourself, you can miss how God can use you, as well as what God has for you.

This was the case with the Israelites when they went to spy out the land in Numbers 13. They saw giants in the land, and the majority of the spies came back with an awful report based on fear and low self-esteem. Their thoughts were reflected in their conversation and inaction: *"We be not able to go up against the people.... we were in our own sight as grasshoppers, and so we were in their sight."* [179]They sounded like the disciples on the boat amidst the storm: *"Lord ... we're going to drown!"*[180] Their thinking caused them to miss their opportunity to go from wanderers to land owners. Because they had a grasshopper mentality, God could not show His might and strength through them.

A lot of men miss their opportunity because of their grasshopper thinking. They think they're not qualified to teach because they lack education and other people have multiple degrees. They think they can't be anything because they come from a rotten background and others come from decent homes. They think they can't excel because they're poor and others have money. These men must change their thinking from a grasshopper to a faith walker. The difference between you and the next person is your thinking.

How can God show Himself mighty and strong if He only uses the so-called mighty and strong? That would give more credit to man than to God. First Corinthians 1:27 tells us that *"God has chosen the weak things of the world to put to shame the things which are mighty."*[181] God loves to take the lowly, weak, uneducated, disenfranchised, imprisoned, criminals, poor, pointless, foolish—the so-called losers—and turn them into winners. When Samuel anointed Saul as king, Saul asked, *"Am not*

179: Numbers 13:31, 33
180: Matthew 8:25 (NIV)
181: 1 Corinthians 1:27 (NKJV)

*I a Benjamite, of the smallest of the tribes of Israel? and my family the least
of all the families of the tribe of Benjamin? wherefore then speakest thou so
to me?"*[182] Saul couldn't understand why God would choose him, being
that he came from the smallest tribe in Israel and that others were much
bigger, stronger, and smarter than him. But God was trying to show
Saul (and us) that He could pick the least and make them the greatest.
He could pick the worst and make them the best. Saul didn't realize
there was a king in him. A lot of men don't realize there is greatness in
them—a preacher in them, a teacher in them, a businessman in them,
a president in them, a great husband in them, a great father in them.
However, if they thought better about themselves, they would be greater.
Greatness starts with the understanding that you have it in you. *"Greater
is he that is in you, than he that is in the world."*[183]

How can you show that you are strong in the Lord and the
power of His might if you don't allow God to use you? The way many
men think of themselves will lead them to disappointment. Many men
are wondering why they don't have the things they want or why they're
not happy or why they can't get the blessing they need. It's because they
don't think that God can use them and they don't allow God to show
Himself through them. How you think has a lot to do with your faith.
Faith opens you up to all the great possibilities that God has for your
life and how God can use you to show Himself through you regardless
of what others think.

DON'T MISS OUT ON PROVING GOD AND INSPIRING OTHERS

Because of many men's low thinking, they can miss out on proving
God strong. They can miss out on being mighty. And when men do
this, they not only disappoint themselves, they discourage others as well.
Somebody is looking for the lowly to rise, the sinner to seek salvation,
because they need inspiration. You could have been that inspiration, that
motivation, that stimulation someone needed to do the unthinkable. If

---

182: 1 Samuel 9:21
183: 1 John 4:4

you had started that business regardless of your low income and your lack of education, trusting that God is bigger than the enemy, you would have encouraged someone else who had little income and education. Someone else would have been inspired and empowered through your stand.

Barack Obama is great not only because he was the first African American president, but also because he encouraged and empowered a mass of people who needed inspiration—young people, old people, black people, white people, hopeless people, Democrats, Republicans, and independents. He inspired people who had lost faith in the political system, judicial decisions, and legislative actions. He came at just the right time to help us regain the optimism that many Americans had lost. He didn't come from riches and glory. He came from a modest beginning. He said that he wanted to run to inspire all the young people who don't think they have a chance.

Your income shouldn't determine your outcome. Your race shouldn't hinder your progress. Yes, there is racism, sexism, and poverty, but there's also a God who is bigger than race, sex, and poverty. God can use racism, sexism, and poverty for His good and your rise. Jesus went from a manger to a mansion in the sky. *"In my Father's house are many mansions: if it were not so, I would have told you."*[184] Jesus worked his way up in spite of his difficult background, family circumstances, and enemies. He didn't use excuses to keep him down; He used the mind of God to lift Himself up.

The helmet of salvation gives you a strong and determined mind, and it also helps you to encourage others who need to be strengthened. Everybody needs a role model. Why shouldn't it be a Man of Armor? Why shouldn't it be a man of God? Handicapped men need to be empowered. If you have a disability and think you can inspire a man with your living testimony despite your handicap, why not inspire him? Lots of young poor boys need inspiration. If you think you can inspire a young man with your story, why not do it? There is a young girl that needs to know there are good fathers out there. If you think you can

---

184: John 14:2

inspire her, why not do it?

That's where the helmet of salvation comes in—to inspire minds with might and fortitude regardless of the visible obstacles. Out of the twelve who went to spy out the Promised Land, only two had on the helmet of salvation—Caleb and Joshua. They were willing to go forward. They had their minds made up and focused on the power of God. They knew that God would deliver them and make them victorious, regardless of the giants in the land. Although it took years for them to see the promise, their thinking prevailed and they were the only two from the old generation who got to see the Promised Land.

DON'T LET THE DEVIL GET TO YOUR HEAD

If you don't transform your mind and keep on the helmet of salvation, you can find yourself only three-quarters dressed with the armor of God and then tearing off the armor because your mind is either weak, confused, or displaced. You're not really dressed if you don't protect your head. Few people have survived a blow to the head. Muhammad Ali was one of the greatest boxers of all time—because of his quickness in the ring, but also because of his braggadocio, articulation, and rhyming: "Float like a butterfly. Sting like a bee. The hands can't hit what the eyes can't see." But the hits to the head eventually crippled him mentally; before he died he could barely articulate his name.

DON'T GET BIG HEADED

Finally you don't want to become big headed. The devil will try and beat you in your head to damage you and make you boastful rather than respectful, arrogant rather than humble. And when the enemy is finished with you, you won't even know how to pronounce your name. Men of God who don't protect their heads can become arrogant and boastful, overconfident and conceited. As the Word of God says, *"Do not think of yourself more highly than you ought, but rather think of yourself with sober judgment, in accordance with the measure of faith God has given you."*[185] Remain humble. Don't use your godly thinking inside God's

---

185: Romans 12:3 (NIV)

house or outside God's house to make yourself bigger and better than anyone else. Use your thinking to help and encourage others. As 1 Peter 5 states, *"God opposes the proud but gives grace to the humble."*[186]

Points to Remember from Step 7

Part 1

1. Step 7 for every man is *Mentally*: He must use his transformed mind to resist temptation and glorify God in what he thinks, says, and does.

2. Salvation is God saving us from afterlife condemnation (hell) and present-life desecration, embarrassment, and death. We could have died in our failure, faults, and sins, but God rescued (saved) us from ignorance, darkness, and disgrace, and brought us into the light so that we can see the wrong we were living and change our ways.

3. The helmet protects the mind from evil thoughts and allows us to think of the goodness of God.

4. You must learn to think differently now that you're saved. The mind of the world is different from the mind of Christ.

5. Being saved requires a made-up mind—a commitment and devotion to always follow God.

6. Don't allow your eyes to lead you to hell. Practice not looking and lusting after women when you're alone, and it will help you when you're with others.

7. People are always watching you, so be careful where you go. Even if you evade the cameras, you can't evade God.

Part 2

8. Mental illness is real. Don't ignore it. Seek help. God is able to heal and restore the mind.

186: 1 Peter 5:5 (NIV)

9. Don't let people, even saved people, drive you insane. Listen for God.

10. The helmet of salvation prepares you for disappointments. Not every goal is going to be in your favor, but God is able to pull you through and help you out. What God has for you is for you.

Part 3

11. Men must live as men, think as men, act as men, speak as men, and raise their families as men. You are no longer a child, but a man.

12. God can bring out the greatest in you. Think of yourself in accordance with the faith God has given you.

13. If you lack wisdom, ask God for it. He will freely give it.

14. Think of yourself in the light of God's love. You are somebody!

15. Be an inspiration to someone by allowing others to see from whence God has brought you. Everyone needs inspiration.

16. Don't think of yourself more highly than you ought. Be humble.

SWORD OF THE SPIRIT

CHAPTER 19

STEP 8: *Effectively—Part 1*

... and the sword of the Spirit, which is the word of God ...

Ephesians 6:17

In 1919, in the case of *Schenck v. United States*, the Supreme Court upheld the conviction of a Socialist party official who had violated the Espionage Act of 1917 by urging young men who had been called for military service to assert their constitutional rights by opposing the draft. Justice Holmes, who wrote the opinion, suggested limitations from government encroachment of the First Amendment's guarantee of free speech:

The question in every case is whether the words used are used in such circumstances and are of such a nature as to create a clear and present danger that they will bring about the substantive evils that Congress has a right to prevent.... When a nation is at war many things that might be said in time of peace are such a hindrance to its efforts that their utterance will not be endured.[187]

The justice concluded that words during war are hurtful and

187: Edward Conrad Smith and Harold J. Spaeth, eds., *The Constitution of the United States with Case Summaries: Bicentennial Edition* (New York: Barnes and Nobles Books, 1987), 109.

can create a danger to others. It is similar to the conclusion the courts reached in *Chaplinsky v. New Hampshire* when it stated that certain words, "by their very utterance, inflict injury or tend to incite an immediate breach of the peace. They're considered 'fighting words.'"[188] Words have power and can be backed by such verbal force that they cut through the very ideals of peace and into the souls of people. Proverbs repeats the condemnation of such words twice when it says, *"the words of a talebearer are as wounds, and they go down into the innermost parts of the belly."*[189]

FIGHTING WORDS

There is no doubt men are at war with demons in themselves and with wickedness in the world. The nursery rhyme that goes "Sticks and stones may break my bones, but names will never hurt me" isn't truthful. Words do hurt and can inflict pain, strife, violence, and death, especially when thrown by Satan. *Gossip, criticism, instigation, rumors, innuendos, threats, insults, obscenities, slurs,* and *lies* are all conveyed by words. Most fights start because of negative words.

The devil is good at inflicting fighting words. In Matthew 4, when Jesus was coming up out of the desert, the devil threw words at him: *"If thou be the Son of God, command that these stones be made bread."*[190] The insulting inference, *"If* you are the Son of God ..." constituted fighting words. The devil then took another verbal shot at Jesus: *"If thou be the Son of God, cast thyself down: for it is written, He shall give his angels charge concerning thee and in their hands they shall bear thee up, lest at any time thy shall dash thy foot against a stone."*[191]

This statement was even more condescending because the devil quoted scripture (although out of context). His wording not only castigated Jesus, but also the holy Word of God. Definitely fighting words. And finally the devil took him to a mountain and showed him all the beauty of the world, and said: *"All these things will I give thee, if*

188: Smith and Spaeth, *The Constitution of the United States,* 109.
189: Proverbs 18:8; 26:22
190: Matthew 4:3
191: Matthew 4:6

thou wilt fall down and worship me.[192] The nerve of Satan to talk to Jesus about worshipping him! No doubt fighting words.

But no word is stronger than the Word of God. God is the supreme Judge who will strike down offensive words from the enemy in times of war.

THE SWORD OF THE SPIRIT

Paul interjected a critical-response mechanism with this piece of armor. It comes swiftly after the helmet of salvation, and is in the opposite hand of the shield of faith: *"... and the sword of the Spirit, which is the word of God...."* In the spelling of *"sword"* is *"word."* God often comes with a sword to convey His Word. In the book of Joshua, a man stood over Joshua with sword drawn in his hand. Joshua asked, *"Are you for us or for our enemies?"*[193] The man revealed himself as host of the angels of the Lord, and Joshua asked, *"What message does my Lord have for his servant?"*[194] God came with a sword to reveal His Word—His message.

Step 8 for every man is *Effectively*:

He must use the Word of God competently to strike down offenses of the enemy.

THE SWORD IS A WEAPON

The sword, as we picture it, is a weapon. While the other pieces of armor are defensive, the sword is offensive; it's designed for attack. While the others are for internal protection, the sword is for external execution. The reason it comes swiftly after the helmet of salvation, and in between the breastplate of righteousness and the shield of faith, is because men must put the Word of God in their heads and seal it on the

---

192: Matthew 4:9
193: Joshua 5:13 (NIV)
194: Joshua 5:14 (NIV)

tablet of their hearts, and use it to the glory of God. As the psalmist says, *"Thy word have I hid in mine heart, that I might not sin against thee."*[195]

The Word of God is the scripture of the Holy Bible. Scripture is the authority of God's spoken word to His people. It gives disciples a manual to develop theological understanding. Theology is the understanding of God and what we believe based upon his Word. Scripture helps us to develop theological interpretation of God in relation to any situation we face. Whether it is personal, political, social, economic, or spiritual, scripture is the answer to what God says about it! The answer then becomes the weapon to *effectively* eliminate any verbal or critical offenses and objections to God's people—thus you get the sword of the Spirit, which is the Word of God.

The Word is the quintessential piece of armor that God has given us to kill the enemy and strike down offensive words while we're at war with him. All other pieces of armor stop the enemy from killing you. But the sword—the Word of God—can actually kill the enemy. To kill the enemy is to strike down with effectiveness the rule that evil has over your life. The sword is actually a carving tool; it effectively cuts out the bad to make room for the good.

STICK THE SWORD WHERE THE ENEMY RESIDES

During our self examination we determined that the enemy is not coming out easily. For some men he's been in there too long to let go without difficulty. If after all the trials you've been through, you're still not rid of all your demons, or haven't even confronted them all, don't worry: this is a lifelong process, which is why you must put on the whole armor of God. You're going to have to fight for the rest of your life. You can get rid of one demon and another kind can sneak in. I've seen many men quit drinking, only to start womanizing. Stop stealing to start smoking.

Our goal is to become expert swordsmen. So no matter what's in us, we can effectively cut out and strike down. That's why the sword of the Spirit is so important. The sword of the Spirit strikes at demons that

---

195: Psalm 119:11

are trying to stay in you and come at you. When you called the enemy out, you called the enemy out to fight. If the enemy is messing with your mind, you have to take the sword of the Spirit, which is the Word of God, and cut him down. Anywhere the enemy can be, you have to cut him down. The Word of God will clear, cleanse, and redirect your path: *"Thy word is a lamp unto my feet, and a light unto my path."*[196]

We do not fight against flesh and blood, but against spiritual wickedness in high places. Since we're fighting against spiritual wickedness, we can't view our battle as physical; we must view it as spiritual. This is why Paul gave us the sword of the Spirit—because in order to fight against the spirit of wickedness, you need the Spirit of God. As I told you earlier, a spiritual problem needs a spiritual answer. The sword of the Spirit is the answer.

REPLACE ONE SPIRIT WITH ANOTHER

The reason for sticking the sword in those areas is to carve out one spirit and replace it with another. Spiritual wickedness works its way to the flesh. The flesh conveys the desires of evil. That's why the Bible says the flesh is contrary to the Spirit of God. Flesh is the weakness of wickedness, and easily submits to its powers. Jesus said, *"the spirit indeed is willing, but the flesh is weak."*[197] The Bible gives us a detailed list of fleshly weaknesses: *"… The works of the flesh are manifest, which are these; adultery, fornication, uncleanness, lasciviousness, idolatry, witchcraft, hatred, variance, emulations, wrath, strife, seditions, heresies, envying, murders, drunkenness, revellings, and such like…."*[198] These seeds were planted in our old man and then sprouted and blossomed, causing wild weeds to strangle our good deeds.

But the sword of the Spirit digs deep into the flesh, cuts out the root of evil, chops down the weeds, and kills the bad seeds. It then plants new seeds for new roots that grow good fruit. The Bible also gives us a detailed list of that new fruit: *"But the fruit of the Spirit is love, joy,*

196: Psalm 119:105
197: Matthew 26:41
198: Galatians 5:19-21

peace, longsuffering, gentleness, goodness, faith, meekness, temperance....[199] The sword of the Spirit is sharper than any two-edged sword.[200] It cuts down weeds with one edge and plants new seeds with the other.

THE NEW CHARACTER

The purpose of this new fruit is to carve out and develop a new character. We spoke about character earlier, but it warrants repeating. Your whole attitude and personality should change as a result of your spiritual conversion. Where there was once hate for whatever reason, there is now love. Where there was depression, there is now joy. Where there was hostility, there is now peace. Where there was impatience and lack of tolerance, there is now temperance. Where there was hard-heartedness and coldness, there is now gentleness. Where there was once mean-spiritedness and deceitfulness, there is now goodness. Where there was once hopelessness, there is now faith. And where there was once arrogance, there is now meekness. With practice the fruit of the Spirit changes your conversation and character to reflect the will of God. So people will know you not only by the role you play but by the fruit you bear.

ROLE AND PURPOSE IN THE SPIRIT

The fruit of the Spirit builds character that ushers in a presence that can't be ignored. Many people say that men have lost their role and purpose. But men have not lost their role and purpose so much as they have lost their divine presence and the Spirit that gives the role and purpose their true identity and worth. Role and purpose absent of the Spirit is insufficient and easily duplicated. When men are not performing their responsibility in the home, roles can be duplicated by others, and men are dismissed and not missed. However, when the Spirit is behind the role and purpose, it is more than a function—it is a divine presence. The presence of the fruit of the Spirit gives substance and significance to the man's role and purpose, and builds a better character. Therefore a better understanding of a man's role and purpose is not just

199: Galatians 5:22-23
200: Hebrews 4:12

212

seen in his performance of cleaning, fixing, and breadwinning, but also felt in his presence—with love, joy, peace, patience, etc. So the work may be duplicated, but the Spirit cannot be imitated, and the man will be missed and hard to replace when absent.

When a father is gone from his children, they will miss him not only because he cooks for them, but because he's patient with them. When a wife goes off on a business trip, she will miss her husband not only because she's lonely, but because he's joyful to be around. When a job has to lay people off, they will have a hard time laying off a spiritual man, not only because he's good at his job but because he has a good attitude and a humble spirit.

This is why men must build their spiritual character, so that their presence can be felt whether they're present or absent. When you do things around the home, do them with joy, not complaint. Nobody wants to be in the presence of a man who's always complaining. It's bad character. When you're teaching your children a lesson like learning to drive, do it with patience. Nobody wants to be around an impatient, grouchy person. The Bible says in Ephesians 6:4 to not provoke your children, which means don't instigate and intimidate them so that they want to fight you rather than embrace you. When you're cooking or cleaning or chastising, do it with love. Nobody wants to be around a hateful and mean-spirited person. Your character built on divine presence will determine whether people miss you or replace you when you're gone. This is why it is important to study the Word of God, so that the role and purpose mixed with spiritual presence can be aptly applied.

STUDY TO SHOW THYSELF APPROVED

The new seeds will manifest the Word of God in you and give you power over the enemy. One thing men must take time to do is study the Word of God. Paul encouraged Timothy: *"Study to shew thyself approved unto God, a workman that needeth not be ashamed, rightly dividing the word of truth."*[201] When you study the Word of God,

---

201: 2 Timothy 2:15

you become analytical and rational, knowing how to rightly interpret and communicate the Word of God for any situation. Studying the Word of God also can improve your reading ability as well as your comprehension and communication. When you study, it is a constant reference to learning and literacy.

As we stated, many have knocked men for their inflexibility to keep up with a knowledge-based economy. The society we live in today requires not just brute strength but thinking and communicating, reading and writing. Many suggest that the reason men don't advance economically and socially is because they're not willing to learn more, go to school, and get a degree of some kind. Reading the Word of God can open your imagination to other forms of education and knowledge for the sake of financial and family stability. That's why you must study to show yourself approved. In the midst of studying, you're not only reading, but also attacking ignorance and rejection from a society built on putting men down.

The sword cuts down shame—because a workman need not be ashamed—and builds up confidence and authority in you. The Bible says that when Jesus spoke the Word of God, He spoke with authority. By studying the Word you're exerting God's authority over the enemy and proving that you are capable of overcoming anything that might make you look bad. The Word of God is your weapon against shame, humiliation, and embarrassment.

BE QUICK WITH THE WORD

Every soldier has a weapon, and the weapon God has given His people is the weapon of His Word. God saw fit that we would not only be prepared for the assault, but also for the attack. Our sword strikes the darts as the shield blocks them, giving us added protection. The armor can take hits, but it can also offer blows of its own.

The Word is your weapon against temptation and false accusations. The writer of Hebrews tells us, *"… the word of God is quick, and powerful, and sharper than any twoedged sword…."*[202] This is no

---

202: Hebrews 4:12

butter knife God has given us. This is the best of the blades, with no other sword like it. How effective it will be is determined by how sharp our minds are when it comes to knowing the Word of God. The more you learn, the *quicker* you'll be. And it's important to be quick with the Word so that you can pull it out when situations arise. Remember the old cowboy movies: the quickest draw won the fight. The quicker you pull out the Word, the sooner you abolish any unnecessary threats against your new existence.

People who are slow with the Word of God often face more difficulty because the enemy knows that they're improperly equipped, so the enemy is going to get you where he thinks you're slow and weak. To be slow and weak is to not know how or when to properly use the sword, which is the Word of God. To be quick is to be ready and to know when and how to use the sword to resist temptation and chop the devil down under any circumstance.

Remember that when Jesus came out of the wilderness, the enemy figured he could tempt Him to test God. The devil said, *"If you are the Son of God … throw yourself down. For it is written: 'He will command his angels concerning you, and they will lift you up in their hands, so that you will not strike your foot against a stone.'"*[203] The devil pulled out his weapon to tempt Jesus, but Jesus was quick with the Word and retorted, *"It is also written: 'Do not put the Lord your God to the test.'"*[204] Jesus won the fight.

If you plan on going up against the enemy, you better be quick. The Word has to be so much a part of your new character that you can sense the devil before he comes. You can smell the enemy before he arrives. You can see the enemy before he sits in that seat next to you. You can quote scripture and analyze stories of the Bible in relation to your situation and slay the enemy with perfection. Because the more you know, the more effective you will be in slaying the enemy.

203: Matthew 4:6 (NIV)
204: Matthew 4:7 (NIV)

EAT IT

The best way to get the Word of God is to eat it. The Word is healthy food. When I say "eat" it, I mean consume the righteous Word of God in your spirit. Digest it. Meditate on it day and night. Psalm 1 says, *"But his delight is in the law of the LORD; and in his law doth he meditate day and night."*[205] Read it over and over again until you get a clear understanding or clear revelation. David wrote in Psalm 34, *"... taste and see that the LORD is good ... "*[206] Again, the Word of God replaces old tastes—like drugs and alcohol, bitterness, strife, hate, and envy—and replaces them with new tastes of love, joy, and happiness. What tastes good makes you feel good. It feels good to know that when death and disaster strike, *"weeping may endure for a night, but joy cometh in the morning."*[207] It feels good to taste a new day without sorrow, regret, and shame. It feels good to know that when everyone else is gone, the Lord *"will never leave you nor forsake you."*[208] The Word of God is a good source of energy. Good source of protein and iron. Good source of spiritual nutrition and vision.

This weapon of healthy living is attained through eating righteously and living holy. The Bible says of Jeremiah that God put the Word in his mouth.[209] And because God put it there, Jeremiah was able to speak it confidently. What goes into your heart will come out of your mouth. You will begin to speak only what God tells you to speak. Jeremiah was used as a vessel to proclaim the will of God.

In order to speak the Word of God, you must eat it for breakfast, lunch, and dinner, and take snacks in between. The Word is your cereal, your burger, and your chicken dinner. In other words you should read the Word of God in the morning when you wake up, in the afternoon on your break, and at night before you go to sleep. When Satan came after Jesus, Jesus said, *"Man does not live on bread alone, but on every*

205: Psalm 1:2
206: Psalm 34:8
207: Psalm 30:5
208: Joshua 1:5 (NIV)
209: Jeremiah 1:9

word that comes from the mouth of God.[210] Every Word of God keeps you alive and strong for battle. Going into battle on an empty stomach means planning to lose before you start. You want to be well-nourished before you battle the enemy. You need *every word* of God to fight the good fight. In Psalm 81, God says, *"open thy mouth wide, and I will fill it."*[211]

210: Matthew 4:4
211: Psalm 81:10

CHAPTER 20

STEP 8: *Effectively—Part 2*

KNOW WHEN TO SPEAK

It is rare to see men pull out a Bible while riding the train or flying on an airplane. Many will pull out a magazine or maybe a book, but hardly ever the Word of God. Just like you pull out a snack, you must pull out the sword, which is the Word of God. The way to get strong in the Word of God is to pull it out and speak it. If you listen to God and speak when prompted, the Word can knock down doors and break down walls you've been trying to get beyond. For example, to get the job you want, you have to know when to speak and what to say. God gave Joshua the word that would knock down the wall of Jericho: *"Shout!"* They listened to God's instructions, and when the time came, they gave a loud shout and the walls fell down. They won the battle because they obeyed God and spoke the right word. You can win a job—if you listen and say the right thing. You can get a good wife—if you listen and say the right thing. You can get a new career, car, health, and strength—if you listen and say the right thing.

KNOW WHEN TO BE SILENT

The Word works, whether with a loud shout or with silence. Some things are better spoken in the head than aloud. When we have the sword of the Spirit, it tells us when to speak and when to be quiet, when to shout and when to shut up. When Jesus was falsely accused and brought before the chief priests and the Sanhedrin, they demanded that He answer their charges. But Jesus remained silent.

There are times when the Word will say "shout!" At other times the Word will say nothing. If the Word of God says nothing, then you say nothing. Many men talk too much, argue too much, and end up indicting and convicting themselves. According to Proverbs, *"When words are many, sin is not absent...."* [212] A lot of men have ended up in prison because of their many words. They put a foot in their mouth by talking too much, giving information that convicted them rather than set them free. A lot of men are out of a job because of their many words. Talking back rather than listening. Talking on the phone at the job rather than doing their work. The mouth can get you in trouble when words are spoken with little thought (no helmet). And with social media everything is in writing, so be careful what you say because you can give people evidence against you with your big mouth. Many words are accompanied by emotion rather than by the fruit of the Spirit. Ecclesiastes cautions us, *"Do not be quick with your mouth ... so let your words be few."* [213] Many men have learned how to train dogs but not their own tongues.

PROFANITY

Some men's tongues are filled with the wrong words because of an old nature. The filth that spews from their mouth is outrageous. For some men every other word uttered is profane—cussing and cursing all the time. Their language is not only a sign of indecency but also ignorance, as if they can't find the proper vocabulary to express their thoughts. I must admit this was my problem for years, and truthfully I'm still working on it—to the degree that I even had some colorful language in this manuscript until the final editing process. It has nothing to do with whether I have the right words or not, as my vocabulary is large. It has to do with an old nature that, when aggravated or frustrated, easily

---

212: Proverbs 10:19 (NIV)
213: Ecclesiastes 5:2 (NIV)

comes out. I've trained my tongue but not killed the old nature with the sword. My goal is to kill it so that my respect for myself and others will be increased.

One thing we men must learn to do is rid ourselves of unwholesome and perverted words. It reveals the corruption in the head and the defilement of the heart. We ought to do as David said in Psalm 141: *"Set a guard over my mouth, O LORD; keep watch over the doors of my lips."*[214] The sword is the guard at the door. Before we say a word, it has to be approved by God or else it shouldn't come out. Before we say a word, it should be acceptable to God. The Bible says, *"Let the words of my mouth, and the meditation of my heart, be acceptable in thy sight, O LORD, my strength, and my redeemer."*[215] God's Word ought to be spoken with authority yet decency. Cut out any cussing, profanity, and disrespect that comes out of your mouth. The sword can cut our tongues before we say the wrong thing. Men, before you speak, ask yourself, *Should I or shouldn't I say it, and is it backed by the Word of God?*

OTHER PEOPLE'S WORDS

It is also important that we don't allow unwholesome language and indecent words to come into our circle or conversation. Men feel free to use profanity and talk vilely in front of other men at the house, barbershop, or street corner. Some have gotten so disrespectful that they do it in front of children and women. Shameful! But if we are truly to rid ourselves of evil, we have to cut it down wherever the source. When people see you, they should know to use better words to express themselves as well as to respect themselves. When vile words are spoken in front of you, use your discretion to cut it down. Say, "Brother, I don't appreciate that type of language being used in my presence. I don't like those words in my house." Use your sword to cut it down.

If you can't cut it down, you can always put on your shoes (the gospel of peace) and walk away. You don't have to stand there and be disrespected by someone's words, filth, or nonsense. If you have to

---

214: Psalm 141:3 (NIV)
215: Psalm 19:14

stand there, you can put on the helmet of salvation and think about the goodness of God. You can also put up the shield of faith and block vile conversations.

I often wonder how men can mouth off at the wrong time, but won't mouth off at the right time to promote righteousness and respect. As I stated before, Paul had been zealous in the world before serving Christ and then used that same zeal to promote the Word of God. Even in front of his old friends—those who knew him as a killer of Christians—he wasn't afraid to speak the Word of God. It's alright to let people know you're saved and to speak the Word of God, just like you spoke the words of filth when you were in the world.

You never know, your words may aid in someone's transformation, inspiration, and spiritual conversion. Some men are waiting for bold men to stand firm on their faith in the midst of gangsters, haters, and debaters of God. Everyone needs inspiration. By speaking out on God's side, you can be the inspiration that someone has been looking for. A lot of men hide their faith, all because they believe they're the oddball on the job or in the shop. But you never know who's itching to talk about the Word of God. I can tell you personally, the greatest conversations as well as surprises come when I'm in the barbershop. I often start a conversation on religion, and before you know it, brothers are jumping up, quoting scripture, and preaching as if it's their initial sermon. It's really hilarious but a great sight to see.

A DOUBLE TONGUE MUST BE CUT

But don't be hypocritical. You don't want to have one tongue that speaks two different languages—one to praise the Lord and another to curse the world. James 3 talks about such men: *"With the tongue we praise our Lord and Father, and with it we curse men."*[216] You can't be duplicitous, using the same tongue to speak two different languages. There is nothing worse than a two-faced man—a man who says one thing to one person and something else to another for the purpose of arousing confusion. Two-faced people are liars and schemers, and full

---

216: James 3:9 (NIV)

of politricks. You have to be real careful with a two-faced man: they're manipulative and can't be trusted. That's why the Bible says the Word is sharper than any two-edged sword, because you're going to need that type of sharpness to cut out duplicity.

If you are the perpetrator of a double tongue, then cut it out. If you are the victim of a double tongue, then cut the speaker off. You will not prosper around two-faced people. Cut out cussing, fussing, gossiping, and speaking filth. Speak words of faith, peace, decency, loyalty, and life. Increase your truth by talking honestly and intelligently to everyone you come into contact with. Stop being manipulative and deceitful; cut out the lies and tricks just to get your way. Speak words that will help you speak the truth and keep your promises.

YOUR WORD IS YOUR BOND

I know you have heard it said: your word is your bond. This is simply to say: keep your promises. If you make a promise to someone, you are making a vow between yourself and someone else in the presence of God. The Bible says, *"When a man makes a vow to the LORD or takes an oath to oblige himself by a pledge, he must not break his word but must do everything he said."*[217] Jesus requires bonds to be even stronger by demanding that everyone keep their word without equivocation: *"Simply let your 'Yes' be 'Yes' and your 'No,' 'No'; anything beyond this comes from the evil one."*[218] People should be able to trust you when you say you're going to do something. The worst thing a man can do is break a vow he has made to others before God. And a vow is not only pertaining to marriage but to any word or deed you make to God, yourself, and others. When you break it or don't live up to it, it is a show of weakness and results in great failure and ruined reputation, not to mention the hurt you cause other people through your failure to keep your word.

A man is known by the words he speaks and the promises he keeps. If you do not keep your word to people who you owe money, to your children, to your employees, or to yourself, it really puts you to shame

217: Numbers 30:2 (NIV)
218: Matthew 5:37 (NIV)

before God. The Bible says, *"Let no debt remain outstanding."*[219] The debt here is not only monetary, but also trustworthiness. Whatever you promise, you are in debt until you deliver on that promise. It not only destroys you if you don't deliver, but think of all the people who are dependent upon your promises. Consider what other people will think of God when you say, "I promise to God I'm going to…." What binds your word is the Word of God. If you can't keep it, then don't make it. If you're not sure you can live up to it, then don't say it. If you say it, no matter how difficult it is, you must do your best to keep it. Only death should stop you from keeping your promises. People will respect you and honor God because you kept your word.

Promises to yourself are even more important, because if you can't keep a promise to yourself, how can you keep a promise to anyone else? Many men make promises to God to never again lie, cheat, cuss, or smoke, and not long after break their promise and ruin not only their connection but their salvation. The worst thing you can do is lie to God. Salvation is built upon promises. God delivered the children of Israel out of captivity based upon a promise that led them into the *Promised* Land. God sent His only begotten Son based upon a promise. When we come into the life of Christ, we come into a binding promise that God gave in Jesus Christ for our salvation from sin and death. The Word of God in Jesus Christ is a manifestation of a verbal promise made centuries before. The Bible says, *"The Word became flesh and made his dwelling among us."*[220] Jesus is a manifestation of the promise that has come into existence to prove that God keeps His word for our salvation. If God keeps His word to us, how can we not keep our word to God and others? Reading and understanding the Word of God will help you keep your promise, because it is binding on your conscience. A promise binding on your conscience will encourage you to do all you can to keep your word.

219: Romans 13:8 (NIV)
220: John 1:14 (NIV)

EXAMINATION

In order to help men become skilled swordsmen, we need to examine how much we know the Word. When in trouble, what scripture do you rely upon? When in pain, what scripture do you quote? When in doubt, what biblical story do you refer to? When angry, where do you go in the Bible? When in need of strength, what scripture do you refer to? When everything seems to be falling apart, where in the Word do you go? When you need to calm down, what verse do you meditate on? When you're about to fall to temptation, what verse stops you? What is your favorite verse that you quote daily? If you don't have one, then get one.

My favorite scripture has always been *"I can do all things through Christ who strengthens me."*[221] I found favor in this scripture because many people I grew up around either said I wasn't smart enough or strong enough to succeed, so to this day that verse has given me the confidence and strength to do things I never imagined. Whenever I'm about to venture into new territory, I take this scripture with me. This examination calls for us to absorb the Word of God. Inhale it, learn it, and live it. *"All scripture is inspired by God and is useful for teaching, for reproof, for correction, and for training in righteousness, so that everyone who belongs to God may be proficient, equipped for every good work."*[222] The Word of God has many roles in our journey. It teaches us how to be faithful. It rebukes us when we're wrong. It corrects us when we're at fault and teaches us when we're out of order.

BEYOND RECITATION

There is a difference between quoting the Word and knowing the Word. Quoting is merely a basic recitation, which can be effective as an initial swing of the sword. But reciting the Word without being able to explain the Word is like using a sword with a dull blade—you're cutting nothing. And the enemy knows whether you're just a reciter or a cutter. You don't want to go up against the devil with a butter knife when he carries nothing but machetes. I know a lot of people who have

---

221: Philippians 4:13 (NKJV)
222: 2 Timothy 3:16-17 (NRSV)

learned to recite the Word of God from Bible study and Sunday school, but recitation can only cut so deep. Knowing the Word goes beyond recitation of Scripture. It's a deeper analysis with relevant Scripture that responds appropriately and swings effectively.

If you don't know what you're talking about, it can make you look weak and the enemy look strong. The enemy loves weak-Worded soldiers. That's like a general without troops. The enemy will challenge you, just to see if you know the Word of God. And you have to remember that the devil knows the Word also, although he will quote it out of context to confuse you. As we already looked at, Satan quoted Scripture out of context when he tried to tempt Jesus. So if you don't know the Word and the devil throws it at you out of context, he can confuse you and make you agree rather than disagree with his analysis. You want to know every grain of God's Word for your own edification and education so you can rid the devil and make him flee.

POLITICS AND THE WORD

You need to know the Word for political reasons. If you're in favor of protecting the environment against hazards, you must not only recite, *"The earth is the LORD's, and the fulness thereof,"*[223] but you also must be able to explain that passage with analysis, references, and additional biblical verses to support your political position. If you say you're against the death penalty because *"Thou shalt not kill,"*[224] then you should be able to explain that scripture with background and purpose to support your political position. We have a host of issues to consider in our society, and some men may be conservative while others may be liberal in their interpretation of the Bible. Whatever the political persuasion, the best swordsman will be the M.A.N. who can exhaustively reference the Word of God with everything from scripture passages to biblical stories to make their case. That's why it's important to attend Bible study. Find a church that is serious about teaching the Word of God. Bible study will help you sharpen your sword so that you can cut effectively.

223: Psalm 24:1
224: Exodus 20:13

DON'T CUT THE WRONG PEOPLE

When you swing your sword, make sure you aim it at the right enemy. Babies with swords are dangerous. You are a M.A.N., so it is important that the sword be used to cut the enemy and not the person. You can make a big mistake and hurt people with the Word of God. Don't be negligent in your usage of the Word. Appropriate use of God's Word is tempered with wisdom. You don't want to use the Word of God recklessly, like driving a racecar on the open road. The Word of God must be used properly and humbly for the encouragement and empowerment of people. At one time the Word of God was used to justify slavery of black people, using passages such as: *"Cursed be Canaan! The lowest of slaves will he be to his brothers,"*[225] and *"Slaves, obey your earthly masters...."*[226] Women have also been reduced to less than and more sinful, and subject to the greatest ostracism as a result of biblical interpretation that is contrary to the will of God, such as women not being allowed to become Bible teachers or pastors.[227] The subjugation and exploitation of people is antithetical to the Word of God. God's Word seeks to empower, discipline, and encourage humanity. As Paul wrote in Galatians, *"You are all sons of God through faith in Christ Jesus, for all of you who were baptized into Christ have clothed yourselves with Christ. There is neither Jew nor Greek, slave nor free, male nor female, for you are all one in Christ Jesus."*[228]

The sword of the Spirit knows what power to dole out, because it is not only for cutting down but also for building up. If someone throws hate at you, you can dispense the spirit of love, because love conquers hate. If your wife happens to be mad at you, you can dispense the spirit of joy because joy is sharper than anger. If insults are thrown at you, you can dispense the spirit of peace from your sword because peace will keep you calm in the midst of the storm. *"Blessed are the peacemakers, for they will be called sons of God."*[229]

225: Genesis 9:25 (NIV)
226: Ephesians 6:5 (NIV)
227: 1 Timothy 2:12
228: Galatians 3:26-28 (NIV)
229: Matthew 5:9 (NIV)

BELIEVE IN THE WORD

More than anything, you want to believe in the Word you speak and study. This is where the shield of faith and the sword of the Spirit work hand in hand: faith in one hand and the Word of God in the other. What good is it to quote something you don't believe in? As a matter of fact, if your words are not backed by faith, what you ask for won't come to pass.

God is true to His word. Many men wonder why they haven't gotten the changes they want in their lives, but many times it's due to lack of faith. You may speak it and pray it, but if you don't believe it, nothing will happen. If you want to receive, you have to believe. God's Word is serious, and in order for the sword to cut, it must be backed by faith. It will cut through doubt and fear and regret and bring you the reward God has for you. Remember that Jesus battled Satan with the Word backed by faith.

JESUS IS THE WORD

Jesus is the Word. John 1:1-2 reads, *"In the beginning was the Word, and the Word was with God, and the Word was God. He was with God in the beginning."*[230] Every word that we speak ought to be backed by the power of Jesus. It assures that our words are correct and righteous. The only way we'll be able to cut down the devil, like Jesus did after coming out of the wilderness, is to know that Jesus is the Word. Then you can go toe to toe, face to face, and Word for word with the enemy.

WORD FOR WORD

Let's end this with the true rumble in the jungle: Jesus versus Satan in the wilderness, which we looked at a bit earlier, but this time let's examine it in light of how Jesus knew the Word and knew how to use it against the enemy. Satan threw his deceitful words at Jesus, but Jesus threw *the* Word right back at Satan. First, Jesus quoted from Deuteronomy 8:3: *"Man does not live on bread alone, but on every word*

230: John 1:1-2 (NIV)

that comes from the mouth of God.[231] Jesus's words let Satan know that we live off of the Word of God.

After Satan's next temptation, Jesus came back with something from Deuteronomy 6:16: *"It is also written: 'Do not put the Lord your God to the test.'"*[232] We don't have to prove what we know to anybody but God. He directs our paths and our actions.

And the final blow, the knockout punch, came from Jesus's last words to the devil, quoting from Deuteronomy 6:13: *"Away from me, Satan! For it is written: 'Worship the Lord your God, and serve him only.'"*[233] Boom! Pow! Bang! Jesus punched him right in the mouth. God always gets the last word.

If you want to step into the ring and beat the devil, you must know and believe in the Word of God. The Word is a powerful weapon. No matter what the situation, crisis, or battle, the sword of the Spirit can answer. Just make sure you pray as you swing.

Points to Remember from Step 8

Part 1

1. Step 8 for every man is *Effectively*: He must use the Word of God competently to strike down the offenses of the enemy.

2. God has given us a sword, which is His Word, to fight the enemy. We do not fight against flesh and blood. We do not fight people. We fight the wickedness behind human actions with the Word of God.

3. The scripture is the authority of God's spoken word. It helps us to develop a theological understanding to effectively and confidently respond to the enemy.

4. The sword of the Spirit can clearly define your role and purpose as a man. It gives you a presence that no one can duplicate or dismiss.

231: Matthew 4:4 (NIV)
232: Matthew 4:7 (NIV)
233: Matthew 4:10 (NIV)

5. The sword helps us to cut out the spirit of wickedness and impart the Spirit of righteousness.

6. You must study the Word of God. Ingest it in the morning, afternoon, and evening.

Part 2

7. Know when to speak and when not to speak. Control your tongue and listen to God before you utter a word.

8. Cut profanity out of your vocabulary. Cussing shows more ignorance and indecency than intelligence and respect.

9. Your word is your bond. When you make a promise, be sure to keep it.

10. The Word of God can be used to justify your political positions.

11. Don't cut the wrong people. A man must cut effectively, not recklessly like a boy with a new toy.

12. The sword is used to cut out and to build up. Conquer hate with the spirit of love.

13. Jesus is the Word. Learn the Word, and you can fight Word for word against the enemy. Take heart: God always gets the last word.

PRAYER

CHAPTER 21

STEP 9: *Prayerfully—Part 1*

And pray in the Spirit on all occasions with all kinds of prayers and requests. With this in mind, be alert and always keep on praying for all the saints.

Ephesians 6:18 (NIV)

The biggest response from America to the bombing of Pearl Harbor on December 7, 1941, came almost four years later. During the final stages of World War II in 1945, the United States conducted two atomic bombings against Japan in the cities of Hiroshima and Nagasaki. By executive order of President Harry S Truman, the United States dropped the nuclear weapon "Little Boy" on the city of Hiroshima on August 6, 1945, followed by the detonation of "Fat Man" over Nagasaki on August 9. The bombings became the ultimate power of the war, changing the landscape and demanding victory for the United States and its allies.

Many people, preachers included, have restricted prayer to a conversation with God, built upon feelings of pity and sorrow, begging for forgiveness and hope for tomorrow. And although prayer encompasses all those aspects, it is not limited to them. Prayer, in its fullest expression, is any words or deeds—whether standing tall or on bended knees, heartfelt or by verbal means—that communicate the passions of people for a powerful response from God. Prayer is indeed a conversation with God, but it is also a power from God. Prayer is a powerful weapon against the enemy. As a matter of fact, prayer is the most powerful weapon we have, because it calls God into the battle. When God intercedes, it's like dropping a bomb on the enemy, which can change the entire landscape of the war and demand victory for the faithful.

PRAYER IS NOT A WEAK MAN'S TOOL

Unfortunately prayer is considered by many men to be a weakling's tool rather than a powerful weapon. If men are to be soldiers, they must also be prayer warriors. The image and perception of those who pray must change from that of pitiful to powerful. References to mighty men of God who prayed must be portrayed and encouraged. Yes, there were weeping women who prayed and slave's prayers, there were sinner's prayers and forgiveness prayers, but there are also powerful unbowed prayers that showed God's might and strength.

The story is told of "Praying Jacob," who was enslaved in the state of Maryland. Praying Jacob resolved that he would pray three times a day, regardless of what anyone said. No matter what Jacob was doing, he would stop and pray. His master, very cruel to his slaves, frequently yelled at Praying Jacob, at times pulling a gun on him so he would get up and continue working. Jacob would look at him and say, "The Bible says 'Men ought to always pray,'" and then Jacob would go back to praying.

The master went home and drank an unusual quantity of brandy so that he might harden his heart and kill Praying Jacob. But he never had the power to strike or shoot him, and he would freely give the world, if he had it in his possession, for what he believed Jacob to possess—the power of prayer.

Prayer is so powerful that it can stop the evil at heart from pursuing their plans and ruining God's people. Praying Jacob dropped a bomb on the slave master's plans and made him realize that a slave's prayer was stronger than a slave owner's hate.

Prayer is not a weak man's tool. Prayer is a tool borne of boldness and faith. It takes strength for men to pray because many are fighting against their own pride and arrogance. Submitting yourself to prayer means that you have acknowledged a higher power than yourself to tackle issues. Prayer is for the hopeful, not the hopeless. Prayer is for the powerful, not the powerless. Many men in the Bible relied upon prayer to change the landscape of their situation. Moses prayed. Joshua prayed. David prayed. Elijah prayed. Jesus, the Son of God, prayed. And all of these were powerful, strong men who submitted themselves to God's will.

ANOTHER PIECE OF ARMOR

Although there are six pieces of armor mentioned in Ephesians 6:14-17, I do consider prayer to be an official piece of armor from God. Prayer is mentioned in verse 18, immediately following the other pieces of armor without interruption: *"praying always with all prayer and supplication in the spirit."*[234] As with the other pieces of armor, prayer serves a specific purpose. Indeed, the purpose of prayer is even greater than that of the others. Just like an atomic bomb, prayer is the blast that can blow up the whole situation and change the course of the war from leaning toward a victory for the enemy to going in your favor.

Step 9 for every man is *Prayerfully*:

He must forever be in conversation with God while battling the enemy.

KEEP IN TOUCH WITH THE GENERAL

Men often downplay or even ignore the importance of prayer, to their own peril. Prayer is both a communicator and a detonator in war. Prayer as a communicator is a weapon that helps us to stay in constant contact with God. A loss of communication can result in tragedy. Prayer is our direct line to God. It is the walkie-talkie, Gmail, cell phone that

---

234: Ephesians 6:18

keeps us in touch with the Master as we engage the enemy. Put simply, soldiers follow the directives of the general. The general tells the soldiers which battles to fight, which direction to walk, and when to retreat. Without the general's orders, the soldiers would be lost.

In 1 Samuel 30, after the Amalekites took David's family captive from Ziklag, he prayed to the Lord before going after his foes. God spoke to David and said, *"Pursue, for you shall surely overtake them."*[235] God is our General. No matter what other armor we have on, if we don't hear from the General, we will not know which battles to fight, what direction to go, and when to withdraw. *"Praying always"* means constantly—continually talking with God. Keep in touch with the General as you fight your battles. Why? Because the enemy is tricky and always hoping that your phone is disconnected or your power is out so he can get you in a vulnerable position and take you down.

Prayer acts as a detonator to the blast that, when released, throws an adverse situation into a frenzy. The battle at Mount Carmel between Elijah, God's prophet, and Ahab, the wicked king, proves how prayer reigns in battle. In 1 Kings 18, Elijah challenged Ahab to call on his god while Elijah would call on his. Ahab brought with him 450 false prophets. Elijah had himself and his faith. The battle took place before a bunch of undecided people who didn't know if they should serve God or serve Ahab's god, Baal. When the time came, the 450 prophets called on Baal over and over, but nothing happened. Elijah then prayed to God, and God answered with such power by fire that all the people who were undecided fell prostrate and praised God. The Lord turned the situation around with the detonation of prayer.

Regardless of who or what or how many are coming against you, prayer can blow up the situation in your favor. Blowing it up is simply to change the enemy's course from one of your destruction to his disaster. When the enemy's assaults start coming after you, pray! A single sincere, faithful prayer can knock out each assault one by one until you're down to none. But as with Elijah's prayer, when you pray and God turns around your situation, it helps you, but there is always

---

235: 1 Samuel 30:8 (NKJV)

an unbelieving, ambivalent person out there who's looking for God to prove Himself. And when your situation turns around, other people start to believe in the power of prayer and the Spirit of God.

PRISON

Many men have changed their lives and become a great inspiration to someone else's transformation, particularly those who were rough and tough and almost atheistic and agnostic in their opinions and actions toward God. When men of disaster become Men of Armor, other men, women, and youth start to take notice. They look at you now in comparison to who you used to be and acknowledge that there must be a God. This is especially true for men who have come out of prison and are doing well socially, financially, and spiritually.

Prison can be the end of one's life, reputation, and social standing, but a praying man can see his life uplifted and transformed. I know of many men who spent decades in prison and then came out and reinvented themselves as hardworking, law-abiding citizens, and they are doing very well, sometimes better than men who've never gone to jail. That's because they prayed and learned from their experience. Their confinement taught them something about life and something about how God answers prayer. God can use prison to corner you and correct your actions and also your spirit—your attitude begins to change and real, uninterrupted conversations begin to take place in confinement, strictly between you and God. So to all the brothers who are confined, don't lose hope—pray. Pray that God will set you free. Pray that God will keep you in the midst of your confinement. Pray that God will speak to you while you're in and give you direction when you come out. Pray that your life will change for the good, and promise to never go back to bad. Pray!

If you're too embarrassed to pray in front of others, you can do it anywhere and anyhow you want: it can be in secret, under your breath, and in private, or it can be open, out loud, and public. And even though many men may not know it, somebody was praying for them. And that prayer with substance turned their lives around. I thank God for my momma's prayer. I can tell you if it had not been for her prayers,

I know where I would be: in the streets or in the grave somewhere. Thanks, Mom.

PRAYER BACKED BY FAITH

When you pray, it has to be backed by faith. The shield of faith and the power of prayer work together to alter conditions. Prayer without faith is a like a bank account with no money—it's good for nothing. Each prayer must be backed by faith so that it can be effective and transformative. A transformative prayer turns any situation around and causes the enemy to flee. With faith you must believe that what you pray for will come to existence. God will give you the words, and the faith will give you the hope that what you pray will come to pass. As long as you pray God's Word, God is true to His Word and will not disappoint.

When we pray, we ought not to have too many specifics, as if we're telling God what to do. We can end up being disappointed if God doesn't do it the way we pray it. And then we lose faith in God because He didn't deliver what we wanted. Jesus at Gethsemane prayed, *"Not my will, but thine, be done."*[236] Our prayers should always be to make sure that things are not done our way but God's way. And God's way is always the best way. This does not eliminate your asking God for what you want. The Bible says, *"Ask, and it shall be given you."*[237] But when you pray, you ought to seek God first so that you ask for what is in accordance with His will for your life. And if God gives you what you ask for, it's a confirmation that you were in tune with what God already had for you. But if God decides to do something else, then bless God because you know that *"all things work together for good to them that love God, to them who are the called according to his purpose."*[238] All you have to do is wait on God and be watchful.

WATCH AND PRAY

As you confront the enemy, you have to learn to be watchful. Paul stressed in Ephesians 6:18 the need to be watchful to this end *"with all*

236: Luke 22:42
237: Matthew 7:7
238: Romans 8:28

prayer and supplication." This is similar to what Jesus told the disciples at Gethsemane: *"Watch and pray so that you will not fall into temptation."*[239] It is important that men watch the enemy and pray to God at the same time. You can't enter a battle and not be aware of your surroundings. The enemy can come from different directions and in different forms in order to tempt you. To *watch* is to *take heed, be aware, pay attention, take notice, be observant, concentrate,* and *focus.* Although the enemy's actions are deceptive, his image is not always the loud, angry, mad monster that we often imagine. As looked at in the first chapter, the devil is crafty and a master at disguise. The devil is shrewd and can deceive you by being attractive and soft spoken, likable and talented. It is easy to recognize the boisterous beast, but acknowledging the silent creep requires a watchful eye. Prayer sees through lies and tricks. When you're aware of the enemy, you can respond with power from prayer. Prayer keeps you humble, yet not gullible or naïve. Watching lets the enemy know that you can't be fooled by evil, deceptive tricks and games.

The silliest notion that comes from others about God's people is that they are naïve, foolish, and easy to deceive, but you ought not allow your meekness to be seen as weakness. Don't let people take advantage of you because you are saved, or let people look down on you because you are humble. David was not weak. Moses was not weak. Jesus was not weak or a fool, or blind to the wicked ways of people. It's good to be nice to people who beg on the street, but everyone who begs is not in need of food. Some of them are using their begging to get your money to buy alcohol and drugs. Why would you want to be foolish and contribute to somebody's demise? You will be held just as accountable as them. Pray so that you're enlightened before you give, act, or contribute. As you watch the enemy, you also must keep an eye on God and His actions in your life. You still may be worried about your past, but remember that things take time to heal. While you're waiting, however, use the power of prayer and watch God open doors as He shortens the time on your sentence. What possibly started out as six years of waiting could be reduced to two years through watching and praying. Pray—and watch God drop a bomb on the situation.

239: Matthew 26:41 (NIV)

CHAPTER 22

STEP 9: *Prayerfully—Part 2*

LEADERS MUST ALWAYS PRAY

You'd be surprised how much danger has been averted in your life, either because of you praying or someone else praying for you. Prayer is a power man's tool, because even when your enemies are plotting against you, your prayers are working for you. Moses was a praying man. When Moses's own brother and sister tried to come against him and call his leadership into question, God remembered the prayers of Moses. And even without Moses praying at that moment, God was able to call his enemies to judgment. God dropped a bomb on them. Aaron began to fear and Miriam was struck with leprosy (see Numbers 12).

If you are a leader in any position, you are a constant target of Satan's threats against your existence. The enemy will throw all kinds of people (including close family members and church folks) and accusations at you to threaten your position and assassinate your character. One thing I've learned is that you can't be thin skinned as a leader; you have to develop strength and faith that thickens your skin and strengthens your spirit. But even then, the enemy can succeed in attacking you. This is where, like Moses, your prayers can work for you. Your prayers call God into the equation to throw a bomb on the situation.

Don't attack the enemy with schemes, plots, and threats, but *"seek ye first the kingdom of God, and his righteousness; and all these things shall be added unto you."*[240] I've had my share of enemies, people who try to diminish me, set me up, and kill my leadership. But I've learned to give the situation over to God by calling out their names in my prayers, and then I watch and wait for God to do His will. And I'm always ecstatic to see God get rid of the person and people that try to come against me. I'm telling you that prayer works, and God is real and effective for those who trust Him.

HOW TO PRAY AS A LEADER UNDER ATTACK

In your prayer you should start by begging God for forgiveness, then seek God for wisdom, and then ask God to take care of the person and/or the situation that's attacking you. And, as Jesus prayed when He was being attacked, always end with *"Not my will, but thine, be done."*[241] Then wait on the Lord to direct you in battle.

BATTLES THAT ARE GOD'S, NOT YOURS

As seen in 2 Chronicles 20, Jehoshaphat was a leader of Judah and didn't know his enemies were plotting against him, until he received notice that armies from other nations were coming after him. Jehoshaphat became afraid and began praying to the Lord. Not only did he pray, he asked all the people of Judah to pray as well. A little while later a prophet of God came to him and said, *"The battle is not yours, but God's."*[242] God dropped a bomb on Jehoshaphat's enemies and caused Judah to gain victory.

Some battles you must immediately surrender to God. Many men will try to fight their own battles out of pride and ego—and lose. But there are some wars, fights, and battles that are stronger and bigger than you. It's hard to fight court judges and corporations; they have more earthly money and power than you alone. It's hard to fight diabetes, tumors, HIV/AIDS, and prostate or colon cancer. Medicines

---

240: Matthew 6:33
241: Luke 22:42
242: 2 Chronicles 20:15

may be prescribed, diets may be changed, and exercises may be done, but battling diseases can leave you drained. Cancer has terrified and taken out the strongest of men. However, even with grim survival statistics, I've seen believing men, praying men, rise up from the hospital bed and be cured from all evidence of the disease when they surrendered the battle to God. He dropped a bomb on the situation.

And *cured* doesn't only mean the disease is gone from the body; it is gone from the soul and the mind, which means it doesn't hinder, trouble, or scare men like it used to. The impact and power of the disease or injury have become ineffective, and men are able to once again live their lives in peace and happiness rather than in fear and dread. In 2 Corinthians 12:7-9, we see that Paul had a pain in his side for years and kept asking God to take it away, but God never took the pain away. Yet God did let Paul know that His grace was sufficient enough to relieve the soul and calm the spirit of fear. God may not take the disease away, but His grace—unmerited love—is enough for you to live comfortably and a lengthy life with a disease.

Many men often wait until they're on their deathbed before they begin to pray. And if God has to take you there for you to realize the power of prayer, then you have to go there. God can show you His power when your life has reached its apparent limits. Hezekiah was on his deathbed when he prayed to the Lord, and God spoke through a messenger and granted him fifteen more years (see 2 Kings 20).

ASK SOMEONE TO PRAY FOR YOU

And don't be afraid or so arrogant that you can't ask someone to pray for you. Jehoshaphat called everyone to pray when he was being attacked. You have to enlist the prayers of the righteous. *"The effectual fervent prayer of a righteous man availeth much."*[243] This means the prayers of the righteous reach God's ear for your help. Call people you know: mother, father, spiritual leader, grandmother, someone that you know who can specifically pray for your situation. Someone that is really concerned about your well-being. It can relieve a world of stress, fear,

---

243: James 5:16

and problems. You'd be surprised what God can do through prayer for us and the world in which we live.

SOCIETY'S PRAYER

Our bodies can be healed by prayer, and our society can also be healed by prayer. Our society is plagued with all kinds of atrocities— from environmental to institutional diseases. In 2 Chronicles, God told Solomon, *"If my people, who are called by my name, will humble themselves and pray and seek my face and turn from their wicked ways, then will I hear from heaven and ... heal their land."*[244] God provides an answer in prayer, suggesting that the reason for the mayhem we experience is wickedness in high places. Prayer, humbly surrendered, can heal the violence, racism, sexism, environmental disasters, poverty, hunger, brutality, and any other vice that exists in the land. Our sin, ignorance, and carelessness are poisoning God's property, and only through conversion of our wicked ways can the earth be saved.

The great assurance of prayer is that it has no geographical boundaries and can reach other countries. If you're in America and pray for Africa, God is there. If you're in Asia and pray for America, God is there. If you are in Europe and pray for South America, Saudi Arabia, and Iraq, God is there. This land is God's land. God was the interconnect before the internet. The healing can begin if we humble ourselves and pray and turn from our wicked ways. A humbled heart in prayer will turn away wickedness and heal the environment.

As men we must do more for the environment—from picking up trash in our community and recycling cans, bottles, and boxes, to fighting against toxins in our water and soil. What kind of man trashes his own community or allows trash and toxins to invade his neighborhood? You have to make sure people pick up garbage and don't allow anyone to throw garbage on the streets in your neighborhood. God gave Adam responsibility to take care of the land. However, with greed, industrialism, oil spills, technology, and inconsideration for God's property, we have polluted the land, air, and sea. As a result not only do

---

244: 2 Chronicles 7:14 (NIV)

humanity and animals suffer, but the earth is sick. If the earth is sick, then it affects our food, trees, water, air, and a host of other bodily and earthly functions. We often wonder how we get incurable diseases, like cancer in various part of our bodies or asthma in our lungs. There is no doubt that some of it can be traced to the toxins in our food, water, and air. The sin of carelessness and recklessness can sicken the land in which we live. Not only do we need to push for better environmental laws and protection, but also spiritual transformation from sin to salvation so that people can be more conscious of how they treat God's property.

Another way we can volunteer our services to our community is to clean it and make sure it is environmentally safe. Every man should find a place in his home, community, or organization that he can commit his time to and assure the cleanliness and elimination of toxins in our world. We have to remember , *"The earth is the LORD's, and the fulness thereof."*[245] When we are careless with God's earth, we are sinning against God and causing problems for ourselves. Prayer can heal the land and wash away wickedness in high and low places.

FAMILY PRAYER

The extension of prayer also reaches family and friends that we can't always reach or speak to when we desire—like those in prison or the hospital, those in another state or country, or those in the military. The Bible says, *"... and always keep on praying for all the saints."*[246] We want to pray for others who are suffering, in need of healing, or just simply on our hearts and minds. At times prayer can say it better than your direct interaction or conversation with the person or people. Your prayers can do just as much as Hallmark cards, emails, and personal letters. Prayer changes things.

NOT ASHAMED TO PRAY

A M.A.N. is neither afraid nor ashamed to pray for himself, for others, and for society, knowing that it is a weapon for the powerful and

---

245: Psalm 24:1
246: Ephesians 6:18 (NIV)

not the powerless. A Man of Armor is never ashamed, even if it means standing in the streets and offering a prayer for the community. Even if it means lifting a prayer at the mortgage agency so he can get a home for his family.

The hardest prayer I ever offered was for a home mortgage. Shortly before I applied, my credit score was low, my money was tight, and the possibility of owning a house was more a dream than a reality. But I can tell you that prayer changes things. Although I had taken the necessary steps to fix my credit and raise the money, how it all came together at just the right time was a result of the power of prayer. God interceded, and by the time the mortgage agency pulled the credit report a couple of months later, my rating had skyrocketed far beyond the minimum needed for a mortgage. The money in the bank was more than enough for a down payment. Even the loan officer was amazed at the increase. As Paul said in 1 Corinthians 3, *"I have planted, Apollos watered; but God gave the increase."*[247] I can personally attest to the fact that prayer can make a great difference in the lives of saints. Prayer works to change things. I'll say it again: prayer changes things.

PRAYER AND BUILDING

Don't be ashamed to pray. If you see prayer as a weapon rather than a weakling's moaning, you will be more inclined to use it in battle while you're rebuilding your life. Remember Nehemiah? While others were taunting him, he kept building the walls. He never stopped except to pray and plant a bomb at the door. He had workers by day and guards by night. God in the battle doesn't mean you can't physically respond. It just means you're waiting for God to tell you *how* to respond. At times God may say, like he said to Jehoshaphat, "The battle is not yours, but Mine." God will then take care of the enemy Himself. At other times God may use our hands (with the sword and shield), our feet (fitted with the shoes of peace), our heads (capped with the helmet of salvation), our hearts (protected by the breastplate of righteousness), and waists (wrapped with the belt of truth) to take on the enemy. God

---

247: 1 Corinthians 3:6

used Saul with his spiritual armor on. God used David with his spiritual armor on. God used Solomon and Samson with their spiritual armor on. God used Jesus with His spiritual armor on. God can use you with your spiritual armor on.

PRAY FOR YOUR ENEMIES

Even when it comes to revenge, we have to pray. This is difficult, because if someone is hurting you or your family, it can cause you to lose all sense of righteousness and to have a desire to respond in the flesh. I know a lot of men who would not hesitate to kill someone if their families were threatened. And I can certainly understand. That is a human response to a human problem. But as a Man of Armor, there is a spiritual (better) way to exact retaliation without making the situation worse: prayer in the Spirit. The Bible says, "*... pray for those who persecute you.*"[248] For those who still doubt the effectiveness of prayer as a powerful weapon—a bomb that can blow up everything around them—listen up. God says, "*It is mine to avenge.*"[249] When you pray, it gives God the discretion to determine the punishment for your enemies.

We have to learn to leave room for God to do what God wills rather than what we want. When you take matters into your own hands, it can cause even more trouble in your life. It can cause headaches and chest pains because you're thinking about how to exact revenge on your enemies. Revenge is not only bad for your spirit, it's bad for your health. Many men have taken revenge and ended up on trial, in jail, fined, or dead. Some things you have to let go and let God handle. Certainly your reaction cannot compare to God's punishment. God will take care of it. And when God drops the bomb, you'd better believe somebody's life is going to be disrupted!

WHEN ALL ELSE FAILS, PULL OUT PRAYER

Prayer is the grenade you throw out when other parts of your armor don't seem to be working. Paul called it praying "*with all kinds of*

248: Matthew 5:44 (NIV)
249: Deuteronomy 32:35 (NIV)

prayer and requests. "[250] C. H. Spurgeon said, "Dear friends, when we are tempted and desire to overcome, the best weapon is prayer. When you cannot use the sword and the shield, take to yourself the famous weapon of All-prayer."[251] There is a prayer for every situation under the sun. When your sword is not cutting, throw out a power prayer packed with the Word of God. When your shield is not blocking, throw out a mighty prayer backed by faith. When the enemy is pulling on your pants trying to loosen your belt, throw out a strong man's prayer backed by the Spirit of truth. When your heart is hurting and corruption is edging in, throw out an earnest prayer backed by righteous living. When your head is hurting and the enemy is stressing you out, throw out a healing prayer backed by God's salvation. When your feet are moving in the wrong direction, throw out a firm prayer backed by peace and just watch God act.

Even if you can't say it the way you want to pray it, God hears the heart. As Paul wrote in Romans 8: *"… We do not know what we ought to pray for, but the Spirit himself intercedes for us with groans that words cannot express. And he who searches our hearts knows the mind of the Spirit, because the Spirit intercedes for the saints in accordance with God's will.* "[252]

DON'T LET THE ENEMY STEAL YOUR JOY

Battles are inevitable because the enemy is relentless in his pursuit of evil and destruction. Prayer gives joy to the battles we fight. James admonished us, *"Consider it pure joy, my brothers, whenever you face trials of many kinds, because you know that the testing of your faith develops perseverance."*[253] Nehemiah 8:10 tells us, *"The joy of the LORD is your strength."*[254] The enemy would love to take your joy, because if the devil can take your joy, he also can take your strength.

Joy is a feeling given by God and received through the Holy Spirit to bring strength and happiness over pain and anguish or any

---

250: Ephesians 6:18 (NIV)
251: Rev. C. H. Spurgeon, "Gethsemane," February 8, 1863, www.spurgeon.org, accessed Oct. 11, 2017, https://www.spurgeon.org/resource-library/sermons/gethsemane#flip-book/.
252: Romans 8:26-27 (NIV)
253: James 1:2-3 (NIV)
254: Nehemiah 8:10 (NIV)

other dismal feeling that you may experience during battle. Joy keeps you in high spirits in the midst of combat. What good is it to fight well and feel bad? Joy is a re-energizer. It puts a smile on your face. Helps you laugh as you go. You're not soft or weak when you smile. You may have had a hard face in the world, but God can transform your soul and facial expression. Let everybody know how good you feel about where you are right now. You lived to see yourself new, improved, better than before. You made it through many hardships and dangers, troubles and backstabbers. You have a reason to laugh. Many of you should be in jail, divorced, diseased, or dead. And even if you are in jail, divorced, and/or diseased, you have a lot to be thankful for if you're still living.

When you stop and think about all that you've been through and where you are now as a M.A.N., a smile should come over your face and a "Thank You, God!" should come out of your mouth. Just the fact that you are even interested in reading this book says something about your transformed reality—your new character and personality. You should laugh and dance at home, school, work, and church. Laughter is good for your health. When you feel good, it resonates all over your body. It keeps you up and ready for whatever comes your way.

It often confounds me how some men can be so stiff during worship service and so expressive doing evil. You can be happy doing good. In many houses of worship, dancing, clapping, singing, and saying "Amen" is a sign of your conversion, and your joy should reflect your salvation. Psalm 98 says, *"Sing to the LORD a new song, for he has done marvelous things; his right hand and his holy arm have worked salvation for him."*[255] We should sing because we're happy and sing because we're saved. If you were drowning and someone pulled you out before you died, you wouldn't come out mad or sad; you'd come out happy and grateful and feeling blessed. As the old song "Love Lifted Me" goes: "I was sinking deep in sin far from the peaceful shore, very deeply stained within, seeking to rise no more. But the Master of the sea heard my despairing cry, from the waters lifted me, now safe am I." You are saved! You have a reason to rejoice!

255: Psalm 98:1 (NIV)

Feeling good brings a whole new attitude to your home. Your family will welcome you in, your coworkers will speak kindly of you, and your friends will notice the difference. Your days will be less stressful. Your health will improve. Your relationship with others will be attractive. You should rejoice, for a great salvation has come and a great injustice has been undone! Joy confuses the enemy about your state of well-being. When the enemy hits you and you're not only standing and swinging, but laughing and singing, you mess the enemy up. He doesn't know what to do with you because your joy is your strength.

You don't want to be a miserable warrior. Prayer drops a bomb on misery and allows for joy and happiness in the midst of battle. You can fight and feel good at the same time. Consider it all joy.

Points to Remember from Step 9

Part 1

1. Step 9 for every man is *Prayerfully*: He must forever be in conversation with God while battling the enemy.

2. Prayer is not a weak man's tool, but rather a strong man's weapon.

3. Prayer keeps us in communication with the General (God) during our battles.

4. Prayer can blow up the situation in your favor.

5. Watch and pray. Be alert, because the enemy comes from all different directions and in various forms.

Part 2

6. Leaders must always pray. Make sure your prayer is backed by faith.

7. Prayer watches over you at all times, even when you're not praying.

8. Pray for your enemies.

9. There are battles that are God's to fight, not yours. Pray so you know which battles are yours and which are God's.

10. Prayer can heal human beings and God's land.

11. Be responsible for God's earth, and better the environment.

12. Don't be ashamed to pray; it's for your own strength.

13. When other parts of your armor don't seem to be functioning, pray so that God can drop a bomb on the situation.

14. Keep the joy of the Lord within you as you fight your battles.

CHAPTER 23

STEP 10: *Boldly*

I have fought the good fight, I have finished the race, I have kept the faith. Now there is in store for me the crown of righteousness, which the Lord, the righteous Judge, will award to me on that day....

2 Timothy 4:7 (NIV)

Hannibal was a black Carthaginian general who lived two hundred years before Christ. With forty thousand soldiers and a caravan of elephants, Hannibal went forth to engage the armies of Rome. Hannibal's soldiers thought that he would lead them eastward, but Hannibal led them westward, up though the straits of Gibraltar and northward through Spain until they came to the foot of the mighty Alps, mountains that had never been crossed by armies or by so many animals. Astride his trusty horse, Hannibal looked back and cried out to his troops, "Do you see the mighty mountains?"

And his soldiers returned the words, "We see the mighty mountains."

A second time Hannibal called back to his troops, "Do you see the mighty mountains?"

Again the soldiers replied, "We see the mighty mountains."

A third time Hannibal shouted back to his troops, "Do you see the mighty mountains?"

251

And a third time the legions responded, "We see the mighty mountains."

Then Hannibal, the story goes, removed his sword from his sheath, pointed it forward, the steel shining in the sun, and cried back to his men, "Forward, march! We are stronger than the mighty mountains!"

And Hannibal, with his thousands of soldiers, a caravan of elephants, and hundreds of horses, climbed the mighty Alps, through ice, snow, rain, and sleet, and stormed the gates of Rome.

FORWARD, MARCH!

M.A.N., forward, march! The day of evil has come. You are mightier than rulers! Mightier than principalities! Mightier than darkness! Mightier than wickedness in high places! You are more than a conqueror. You can do all things through Christ who strengthens you. The joy of the Lord is your strength! Greater is He that is in you than he that is in the world. Put on the whole armor of God! Go through the snow and the rain, the heartaches and the pain, and storm the gates of hell and be set free. Fight the enemy with truth, righteousness, peace, faith, love, and joy.

Step 10 for every man is *Boldly*:

He must go forward courageously.

Be strong in the Lord and the power of His might.

Declare war on the devil. No longer will you be a slave to sin. No weapons formed against you will prosper. No more will you fail. No longer will your reputation be ruined and your family suffer. No longer will you be put to shame and blamed for your past mistakes. No longer will you fall to temptation. The devil will flee. You will succeed. The devil will fall. You will rise. The devil will lose. You will win. You are a champion!

M.A.N., this is the moment of truth—the moment you've been preparing for. The Bible says that when Jesus came up out of the desert, the tempter was there to tempt Him. As soon as you step out of the dressing room, the devil will be waiting for you. He's waiting to tempt and test you, harass and beat you, use and abuse you, until he kills you—physically, emotionally, and spiritually.

However, you don't have to wait for the enemy to come to you. Just as Hannibal showed boldness, put on the whole armor of God and go to the enemy. Knock down doors, break down walls, and engage the enemy. As you go forward, remember, *"… be strong in the Lord, and the power of his might."*[256]

256: Ephesians 6:10

THE ARTICLES OF ARMOR

THE PLEDGE OF ARMOR

I, Man of Armor,

promise to live in Truth,

walk in Peace,

have Faith in Christ,

and execute the Word of God

with Justice and Righteousness

for the Salvation of all people.

THE PRINCIPLES OF ARMOR

Truth, Righteousness, Peace, Faith, Salvation, Prayer, Courage,
Love, and Joy

THE PURPOSE OF ARMOR

To effectively dismantle the enemy from my life, community, and
family as I live by the principles of armor

THE PRACTICE OF ARMOR

To fully practice the purpose of armor, based upon the principles of
armor; to apply understanding through my daily living so that my life
is not in vain

THE PRAYER OF ARMOR

"Create in me a clean heart, O God; and renew a right spirit within me."
(Psalm 51:10)

THE POWER OF ARMOR

To resist temptation through the power of the Holy Spirit,
believing I can do all things through Christ who strengthens me

THE PENALTY AND PROMISE OF ARMOR

To live my life to avoid the punishment that comes with falling to
temptation,
and to receive the promise that comes with overcoming temptation
"For the wages of sin is death; but the gift of God
is eternal life through Jesus Christ our Lord."
(Romans 6:23)

THE SONG OF ARMOR

Man of Armor Nation, looking for the perfect peace!
I'm a Soldier in the Army of the Lord!